DRAG QUEENS AT THE 801 CABARET

T0385610

Leila J. Rupp

DRAG

and Verta Taylor

QUEENS AT THE 801 CABARET

The University of Chicago Press • Chicago and London

The University of Chicago Press, Chicago 60637
The University of Chicago Press, Ltd., London

© 2003 by The University of Chicago
All rights reserved. Published 2003.
Paperback edition 2015
Printed and bound by CPI Group (UK) Ltd,
Croydon, CR0 4YY

22 21 20 19 18 17 16 15   2 3 4 5 6

ISBN-13: 978-0-226-73158-2 (cloth)
ISBN-13: 978-0-226-32656-6 (paper)
ISBN-13: 978-0-226-33645-9 (e-book)
DOI: 10.7208/chicago/9780226336459.001.0001

Library of Congress Cataloging-in-Publication Data

Rupp, Leila J., 1950–
   Drag queens at the 801 Cabaret / Leila J. Rupp and Verta Taylor.
      p. cm.
Includes bibliographical references (p.   ) and index.
   ISBN 0-226-73158-8
   1. Transvestites—Florida—Key West. 2. 801 Cabaret (Key West,
Fla.)—Employees. 3. Sex role—Florida—Key West. 4. Marginality,
Social—Florida—Key West. 5. Gay liberation movement. I. Taylor,
Verta A. II. Title.
   HQ77.2.U6 R86 2003
   306.77—dc21
                                                                    2002013751

To Sushi,
WHO MADE IT ALL POSSIBLE

CONTENTS

SECTION III: "LIFE IS A CABARET"

SECTION IV: "WE ARE FAMILY"

SECTION V: "FREE YOUR MIND"

ILLUSTRATIONS

PREFACE

The first time we walked into the 801 Cabaret, we could never have imagined how immersed we would become in that world and how much we would come to think of the bar as home. Writing about the drag queens at the 801 Cabaret has been an extraordinary experience for us. As non–drag queens and non–gay men, we feel privileged to have been let into their world (although it has not escaped us that the classic work on American drag queens was also the product of a lesbian woman, Esther Newton). First and foremost, we want to thank the 801 Girls, who shared their time and thoughts and feelings with us with boundless generosity. Somehow, from the first time we met Sushi, she took us seriously, despite the fact that, as we came to learn, people are always trying to get close to the drag queens by claiming that they are writing a book about them. Sushi believed in us, she urged us to "tell the truth," and she made it all possible. To Sushi, Milla, Kylie, R.V., Margo, Inga, Scabby, Gugi, Desiray, Mama, and Lady V, all of whom we interviewed, and to all the other drag queens who graced the stage at the 801 Cabaret while we worked on this project, we say thank you from the bottom of our hearts.

So many others also helped to make our work possible in different ways. Betsy Kaminski and Stephanie Gilmore, our research assistants and so much more, not only transcribed and coded interviews and shows, coded articles in *Celebrate!*, turned photographs into transparencies and computer images, conducted formal and informal interviews, researched the music, read and commented on our work, observed and commented on the shows—they also fell in love with the drag queens and, happily, with each other. About them we can truly say, "We Are Family."

Josh Gamson worked with Verta in writing a successful joint proposal for a Wayne C. Placek Small Grant Award from the American Psychological Foundation, and he played an active role in the focus group portion of the research. He also coauthored an article with us and in so doing provided incredible insight that has much improved this manuscript. We are extremely grateful not only for his help and advice, but for the pleasure of his company on several occasions in Key West.

In addition to the American Psychological Association, the Coca-Cola Foundation (through the Department of Women's Studies), the Department of Sociology (particularly Betty Menaghan), the College of Social and Behavioral Sciences (through a program administered by Toby Parcel), and the Department of History, all at Ohio State, provided generous support of various kinds. Jim Gilleran, co-owner of the 801, graciously allowed us to hold focus groups with audience members in the cabaret and provided a free drink to each participant as an incentive and reward for volunteering to show up.

Many others played a part in making this research possible. Ann Paxton did yeoman service on the difficult job of transcribing the focus group tapes. Gail Summerhill, associate to the chair in the Department of History, in addition to her regular role of helping to keep Leila's head above water, produced the first "Cast of Characters" on her computer and, more importantly, loved hearing about the drag queens. Ron Aminzade, Kathleen Blee, Elizabeth Clemens, Myra Marx Ferree, Mary Margaret Fonow, Josh Gamson, Stephanie Gilmore, Joan Huber, Elizabeth Kaminski, Joanne Meyerowitz, Deborah Minkoff, Ann Mische, Carol Mueller, Peter Nardi, Esther Newton, Pam Paxton, Vincent Rosigno, Steven Schacht, Beth Schneider, Carroll Smith-Rosenberg, Birgitte Søland, Jennifer Terry, Barrie Thorne, Nella Van Dyke, and Nancy Whittier commented on presentations or versions of the text, providing both encouragement and astute criticism. A whole slew of friends and family, including a number of noted gender scholars, went to see the shows, either with us or by themselves, and they, too, provided encouragement and shared their responses. For that we thank Chris Bose and Edna Acosta-Belén, Paula England, Myra Marx Ferree and Don Ferree, Judy Howard and Jodi O'Brien, Birgitte Søland and Nancy Guzowski, Mike and Renée Ako, Leslie Bomar and Steve Salyk, Jane Brannigan, Nancy Campbell, Tania Cole, Richard Dennison, Dana Fisher, Darryl Fohrman, Darrell Goddard, Leo Gullick, Brian Holden, Betsy Kaminski and Stephanie Gilmore, Victoria Lesser, Gwen Longbotham and Melinda Simonds, Debbie O'Donnell, Carla and Don Pestana, Jeff Polawski, Ann Reynolds and Tom Kirschbaum, Jenn Rosen and Maria Nielsen, John Rule, Eric Selby, Steve Shapiro and Donna Stark, Jim Smith, David Symons and Caroline Lacy, Linda, Jason, and Sara Taylor, Griff Tester and Chad Schone, and Elmer and Kimberly White.

We also thank everyone at Antonia's in Key West, where we so often dined before the shows, for the culinary, intellectual, and musical nourishment we enjoy there. We should also mention Seven Fish and Camille's, both places where we shared some wonderful meals with various 801 Girls. And speaking of nourishment, we are enormously grateful to Doug Mitchell, who expressed enthusiasm for this book from the beginning, listened patiently in person and over e-mail to drag queen tales, took us to marvelous restaurants in a variety of conference sites, and kept promising that he would come see the show. We wish we could bring with us all of the wonderful University of Chicago people who helped along the way, including Doug's assistants, Robert Devens and Tim McGovern, promotions manager Mark Heineke, designer Mike Brehm, and especially senior manuscript editor Erin DeWitt, whose skill with a red pencil is matched by her sense of humor and ability to make last-minute corrections and thus save us from embarrassment.

Finally, we note the death of Emma, our diva dog, who made her debut on the 801 stage. She liked the 801 much better than does Phoebe, our new Maltese, whose youthful ears find the music a bit too loud. With this book completed, and having moved after long, happy years from Ohio State to the University of California at Santa Barbara, and in the aftermath of September 11, our world is a different place in more ways than one. But more than anything, the 801 Girls have made sure that we shall never again think about gender and sexuality in quite the same way.

CAST OF CHARACTERS

All photos by authors, unless otherwise indicated

Sushi

Gary

Kylie

Kevin

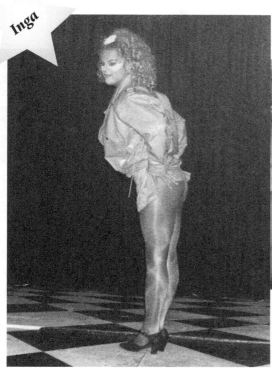

Inga

Roger

Milla

Dean

Margo

David

Timothy

Matthew

Gugi

Rov

Joel

Desiray

ONE

INTRODUCTION
"What Makes a Man a Man?"

It's Saturday night in Key West and the "Girlie Show" is about to begin at the 801 Cabaret. The 801 Girls have been outside on the sidewalk, in drag, handing out flyers and inviting everyone who walks or drives by to come see the show. The room is packed, the house music is loud, and it's getting smoky. At the top of the stairs is a throng of gay men. If you push through, it is possible to get up in front of the bar, which fills the center of the room, but all the tables and chairs in front of the stage are taken. The crowd there includes women, some with other women, some with men. We scoot over to the windows, which remain resolutely shut against the tropical evening air because of a city noise ordinance. People say "hi" and reach out to pat Emma, our Maltese who always comes along and who performs an occasional number with Milla. We settle in on bar stools at the counter that runs along the wall. Kylie's voice booms over the sound system, telling the audience the show will begin in just five more minutes.

And then the house music goes down, the spots illuminate the stage, and En Vogue's "Free Your Mind" fills the room. Inga, Kylie, Sushi, and Milla come out from behind the curtain one by one. Inga, a statuesque blond, wears a black leather minidress, high boots, and dark glasses. Kylie has on a red satin bustier. Sushi sports a black bra and miniskirt with red fringe. Milla is wearing a long-sleeved, floor-length, black see-through garment over hot pants. They perform a choreographed routine, the product of Inga's expertise, as they lip-synch the words: "Free your mind, the rest will follow. Be color-blind, don't be so shallow." The show has begun.

At the end of the show, R.V. Beaumont performs "What Makes a Man a Man?"—a plaintive ballad about the difficult life of a drag queen. R.V. comes out of drag onstage, removing her wig, makeup, and falsies, stripping off her dress, and pulling on jeans and a T-shirt. It is a performance that visually questions the meaning of gender, making explicit what is central to drag shows.

This is the story of an evening at the 801 Cabaret, the story of drag and what it means in contemporary American society. At the turn of the twentieth century, it seemed as if everywhere one turned in the world of popular culture, men were donning women's clothes: basketball star Dennis Rodman, off court; RuPaul on television's *Hollywood Squares;* Lady Chablis playing herself on the silver screen in *Midnight in the Garden of Good and Evil; Hedwig and the Angry Inch* rocking Broadway. Public fascination with the meaning of gender-crossing has its counterpart in the world of scholarship, where feminist and queer theorists contemplate the instability of the categories "woman" and "man," "feminine" and "masculine," "heterosexual" and "homosexual." Drag and other forms of gender transgression inspire intense public and scholarly interest, yet not since Esther Newton's classic 1972 book, *Mother Camp,* has anyone written the kind of in-depth exploration of the world of drag queens that we present here.[1] *Drag Queens at the 801 Cabaret* clothes the theoretical bones of the scholarship on gender and sexuality in the finery of actual drag queen life.

Perhaps the central question that drag elicits is whether the spectacle of men dressing in women's clothes (or women impersonating men, as in the case of contemporary drag kings[2]) challenges the concept of female and male as distinct, opposite, and nonoverlapping categories. There are those—especially gender theorists, who are drawn to drag because they see precisely this phenomenon—who would say yes. But there are others, also believers in the project of breaking down the rigid barriers between our ideas of "men" and "women," who see drag as confirming traditional notions of femininity and masculinity. And of course there are those who see both phenomena at work at the same time.

It is in this context that we came to study the drag queens at the 801 Cabaret. We knew that drag has a long and rich history in American communities of people with same-sex desires, and we knew as well that drag shows in tourist destinations such as New Orleans, San Francisco, Provincetown, and Key West have long served as a unique window through which straight women and men can view gay life. So we asked not just what meaning we might see in the drag queens' performances, but what the drag queens intend and what impact drag performances have on audience members, both gay and straight. We suggest that drag as performed at the 801 should be understood not only as a commercial performance but as a political event in which identity is used to contest conventional thinking about gender and sexuality.[3] The drag queens intentionally throw out this challenge, and their performances both create solidarity among gay audience members and draw straight viewers into a world they seldom experience.

This leads us to the broader question of what makes a cultural performance such as drag serve as social protest, a question that has vexed scholars of social movements, if not so much scholars of cultural studies, who tend to find the connection between culture and politics unsurprising. To answer this question, we draw upon three bodies of scholarship. The research on gender and sexuality has pointed to the role of external markers such as dress, gestures, and other behaviors, as well as language and interaction, in creating a polarized and hierarchical gender and sexual system consisting of male/female and heterosexual/homosexual.[4] This rigid binary system of gender creates cultural barriers to social acceptance of homosexuality and to self-acceptance among lesbians and gay men. Scholars have acknowledged the significance of transgressive tactics such as cross-dressing, drag performances, and the adoption of transgendered identities for disrupting those divides because they highlight the social basis of gender and sexuality.[5] Most of this work, however, fails to consider the extent to which cross-dressing both emerges from and contributes to the ideas and collective identities of the lesbian and gay movement.

Social movement theory adds the missing element by providing insight into the varied forms of protest or collective strategic action that groups use to challenge stigmatized identities and to create new forms of identity and community.[6] If social movement scholars have tended to separate political from cultural repertoires of action and to treat cultural events as inconsequential, research in performance studies questions the conventional distinction between commercial entertainment and politics.[7] This body of research allows us to understand drag shows as political events that are capable of winning a hearing for serious political purposes precisely because of their entertainment value. Applying these three perspectives to the study of the 801 Cabaret, we offer a framework that allows us to understand when and how cultural performances are political.

In order to understand the complexity of drag, we collected a wide variety of data. We did intensive interviews with twelve drag queens, and we also interviewed the owner and manager of the 801, the boyfriends of two drag queens, and the mothers of two others. We attended rehearsals, weekly drag queen meetings, and various social events, and we taped and transcribed fifty shows. We also analyzed publicity in the local weekly Key West media. Finally, in order to explore what audience members take away from drag shows, we held focus groups, recruiting participants at the shows and facilitating group conversations the next afternoon about their reactions to what they had seen. We also talked more informally with other audience members. We began our study in 1998 and continued to add new information until the summer of 2001, but we did our most intensive research from 1998 to 1999. For those who are interested, we describe the methods in more detail in the appendix.

We see the 801 Girls as unusual, since they perform in a gay tourist destination also known as a drag queen mecca, but we are also convinced that what happens on the stage at the 801 Cabaret has something to tell us about contemporary American drag performances in general. It is clear from our own observations and from those of audience members that there is a national drag queen repertoire of songs and talk exchanged from place to place. Focus group members who had attended numerous drag shows in different places tended to comment that what was different about this show was the extent of audience interaction. So this is both a story about a drag show in a very particular place and a broader analysis of drag in contemporary American society.

The 801 Girls are full-time drag queens who perform every night of the year to mixed audiences of men and women, gay or bisexual people and straight people, tourists and locals. The roster has changed somewhat over time, and there are almost always some occasional performers who may or may not eventually join the troupe. Our cast of major characters includes eight core performers. Six (Sushi, Milla, Kylie, Margo, R.V., and Scabola) have remained part of the show since we began the study in 1998 (although Milla left Key West late in 2001). Two (Inga and Gugi) left to perform in another venue (and then Gugi returned just as the book went into production). We also include Desiray, a performer who came on after 1998, because she took over Gugi's role in the show and also plays an especially interesting part in our research, as you will see. Many other Key West drag queens— including Lady V, Destiny, Mama Crass, Mama, Ma Evans, Miss Q, Nikki, Baby Drag, LaLa Belle, Krystal Klear, Ms. D, Vogue, Mr. Randy Roberts, Christopher Peterson, BellaDonna, Charlena D. Sugarbaker, the Bitch Sisters, D.D.T., Hellen Bed, Raven, Ice, Gina Masseretti, Angelica Duval, Mona Celeste, and Colby Kincaid—make guest appearances in the story.

Perhaps we should add a word here about our use of names and pronouns. The vast majority of the time, the girls call each other by their drag names and use the pronouns "she" and "her." But not always. And there is almost no consistency, in contrast to the common practice in the transgender movement, between appearance and linguistic gender. As a result, in both life and this book, we use pronouns and names somewhat randomly. Some of the girls have preferences about their names, and we have honored that. Dean, Matthew, and Roger seemed to want us to use their boy names, at least when they were out of drag, and we have always moved back and forth for them. Gugi, on the other hand, never uses "Rov," so we don't either. We have always called Sushi "Sushi," because that just seems like who she is, and we always call Kylie "Kylie" and R.V. "R.V." because they seem androgynous names that fit them as both drag queens and men. David/Margo, because of his role as columnist for the local gay newspaper as well as drag queen, is the only one with a public persona in both names, so we move back and forth too.

One other caution about language: although we argue that drag queens and drag performances break down the boundaries between woman and man, gay and straight, we continue to use these categories, however flawed they might be, to identify people. In part, the language gives us no choice. But, in addition, this seeming contradiction, as we shall see, mirrors the methods the drag queens use to accomplish their goals. We simply want to acknowledge that we recognize the ambiguity.

Drag Queens at the 801 Cabaret takes you through a night at the 801 Cabaret, from the process of getting dressed to the final curtain call. In the process it delves into a whole raft of issues, from what we call "drag-queenness" as a gender category outside femininity or masculinity to the role of drag queens as both celebrities and outcasts in the Key West community to the work life of drag queens to the performance of protest to the complex construction of collective identity to drag as an important strategy of the gay and lesbian movement. We argue that drag does, as gender scholars put it, "trouble" gender and sexuality by making people question the naturalness of what it means to be a man or a woman and what it means to be heterosexual, homosexual, or bisexual. Drag embodies ambiguity and ambivalence. When straight women exclaim that they are attracted to the girls and they aren't even lesbians, when straight men are aroused by gay men in dresses, when lesbians find it erotic to see two drag queens doing the lesbian number "Take Me or Leave Me" from the hit Broadway show *Rent*, the conventional divisions between female and male, straight and gay, become almost meaningless.

Furthermore, we argue that drag is an important strategy in the gay and lesbian movement's struggle. Weaving together the fascinating life stories of the drag queens, their costumes and music and talk during their performances, their interactions with each other and their audiences and community, and the reactions of spectators to what they see and hear and feel, we suggest that drag can serve as a catalyst for changes in values, ideas, and identities in twenty-first-century American society.

Drag attracts diverse audiences. At least one of our focus group members, having studied with Esther Newton, a major scholar of sexuality, could discuss the theoretical literature on drag with great sophistication. Others enjoyed the shows with no clue that academics have written about "liminal figures" or "transgressive sexualities" or "the category crisis" or "performing gender." Like the drag queens, we hope to reach readers where they live. So we trace the scholarly trail in the notes, leave an explicit discussion of theory for the conclusion, and turn now to where the girls are getting dressed for the evening.

SECTION I
"I'M BEAUTIFUL, DAMMIT!"

One of R.V.'s favorite Bette Midler numbers, "I'm Beautiful," expresses the drag queens' confidence in the face of challenge. Expressing comfort with her physical appearance, Midler sings of her right to be herself. "Ain't this my world to be who I choose?" Midler/R.V. asks.

We're back at the show. Or, rather, we've backed up to about eight o'clock, when the girls begin to arrive at the 801 to get ready for the evening. Off to the side of the stage, under the eaves, is a tiny windowless dressing room, no bigger than six by ten feet, and here the four or five performers for the evening, while sipping their cocktails and powdering their noses, somehow manage to get dressed and made up. Each regular girl has a stool, a shelf for makeup and props, and a section of the mirror that runs all around the room. What wall is not taken up by mirrors and the low-sloped ceiling is papered with photographs and flyers and adoring fan letters. It is here that Gary, Dean, Kevin, Roger (replaced by Rov, and later by Joel), David, Matthew, and Timothy transform themselves into Sushi, Milla, Kylie Jean Lucille, Inga (replaced by Gugi Gomez, later by Desiray), Margo, Scabola Feces, and R.V. Beaumont. This section tells the story of how and why this happens.

TWO

GETTING DRESSED

Getting into the dressing room to see the whole process was not so easy. One Saturday night Sushi arranged for us to come, under the condition that we sit quietly and not talk. But when we arrived Sushi wasn't there, and she hadn't told the other girls we were coming. Roger threw a fit. He didn't want anyone watching him get dressed, and that was that. (Apparently Leila threw up her hands in what neither of us had noticed was a characteristic gesture and exclaimed, in a slightly hysterical fashion, "What are we going to *do*?" Dean later told us that this had become a favorite expression among the girls, and then it became a favorite of ours, as well.) So we didn't get in that night. Later Roger told us he'd never let us see him get in or out of drag.

Several months later Roger went to work at Diva's, the club down the street that pays more, although he continued to perform occasionally at 801 and often came around during the shows, both in and out of drag. So finally one Sunday night, Sushi said it would be all right for us to watch. We decided just one of us would go, since the space was so tight. That night Verta was running one of the focus groups with audience members, and then we had to go grab something to eat, so by the time Leila got to the dressing room, they were all in the midst of putting on their faces. They arrive in shorts and T-shirts. All except Margo, who could be their father (or mother!), range in age from late twenties to mid-thirties.

Sushi, whose mother is Japanese and late father was from Texas, has a beautiful tall slender body, with thin but muscled arms and a dancer's legs. He never really looks totally like a man, even when he is dressed as Gary. One year at Queen Mother, the annual drag queen pageant and fund-raiser, he wore white shorts and two tank tops and put his shoulder-length jet-black hair in a bun wrapped in pink feathers. His dog Aurora sported a matching ruffle of feathers. Other times he ap-

The dressing room (photo by Gwen Longbotham)

pears in tight red plaid capri pants, or overalls cut off at midcalf, wearing thongs, with his hair in pigtails.

Milla, like Sushi, is beautiful. Dean's mother is Italian and his late father was a military man from Florida. He has short wavy black hair, expressive eyes, and kissable full lips. He is the only one in the group who has altered his body in any way, getting black-market silicone injections in his cheeks and forehead, mostly to get rid of the wrinkles they all fear so much. When he read our book prospectus, he got stuck on the phrase "black-market silicone" and kept repeating it over and over. The others seem wary of such procedures, and recently Dean reported that his source (herself transsexual) was cutting him off so he wouldn't overdo it. With her olive skin and dark eyes and her fondness for Erykah Badu and similar numbers, Milla is often taken onstage for African American.

Kylie, Sushi's best friend from high school, is much shorter than Sushi and Milla. Kevin is a very handsome preppy man with straight blondish hair that falls over his eyes. His teeth are a little crooked and lend warmth to his engaging smile. The other drag queens are convinced that Kylie could go in drag to one of the straight bars at the other end of Duval Street and easily pass herself off as a woman. Most women don't think so, despite Kylie's gorgeous legs, shapely ass, and California valley-girl ways. As one young lesbian put it after meeting him out of drag, "Jeez, did you ever think he would look like that?" And her girlfriend replied, "He's a better-looking man." Still, one day when we were at the beach waiting for him to meet us, we kept spotting men in the distance and asking "Is that him?" until suddenly we recognized his walk. Barefoot and out of drag, he still walked as if he were wearing high heels. But this is clearly something learned, as a drag queen, not a long-standing effeminate way of walking. One night we went to dinner at Antonia's, a favorite restaurant, with Kylie and Sushi, and Verta was surprised to see Kylie shake hands with Phillip, Antonia's husband, and say "Hello" in a deep masculine voice. Verta commented that she'd never seen Kylie in such a boy role, and he responded, "I act like that when I'm wearing men's clothes."

R.V., who grew up in a small town in Ohio and used to split the year between Key West and Provincetown, is short and stocky. The other girls call her "fat girl" onstage. One of them commented that Timothy always looks so much thinner dressed in men's clothes, and in fact he is an attractive man. He has a redhead's complexion with short curly bleached-blond hair. He wears T-shirts that say I'M NOT AN ALCOHOLIC, I'M A DRUNK or BETTY FORD CLINIC ALUMNAE. In drag R.V. looks like a drag queen playing Bette Midler, for Bette is her favorite character and she did, in fact, learn how to do Bette from watching another drag queen rather than Bette herself.

Margo is a sixty-something New Yorker with a deep voice. David is painfully thin, having struggled with anorexia after a fat boyhood, and he is balding on top with graying short hair around the sides. He looks older in drag than out. He is, in fact, not in good health, having suffered a recurrence of bladder cancer and a heart attack during the latest surgery, for which he had to be airlifted out of Key West as Hurricane Georges hit. He's a local celebrity both as Margo, "the oldest living drag queen in captivity," and as David, a columnist for the local gay newspaper *Celebrate!* He arrives at the bar on an adult tricycle, the handlebars strung with beads.

Scabby, from Providence, Rhode Island, has no intention of looking beautiful, although as Matthew he is a handsome man. He is very thin, has large expressive eyes, a raspy smoker's voice, and a big evil-sounding laugh. He puts together outlandish costumes and crazy headdresses that he Super-glues onto his shaved head. One of the other queens says he is afraid of pretty-girl drag, but that twice when others put him in it, he looked as stunning as Milla. Over time he has looked prettier and prettier in drag, which he blames on pressure from the other girls.

Gugi took the place of Inga, although they couldn't be more different in most ways. Inga, the "Swedish bombshell," is tall, blond, big, soft, and adorable, with deep dimples. She was the youngest of the troupe at the 801, just twenty-five. Out of drag as Roger, he favors long baggy shorts and T-shirts, wearing his hair in a thin ponytail. In drag, it's hard to believe that Roger is inside that voluptuous body. Inga is curvaceous and icy, prone to giving audience members the finger. Gugi was an occasional performer who took over Inga's show when she moved to the new club. Gugi is Puerto Rican, from Chicago, and as Rov he's stunning, with black curly hair, beautiful dark eyes, and an unbelievably sweet face. He's pretty shy, while Gugi is aggressive and outgoing. Because she's short, Gugi really looks like a woman. She moves and dances seductively. She's gorgeous, too, but the first time we saw her out of drag, we couldn't stop looking, because it was impossible to see Gugi in Rov. When a regular visitor, a businessman from Denver, invited and escorted her to the Imperial Court of the Rocky Mountain Empire (a western drag extravaganza that draws men from all over the country), Gugi tells us that the Empress was so impressed with her that she had her close the out-of-towners show, even though she didn't have a "royal title."[1] Gugi followed Inga to Diva's, but both were central to the lineup during the time period on which we concentrate.

But back to the 801: So the guys come into the dressing room, take off their shirts, and begin the transformation. It's a lot of work. One gay male audience member who occasionally dresses in drag expressed appreciation for the effort, since he refuses to tuck and shave anywhere that doesn't show. "It's just too, too much." His lover, who did drag once, commented that it took him four hours to shave his legs. Shaving does come first. Some of the girls shave all over their bodies, some their faces, chests, legs, and arms, some just their faces. Kylie shaves his entire body and once had electrolysis on his face, but, he says, "it feels like you light a match, blow it out, and then put it to your skin. . . . It was just too painful." He's interested, however, to hear about Verta's Epilady, which pulls the hairs out and doesn't leave stubble. Scabby paints on warpaint-like eyes, wide swaths of color up over his forehead and into his temples, but the rest work to make their faces look like women's. They powder their faces, necks, and chests, using a thick base to hide their beards. Dermablend, a kind of makeup designed to hide scars, covers blemishes and wrinkles as well as beards. Some of them use Erace, a cover stick. They deftly (some more deftly than others) use blush and powder to create cheekbones and hollows and other desirable features. Some of them shave or partially shave their eyebrows and draw on new ones. Even with eyebrows, they can create new higher ones and use color and powder to hide the real Mc-Coy. Eyeliner, eye shadow, mascara, false eyelashes, lip liner, and lipstick are painstakingly applied, and beautiful women's faces begin to appear. When they are finished, some of them spray their faces with aerosol hairspray to fix the makeup. It's hot in Key West, and they work hard, so they are inclined to sweat a lot. The air in the room is thick with cigarette smoke, powder, and hairspray. Early on we got lectures about kissing or touching them when they are made up. Inga taught us to air-kiss them, and Milla instructed us that it was not proper to touch a drag queen in makeup above the shoulders.

The girls learned to do their makeup in different ways. Milla, as a boy of eleven or twelve, shut himself in the bathroom and used his mother's or sister's makeup to try to copy photographs of models from *Vogue* "or Boy George himself or pictures of anybody androgynous." He would "lay the pictures down on top of my sink and then I would look, then I would follow until I got it right. I would spend hours, literally hours back then, just perfecting. . . . If I made a mistake, I would wipe it off and I'd start over again and over again and over again." Kylie, too, tried to re-create the effects he found in photos he admired. Scabby learned from the film *The Adventures of Priscilla, Queen of the Desert,* about Australian drag queens. He watched it time after time and hit the pause button and thought, "Ooh, I can do that." Over the years, Dean (Milla) says, he's had to change his approach. Now in his thirties, he needs to wear thicker makeup because his beard is heavier. He used to use the same water-based makeup that Sushi, who barely needs any, favors. "I had to go back to theater makeup and learn how to contour and make it look soft onstage." He is critical of the results of some of the other girls' efforts: "They don't know the art of makeup."

As Dean's comments suggest, experience with the theater is another

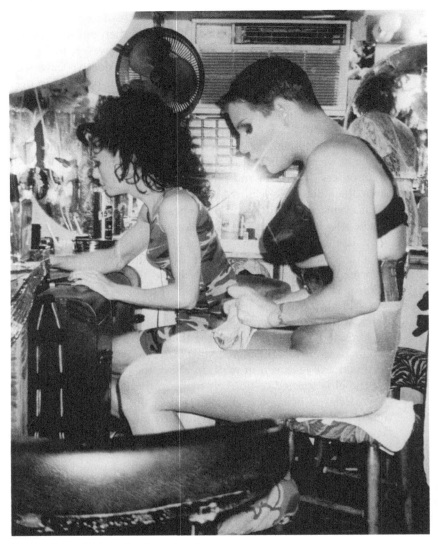

Getting dressed (photo by the authors)

important way that the drag queens learned to do makeup. Almost all of them had been involved in theater from an early age. Inga, R.V., and Scabby had different kinds of professional theater experience—Inga in Sweden, R.V. at Disney World, Scabby with an avant-garde "cyber-sex fetish" troupe—and so learned theatrical makeup and adopted the technique for drag.

Several also worked in the beauty industry. Dean was a hairdresser who got so sick of clients at Van Michael's, the prestigious Atlanta salon where he worked, that he became a dog groomer, "because I was going to put a knife in my client's back, my next client who sat in my chair. I couldn't handle it anymore; it was just too much." Kevin Truehart, who as Lady Victoria performed with the troupe for a time, went to hairdressing school right after high school and began doing the wigs for drag queens at the salon where he worked. One day the queens challenged him to do drag himself, and he was such a success that he eventually rated a one-woman show in Provincetown. When he was first starting out, he says he realized that "this is like everything I learned in hairdressing, everything that I had learned in makeup, and working with women, learning, studying women all those years of doing their hair—it was like everything I had learned all of a sudden had compiled for this one thing. . . . So I had fallen into my destiny."

But he, like others of the girls, also learned a lot from other drag queens. One queen, he explains, "gave me the secret of drag. How to get that eye to make it look right, like an eye, the glamour eye." She painted one side of his face and told him to do the other. "So once I learned how to get there, I developed it. You know, of course, blending, getting the softness and the sweetness, and just really getting the feminine look." While performing in Key West, Kevin continued to do hair, nails, and makeup professionally. Both he and Roger (Inga) sometimes still make up other drag queens for pay, Kevin at Headlines, the salon where he works, and Roger for Mama, a Brazilian drag queen in her early fifties who is part of the 801 family but doesn't perform. Mama pays Roger $20 for a half hour's work. Mama complains: "In the United States, you have to have a very high degree to make twenty bucks in half an hour. Maybe New York, but not in the South. I complain, but she says she makes me twenty years younger. I say 'so?' But it's OK." Roger is, in fact, very good at what he does.

Toward the end of our research, Sushi announced that we could never really understand drag unless we let them dress us as men dressing as women. He wanted us to perform a number but we begged off, offering instead to go out on the street with them as they "hook" for potential audience members and help them do whatever they needed during the show. He gave us instructions: "Come clean-shaven, with eyelashes, panty hose, and black undergarments." We did. (Well, sort of. When we showed a group photograph from that night, someone commented, "The dykes are the ones with the underarm hair, right?") It was amazing what he was able to do with our faces. He took about half an hour to make up each one of us, using foundation and powder to contour our faces. He made our features look bigger so that we would pass as men. With the heavy foundation, exaggerated eyes, and enlarged glittery lips, we actually fooled people into thinking we were drag queens. Sushi loaned us dresses and wigs: Verta, a green, slinky, crushed-velvet dress over a black bustier, with a frosted wig in a shag style that she actually used to wear when she was a majorette; Leila, a black mesh one-shoulder dress with feathers around the neckline, a black boa attached to one wrist, and a blond shoulder-length Marilyn Monroe–style wig. Before even donning her wig, Verta went out of the dressing room with her hair slicked back, in shorts and a silk tank top, and although she is short even for a woman, no one would believe that she wasn't a man wearing makeup. She had to show a breast to convince someone. It was a lesson, if we needed one, in the power of makeup. It also said something about breasts as the defining feature of women.

While the girls put on their faces, they concentrate, relax, drink, and gossip mercilessly, all at the same time. Gugi says she goes in early: "Just so I can sit around and talk." Roger likes "to have a good time, maybe sit down, have a drink before." They talk "about everything and anything." They are alternately silly, catty, bitchy, supportive. They talk about sex; they tease each other; they discuss their makeup and their performances. Sushi says he doesn't really talk to the girls, that he likes to be left alone until he gets out there, and he is quieter than the others. Sometimes they all talk at once:

> Milla: R.V.! Those pieces of junk you bring home every night.
> R.V. I don't bring . . .
> [Everyone laughs.]
> Milla: I sat there today and figured out how many people I've brought to my room. You know how many? Two!
> Gugi: I'm sorry.

A little later:

> Kylie: I keep thinking of words to call R.V., because she takes offense at me calling her fat [they all laugh], so I started using "portly." Then one night I was trying to go to bed, but I was high, and I kept thinking "porkly" would be a great word for her.

Scabola laughs her big wicked laugh. Gugi says something.

> Sushi: Shut your mouth, Puerto Rican slut.

Scabby laughs again. They move on to other subjects, then:

> Milla: This black man, when I was walking through Bahama Village?
> Scabby: What was he trying to—

Jinxie and Blackée (photo by Jim Smith)

Milla: . . . and I'm walking up to him, and he says [Milla takes on a low masculine voice], "When can I suck your dick?" And I look down and he's got a cross and a Bible in his hand! And I thought, this is too much for my gaydar.
Scabby: Whoo!
[Everyone laughs.]
Milla: I just looked at him, and I was like . . .

Scabby: So she scored a baggy off of him.

Milla: . . . at least drop the Bible!

Kylie: They say the devil will come to you disguised as an angel, darling.

Milla: Well, that was no angel, that was a black man in Bahama Village.

[Everyone laughs again.]

Milla: I was horrified.

Kylie: Suck your dick! [She laughs.] Are you sure you heard it right?

Milla: I heard it, you know why, 'cause when we stand on the street, he's come by many a time.

Scabby: A couple of times.

Sushi: He's not the guy in the big red convertible Cadillac?

Such chatter continues:

Sushi: I had some guy last night, when I was walking home finally, I had some guy, he was like across the street and he came over, you know, and I was out of drag, you know, and he was like . . .

Kylie: You look like a girl sometimes out of drag too.

Sushi: And he came up to me and he looks at me and "Ooh," and he turns around and walks away. [He laughs.]

Kylie: It's just like the guy who came up to me, and he said, "How beautiful!" And then he goes, "You've got a great body!" [He laughs, too.]

Sushi: Then what does it all mean?

Kylie: It means that he was going to say that I was beautiful and then he got a good look at me.

The talk isn't all about sex. They discuss a booking that Milla arranged for three of them to perform at a furniture show in North Carolina, where they were well paid for very little work. Milla insists she is good at such things; some of the others give her a hard time.

Milla: Oh shut up, you dumb whore. What do you do except sit around and complain about what everyone else does?

Kylie: You mean you can't take criticism?

Milla: I can take any fucking criticism, I just can't take your fucking—

Kylie: Always defensive, always defensive.

Milla: You're telling me that I'm defensive?

Gugi: Yeah.

Milla: [In a small cheerful voice] Yeah, OK, I am.

But they inevitably return to sex. Milla couldn't take the living situation at her house one night:

Kylie: And she ends up having to [she laughs] . . . walking down the street barefoot, with a face of makeup on, in the middle of the night, to my house, to escape, and ends up hooking herself out for a place to sleep.

[Scabby laughs.]

Milla: I had sex—

Kylie: You had sex with someone for a place to sleep!

Milla: I felt like I had to, I mean, I couldn't just sleep there!

Sushi: She was escaping her emotions.

Milla: Escaping?

Kylie: And she fucked him! And Milla is not a top, so when she starts becoming a top, you know something's wrong!

[There's a pause.]

Kylie: It all makes for good fun, girl, I'm telling you.

The talk goes on for a while.

Sushi: Milla was really a prude when I first met her.

Kylie: No, she wasn't.

Milla: Yes I was; I still am.

Kylie: She was?!

Sushi: She was sexually active, but she was—

[Everyone talks at once.]

Sushi: You were a what? A prostitute! [In mock horror] Oh!

Kylie: The story she told me, she's full of shit, girl.

Sushi: She never did it in drag. She never prostituted herself in drag. . . . She had a customer who wanted to pluck every pubic hair out of her with his teeth. Now that is not a prude, OK?

[Everyone laughs.]

Milla: Actually, that was my first.

Kylie: You got two hundred dollars for it, though.

Leila's supposed to be quiet, but she can't resist. "You did?"

Milla: Yeah, I did. But that was my first time ever—

Leila: But I mean, did he pluck all your pubic hair—

Milla: Yeah, I was like—

Kylie: The way she described it was so hilarious. I just, how did
   you put it, "Girl, I just lay there, I couldn't bear it, I was just
   like, would you just do it, get it over with."
[They all laugh.]

After finishing the makeup, they begin to get dressed. This is an
elaborate procedure, involving many layers of undergarments that,
piece by piece, create the illusion that they have breasts and women's
waists and hips. First they (or most of them—Scabby doesn't) tuck
their penises and testicles between their legs, using a gaff, or several,
to make sure everything stays out of sight. Gugi has trouble tucking
with his long acrylic fingernails:

Sushi: Girl, you need scissors?
Gugi: These fucking nails, I can't get it fucking tucked.
Sushi: You're going to cut your nails 'cause you can't tuck your
   cock?
Scabby: Well, hello!
[They all laugh.]
Kylie: Sushi'll do it for you. Or I'm sure Scabola would do if for
   you; I'm sure she'd like to help. Let's get R.V.! Now that's the
   one I know you'd like to touch your dick.
Gugi: Oh yeah, big time.
Kylie: [calling] R.V.?!
Gugi: If I want a pink dick, or . . .
Kylie: [to R.V.] She needs you to help her tuck.
Gugi: . . . scabies or . . .
[They laugh again.]

After the gaffs they put on panty hose, sometimes several layers of
thick ones. Then even those who don't shave their legs have no visible
hair. Dean (Milla) stopped shaving his legs, although he had earlier
told us that he felt dirty if he didn't. Matthew (Scabby) talked him into
it, and, perhaps because he was in a new relationship, he started to
feel sexy with hair on his legs. Over the panty hose go corsets and waist
cinchers; some lace more tightly than others. Sushi and Scabby don't
wear corsets. They certainly don't need them, but Margo, who doesn't
need one either, wears one. Milla's corset is old and ratty and held
together with duct tape. She also ties a string around her waist, very
tightly. R.V., who is not svelte, doesn't believe "in putting my liver
somewhere else where it should be and my stomach . . . They should
stay where they're at." Although he wears a waist cincher, he describes

himself as a "truck driver in drag." He doesn't like tucking, wearing the tits, or sweating so much.

They all, of course, wear bras. Milla wears two, both very tight, which gives her an impressive cleavage, further enhanced with powder and blush. Nikki, an occasional performer, uses duct tape across her chest to make cleavage. They all use something different for breasts: water balloons (the tied end makes an amazingly realistic nipple), half a Nerf football, lentil beans in a pair of nylons, foam or silicone prostheses. Inga has a professional corset with breasts built in.

All of this tucking and squeezing makes rolls of flesh appear here and there over the top of a corset or under a waist cincher, even when they are very thin, so what is most amazing is how they make that all smooth out. Milla wears a corset, panty hose over the corset, and a waist cincher on top of the panty hose "to help soften." Gugi pulls a pair of panty hose over her corset, tucks them into the top just under her bra, draws a navel on the panty hose, and can wear a dress with a see-through middle looking as if it is skin and her real navel that we see through the black mesh. When you hug Milla, you can feel the corset and a small roll of flesh just under her bras, but looking at her onstage, you'd never know that she didn't really have that hourglass figure. "I'm like almost insane about the idea of creating that figure and having all the form. And I don't like to see little marks when I put on a dress. When I put on a dress, I don't like to see lines, and my tits and my cleavage, it's all so important." Gugi proclaims this part of the process "the art of illusion."

Then they put on their dresses, which hang on a long rod behind the stage. Sushi makes most of them and is known all over town as a talented seamstress (the word he uses to describe himself). He once even worked for local designer Victoria Lesser, although he lasted only three days because he prefers creating costumes to sewing perfect seams. He, with help from Kylie and Milla, created all of the elaborate costumes for the play *When Pigs Fly*, which came to town during the 1999 season. They do buy some things, especially accessories (boas are a big item, of course). There's a drag queen store in Key West, called Sweet Mischief, but Kylie complains that it is overpriced. Because he is relatively small and wears a size ten women's shoe and size eight or ten dress, he can go to regular stores to buy things. Sushi is small, too, and Margo is, according to Kylie, "hardly anything, just a bag of bones." R.V. wears drag queen hand-me-downs, buying only shoes. Gugi says women and other drag queens give him things. A man who picks through the trash stops by regularly and sells them items, sometimes for drag and sometimes for their own personal wardrobes. As Dean says, "We know how to make something out of nothing. . . . You know, we'll go right up to a garbage can and pull something out of the fucking trash."

The shoes they wear have, of course, ridiculously high heels in most cases, although Margo is inclined to wear pretty moderate ones. After Sushi decided we had to get into drag, he brought out a pair of heels for Leila to try at a drag queen meeting. They must have had five-inch heels. She put them on and tried to walk. "Come on, darling, walk," says Sushi. Then he shouts, "*Oh no*, don't walk on the heels, girl! Walk on your toes! Walk like this! Walk on your toes!" Everyone else starts calling out advice. Sushi explains, patiently: "The only time you put weight on your heels is when you stand, to balance. Walk like this." Margo offers: "Like toe dancing." Leila tries, holding on to the back of the bar stools for support. Gugi starts to imitate her wobbly stride and calls out, "Stop walking like that!" "How do you do it?" asks Leila. "Move your hips! Small steps, girl!" Kylie can't believe they have to teach us how to walk in heels. "You don't have any high heels? [Incredulously] Not even at home? You wear Doc Martens?!"

Sushi finally realized that Leila would never get the hang of it in such high heels, so she found a pair of open-toed lower ones, and those worked. Verta's feet are too small for drag queen shoes, so she had to borrow a pair from Kimberly, a regular at the bar, about whom more later. Hers were gold lamé, pointy-toed, and a bit too small, and they fell apart by the end of the evening. When Verta was first getting dressed, Mama advised her not to put the heels on until the absolute last minute. "Save yourself, honey. It'll be a long night in those shoes." It was a relief to know that someone else thought they were uncomfortable, since they can all not only walk but dance with complete ease in shoes we can't even stand in for a minute.

Getting dressed can be simple or elaborate. Sushi might just slip into a long velvet dress, while Scabby can take a long time getting into a dominatrix outfit, latex with a leather boned corset. She spends a lot less time on makeup than the others but pays a great deal of attention to detail, getting the feathery edge of a *Priscilla, Queen of the Desert* outfit just right. Although she claims to be able to go from shaving to ready in fifteen minutes, it's a little hard to believe. Margo describes her as taking a long time to get dressed and occasionally becoming hysterical about having to go out and talk on the microphone when she's in the middle of fixing her costume.

Last of all they put on their wigs, which Milla takes responsibility for washing and styling. Sushi sometimes wears her own beautiful long hair, and sometimes just adds an abundant black fall. Kylie is always blond, Margo always white-haired, but the rest of them switch around colors and styles. Scabby often does not wear hair, substituting a pony-tail stuck on her shaved head, a headdress made of Slinkys, a molded yellow plastic wig, or other equally outlandish creations.

The whole process of getting dressed takes anywhere from about half an hour (Scabby) to two hours (Lady V). Matthew says that Dean "used to start painting the face at one o'clock in the afternoon" when he didn't have to be ready until eleven. Roger says he can do it in forty-two minutes, so you know he's timed himself! They primp and stare in the mirror and worry about how they look. "Everything has to be perfect," says Milla. "Not one person can tell me that I don't look right. That one person tells me that I don't look right, I'm going to fall apart."

David puts the whole process in perspective in his column in *Celebrate!*, Key West's gay and lesbian weekly paper:

> You must give them credit. They take parts of their body and push them where they were never meant to be pushed. They add protrusions to other areas that were never meant to protrude on males, and wear layers of makeup under stage lights in addition to girdles, bras and as many as three pair of pantyhose. They parade around in those shoes that real women don't even wear anymore, and do it all with a smile. It ain't easy being pretty![2]

Finally they are all dressed. Sometimes there's a last-minute addition: Sushi: "Put on the lashes and let's get."

It's an elaborate process that takes a lot of creativity and practice. And it isn't comfortable being tucked and squeezed and slathered with makeup. So why do they do it? How did they get to this point?

THREE

BECOMING DRAG QUEENS

It's hard, watching the girls get dressed, to imagine how they learned so much about how to look like women. Some of them started early, and their stories, like so much else about them, are filled with ambivalence, with both joy and pain. We first heard some of their stories when Dean (Milla) and Matthew (Scabby) came to dinner. Dean offered, "I'll start, I guess," and Matthew encouraged him: "Go ahead, girl." Dean explains:

> OK, let's see, growing up as a child, I was, it's not that I started out being effeminate, I was just always very comfortable with the female side and, I don't want to say that I was a sissy, but I was always, I *loved* women, I loved the female figure, I loved the female body, I always played with Barbies, I wanted to make everybody pretty, I used to do my mom's hair and, you know, my sister and I, which I learned later in life, my sister had all these disgruntled feelings about my relationship with my mother and how, she'd sit there and, you know, "You used to do Mom's hair and she'd *never* let me do her hair," and I'd say to her, " 'Cause you couldn't do it."

Dean goes on to say that he loved beauty, found women to be beautiful, although on a sexual level he thought men lovely. Matthew interrupts: "Whore," and Dean comes back quickly with "Slut, trash." But he then goes on quite seriously to explain that it was that women were allowed to be creative with their bodies, and that women's bodies are gorgeous, that he loves the shapes "as much as I love the shape of a man, honey." Referring to his current boyfriend, who has come along, he says, "when I see his body, I just want to, I, it's like Jell-O."

Getting to the question of how he came to dress in drag, Dean says that he's thought hard about why, that he was just always very comfortable with it, and "it's the same story that everybody tells you." (Matthew at another time says, "It seems like every fag I've ever met" has dressed in his mother's clothes as a kid, and in fact almost all of the 801 Girls, even if they didn't get into drag until late, acknowledge having done this.) "Growing up, Mom and Dad would leave the house for a second, and I just had that hour to get in her drawer and put on her panty hose and put her shoes on."

Matthew interjects: "Oh, girl, I used to do the same thing!" He tells how his parents used to go out on Friday and Saturday nights to a cocktail lounge, and he and his older sister had responsibility for their younger siblings. "So that was the perfect opportunity for me [he giggles] to go raid my mother's closet." He had a favorite dress—"Well, it really wasn't a dress, it was a negligee. It was lime green, because you know I like those Technicolors, with ostrich feathers around the collar and around the sleeves, full length to the ground, and she even had the little slippers with the ostrich feather plumes." He added a fall and went down to the local pharmacy to buy cigarettes.

Dean picks up. He was about seven or eight, living in St. Petersburg, Florida, when he began wearing his mother's clothes. His favorite was a polyester maxi dress with cutout shoulders, yellow, black, and white swirls. He'd add her wiglet, sit on the patio, smoke cigarettes, drink his father's bourbon, walk up and down the sidewalk, "thinking I was grand." But then "I'd see them, I could *feel* them almost coming back down the road and into the driveway. And I'd [he screams] rip off the panty hose, throw the shoes back in, and I'd put runs in the stockings and stuff them back in her drawer."

We get back to Matthew, who's at the pharmacy in his small Massachusetts town trying to buy cigarettes, pretending to be his mother. Pete, the pharmacist, would say, "Oh, Matthew, what are you doing here," and he'd call the police, who would drive him back home. Matthew claims in a newspaper interview that he successfully passed as his mother when his brother was caught shoplifting at a local store.[1]

Gugi, too, admits to liking to dress in his mother's clothes, although he didn't do it as regularly as Dean and Matthew. "I would like to wear dresses. I would put dresses on." Since he had said he basically just locked himself in his room most of the time he was growing up, we asked if he did it in front of anyone. "One time. I was about seven or eight. I stayed over at my stepsister's mom's house with them. And her mother went out somewhere. Actually we'd do these little skits with my two stepsisters and their half-brother and -sister. . . . We would do commercials, TV shows, talk shows and record it on tape. . . . So one night, they had tucked me up in a dress and I walked down the street in a dress. No one knew the difference." Asked what he liked about it, he says, "I'm not quite sure. I never asked myself that question. I don't know, I guess I felt comfortable. That's what I wanted to be."

For Dean, dressing in women's clothes was about hiding from an unhappy childhood and distancing himself from being a man like his father. His father spent thirty years in the navy and then, when it was time to retire, married an Italian woman. When Dean was growing up, his father was drinking and abusive. "I never wanted to be like my father. . . . And I think that's what almost pushed me to being more effeminate. . . . This man I saw early on as something that I didn't like, all of the idea of what a man was supposed to be about was nothing that I wanted to be." Matthew chimes in, "I agree with exactly what you're saying." Sounding like a textbook on what makes boys gay, he adds that his father was so distant, that he just worried about what the neighbors would think. Matthew sounds pretty hostile, and Dean says, quietly, "Umm, I think your father's probably a good man, girl, from what you've told me." Matthew agrees that he's a good man but complains that he never gave him the time of day. Like Dean, Matthew was very close to his mother, who had five children and two heart attacks before she was thirty-five. He describes his favorite photograph of her—"a big ol' fat blob sitting in a lawn chair, big glasses, and she's got a fly right on her knee"—and it could be a description of one of Scabby's characters.

Not wanting to be like his father and needing to hide from the fat, unhappy sissy self he was, Dean sought to create a life, a place where he was comfortable. "I was just like, from day one, everybody knew, I was basically gay. I was a sissy. . . . So it intrigued some; it [pause] horrified others. . . . And the fatter I got especially and the more uncomfortable I got with my home life and my body, the more I started to hide it and become a character."

Because it was the beginning of the 1980s, with the "English invasion" and Boy George, Dean says, "I found a place where I could be, I could hide, I could mask myself behind wacky makeup, crazy hair colors, the wildest outfits, and feel strong, feel good. Overpowering." So he hid behind his characters. He says there was a time in his life he wanted to be black, to be German, to be a girl, and he wonders why he was such an unhappy person that he always wanted to be something else. The first time he ever did drag professionally was because he was ending a relationship. "I'm in pain, so I'm creating something. I'm going to become a drag queen. So there's Milla. What a great way to get over all this shit." The first time he dressed in drag in Key West, "people gave me love, I got all the attention, all the things I never got from a man."

All of their stories include some kind of effeminacy as a boy. Dean describes playing with Barbie dolls, taking the role of Princess Leia in *Star Wars* games. Even before he did drag professionally, he had "a face full of makeup with the long hair" and was "so soft and pretty" he looked like a "butch lesbian" when he married a woman for immigration purposes. Matthew, too, always wanted the female roles as a child. David (Margo) says he never liked doing the things boys were supposed to do. He says he was a "fat, unpopular kid," and he remembers tossing away the baseball glove his father gave him. His mother died when he was sixteen, and he then took over the care of the house and his womanizing father.[2] Timothy (R.V.), like Dean, played with Barbie dolls—his sister's—and baked in her Easy Bake oven as well. He says his mother "knew when I was a kid what I was going to be." Matthew's parents bought him G.I. Joe dolls, and he remembers being upset because his sister's Ken doll "had a bigger bulge than G.I. Joe." Doing exactly what one can imagine Scabby the drag queen doing as a child, he bit the tip off a Hot Tamale candy and stuck it on his G.I. Joe to "give him a big old boner." Jim Gilleran—the owner of the 801 and, according to David, "the gayest straight man I've ever met"—says that expressing themselves in drag is a way for these (he hesitates slightly) men to show an effeminate side, a "way for their personalities to evolve."

For all of the drag queens, doing drag is intimately connected with having sex with men. They all identify as gay, and most of them never felt any other way. David (Margo) remembers that when he was seven, a female cousin brought home her boyfriend, and David took one look at him and fell in love. Like David, Gugi says, "I've always known I was gay. I always knew I was attracted to men; I just hated the word 'gay.'"

Roger (Inga) says directly that he started to do drag because of "coming out being gay." Although he knew he was gay from the time he was fifteen or sixteen, he didn't deal with it until he was twenty-one, and it was a fag-hag girlfriend who introduced him to the gay world and talked him into doing drag.[3] It was striking how many of them answered the question of how they began to dress in drag by talking about first having sex with other males. Dean starts to tell about a painful relationship he had with the director of the children's theater group he was in from when he was eleven to fourteen, then goes back to explain: "I always knew what I liked, which was I knew I liked boys." The neighborhood boys all came to him for sex. "They still come to me; I'm thirty years old and the neighborhood boys still come to me," he says. The theater group director was eighteen and Dean felt so special that he was loved, and he craved the sex, but then he found out that his lover was sleeping with everyone he could get his hands on, male and female. He relates this to creating Milla, striving "to be that exceptional, because at one time I thought I was and then found out I wasn't."

Matthew says he started having sex with other boys in kindergarten. He tells about walking along at summer camp with the son of his parents' best friend when he was twelve or thirteen and starting to lick his ear. He got picked on constantly in school because he never hid from anyone. When we ask him how he started to do drag, he says, "I've always been gay, always been attracted to men. I used to do all the boys in the neighborhood."

Sushi describes himself as not a very sexual person until about the time he met Kylie in high school and began to dress up. He had his first sexual experience with a presumably straight football player who gave him a ride home after a school dance. Kylie, on the other hand, says he knew he was gay in the second grade. Yet he didn't have sex with a man until he was nineteen or twenty; he was molested earlier, but, as he explains, "I don't consider that sex." He remembers distinctly riding his bicycle down a particular street and thinking about twins, a boy and girl, who were his friends, and realizing that the girl had a crush on him but that he liked the boy better. He knew that meant something, but he was afraid for years to try to meet a man who was also interested in sex.

Although trying on their mothers' clothes, being effeminate, and having sex with other boys are part of their stories, most of the girls describe doing drag as coming much later than early experiments with cross-dressing. Even Matthew, who loved to dress in his mother's clothes, only identifies as getting into drag in his thirties. But most of them transitioned into drag from being "club kids," wearing wild clothes for fun and to get attention. Matthew would wear women's clothes and a wig and run around the streets, "but I never actually *did* drag." For many of them, the media and popular culture had an enormous impact. Dean remembers the inspiration of going to see the *Rocky Horror Picture Show* at fourteen. Boy George and the gender-bending style of the 1980s, as Dean has already suggested, come up often. At sixteen, Dean started to dress as a woman, and this he describes as drag. "I went from being very progressive punkesque into being more of the gay life . . . taking that freaky look, that '80s punk freaky thing into more of an effeminate pretty thing." For Matthew, being a club kid turned into drag when he saw *Priscilla* and added makeup to his repertoire for the first time. He was hooked. "Whoo-whee, look at these girls, they are *horrifying*," he thought, "and I was like, if they can do it, why can't I?"

Kylie, too, begins with Boy George. "We started dressing like Boy George. . . . You know, when you're in high school, the musicians you idolize, some musicians you used to dress like and like had posters of, and that's how it was for me with Culture Club and also with Sushi." Kylie says it wasn't really drag, it was offbeat, but he would make the clothes, and "suddenly I remember one time I was making a dress. And it just dawned on me, 'This is a dress, this is like completely all the way into dressing like a woman.'" To dress like Boy George was one thing, but to wear a dress to a club was something else. He did it, he says, because "I wanted attention. I wanted love, really." Roger, echoing Kylie, talks about dressing in drag to get attention. "When I was younger, I always had a need to get all the attention, so I was dressing in freaky clothes during the daytime, hats, capes, but never in drag." But then he realized that performing in drag, "with all this makeup and this fake costume . . . I got attention this way." A young Latino man who lives in Key West sees this need in the girls: "I think a lot of it is this extravagance that's within their personality that's allowed to be expressed and want and possibly need for attention."

Gary (Sushi) first got into drag when he, as an honor student, musician, Eagle Scout, met Kevin (Kylie) in high school in a small town in Oregon. Gary's father, an American soldier stationed in Japan, met and married a Japanese woman who disgraced her family by running off with a foreigner when she was betrothed to another man. Gary spent his first years in Japan and Thailand and was fluent in both languages when he was very young. When he was fourteen, his father suddenly died of a heart attack. It was very traumatic: "I can't shut my eyes in the shower. Because that's when he died, when I was in the shower washing my hair and I was closing my eyes, you know, the shampoo. And I heard my mom and my brother screaming and yelling."

Perhaps in reaction to the loss of his father, the Eagle Scout went wild. "Kylie came into my life and we just went crazy," he says. Following Boy George, they began ratting their hair, wearing eyeliner, and doing crazy things. They dressed up to "have fun" and "be this other person." By his senior year, Gary was a "flaming queen," wearing full makeup and platform shoes. He was causing such a disturbance that his mother talked the school officials into letting him graduate early. "The more people hated me for it, the more I wanted to do it." His mother put him on a plane and sent him to Tokyo to live with his uncle. Much later he found out that his mother's family, which had totally disowned her, wanted to buy him or one of his brothers to continue the bloodline.

Living in Japan was supposed to straighten him out, but his uncle was an alcoholic, and Gary experienced total freedom. Working in his uncle's restaurant, he started drinking and going to gay bars. He met his first transsexuals—"drag queens with teeny titties"—and "discovered myself. That's when I knew I was gay." He started to do drag shows after he came back to the States and got a job at a cannery in his hometown. He saved his money, moved to Portland, the big city, and began dealing drugs and doing drag. He lived in a house with a group of other queens (and a house "mother") and learned a lot about what he does now. In the meantime, Kevin had moved to Los Angeles with his parents and become "normal," as Gary puts it, working in a grocery store. "The only time he did drag was when I went down there." Gary moved to L.A. to be near Kevin and ended up living on the streets and selling sex in drag. Eventually he moved back to Portland and began working as a drag queen cocktail waitress.

Kevin's (Kylie's) parents put up with his dress in high school because his brothers and sister had been more trouble, getting into drugs. He didn't do drugs or drink then, although Gary did. After Gary left for Japan and Kevin's family moved back to Los Angeles, Kevin started dressing like a woman, because the only people he could relate to, now that Gary was gone, were drag queens. "You know, birds of a feather . . ." But Kevin stopped doing drag for a long time, until a friend who was feeling neurotic about his looks decided that he would feel and look better if he went out in drag. Kevin thought this was crazy, but he went along and dressed in drag to keep him company, and "I thought, god, this is fun, I forgot how it was." Although he never performed professionally until he came to Key West, he did make an "art movie" and model in drag for a series of humorous gay greeting cards in Los Angeles.

So despite the different stories, certain common themes emerge in the making of a drag queen. Effeminacy, gay sexuality, and a love for wild dressing all play an important role. The cultural styles of the 1980s—like the foppish dress of earlier centuries—made room for flamboyance that could easily edge into true drag. Dressing in drag allows one to hide, attracts attention, and expresses an in-your-face attitude. Those contradictions—hiding while flaunting—mirror the pain of being ridiculed as girly or faggy or fat joined to the joy of expressing oneself and satisfying sexual desire. But what does it really mean to be a drag queen?

FOUR

BEING A DRAG QUEEN

First things first: not all men who dress as women are drag queens. The day after we first went to a regular Monday afternoon drag queen meeting, we went to observe a planning session at the pool of the place where Margo was house-sitting. David (Margo), Sushi, and Roger (Inga) began to make distinctions among different kinds of men who dress in women's clothing, but they said nothing about straight cross-dressers who do it for the erotic (heterosexual) thrill. When we talked to R.V., he identified cross-dressers or transvestites as straight and drag queens as gay. So the first distinction is on the basis of sexual identity.[1]

Then there are categories based on physical transformations of different degrees. Titty queens get breasts through either hormones or implants but keep their penises. Sushi describes them as "in-betweens." Transsexuals have sex-reassignment surgery. In contrast to these, drag queens keep their male bodies (although as we have already seen some facial transformation is acceptable). David tells of first reading about Christine Jorgensen's famous transformation from a man to a woman.[2] David was at the time a young gay teenager in New York, and it scared him. "I did not want to be a woman, and here it is in the paper that this may be what I have to do." It scared a lot of gay men, he says. "Is this what you're supposed to want? And I knew I didn't want this. I mean, I would like to have the mink coat, but I don't want to be a woman." Kylie says he wouldn't mind having tits just for the show, "Like if I could take a pill to have them . . . and then take another pill to make them go away. I would do that. . . . They would be good for the show." In one show Sushi asks the audience whether she should get tits. "You think I should get some big bazoongas, you know, like a size D? I'd have to sleep with them. These I can take off, as you've already noticed." R.V. says he likes his tits being machine washable.

So drag queens are gay men who dress as but don't want to be women or have women's bodies. The girls will occasionally announce in the show that "drag queen" means "dressed roughly as girls." Within the category of gay men who dress in women's clothing but keep all of their male bodies, there are further distinctions based on performance style. Female impersonators keep the illusion of being women. Kevin Truehart, who performed at 801 for a time as Lady Victoria or Lady V, identifies as a female impersonator, not a drag queen. He hates the term "drag" because "over the years, it's been made out to be something very trashy and tacky." His take echoes the distinction between "stage impersonators" and "street impersonators," the latter, like Sushi in his days on the streets in Los Angeles, young men who sell themselves on the streets and live a marginal life.[3] Lady V does celebrity impersonation: Barbra Streisand, Lucille Ball, Cher, and Liza Minnelli. "I started with Lady Victoria first and she spawned them all." If he did Lady Victoria full-time, he says, then he would be a drag queen. But there's no uniform understanding of such a distinction. A gay male dancer at one of the local clubs describes female impersonation as "just a job. It's getting up and singing Cher songs dressed up as Cher." Adding creativity to motivation to explain the difference, he says, "A drag queen is somebody who goes out, puts an outfit together, puts a routine together by themselves, their act, their dance and all that stuff, picks a song that they're gonna do it to, and comes out and does it. Not as Cher. Not as somebody." On the other end of the spectrum—if there even is one—from Lady V is Scabby, who mostly doesn't try to look like a woman at all. Lady V describes Scabola as a cross between a drag queen and a club kid, others describe her drag as "camp." Although the 801 Girls have different styles, they all identify as drag queens. "Did I tell you that I'm a drag queen?" Sushi asks the audience. "I'm a drag queen. I'm not a female impersonator; I know that I don't have a pussy yet. Yet. I don't have a pussy yet." Onstage another night Sushi explains, "A drag queen is somebody who knows he has a dick and two balls."

Being a drag queen requires having a drag name. When Sushi announced at a Monday meeting that he was going to put us in drag, they told us a trick for coming up with a drag name: take the name of your first pet for your given name and the name of the street where you lived, or, if that doesn't sound right, your mother's maiden name, for your family name. Voilá, Leila became "Jinxie Dogwood" and Verta, "Blackie (transformed in the course of the evening to 'Blackée') Warner." None of the girls use names made up in this way, although John "Ma" Evans, who has become an 801 Girl, concocted his first, "Joletta Bridgeway," which he still uses occasionally, with this method. The name "Ma," we should say, is not his drag name; local author June

Keith reports that as the middle child in a family of eleven, he baby-sat so often, his younger siblings started calling him "Ma."[4] When Ma first came to the 801, he used "Arlene Goldblatz," then he became "Ma-jongg" or "MaJon." Margo, originally "Margot," "just happened," says David. He dropped the "t" because he realized that everyone would mispronounce it. Sushi was once "Soy Sauce" and obviously plays on her Japanese heritage. Kevin couldn't think of a name, but a friend came up with "Kylie Jean Lucille" and he liked it. Gugi, too, got his name from a friend. He entered Miss Firecracker, the amateur drag queen contest in Key West on the Fourth of July, and his manager at the bar suggested "Gugi Gomez," a character played by Rita Moreno:

> I'm like, "'Gugi Gomez!' That doesn't roll off the tongue!" And he goes, "No, you have to see this movie, The Ritz. It's with Rita Moreno; she's launching to sing in a gay men's bathhouse. And so people think, the guys here think she's a drag queen." . . . And he goes, "OK, why don't you rent the movie, and if you don't like it, I'll pick out another one for you." So I saw the movie. She had this little number she did, "I Had a Dream" [he sings it]. Only in a thick Spanish ac-cent. . . . And then she's walking down the hallway—that's where I got the idea that this was going to be my name—this gay guy goes up to her and says, "You did a fabulous performance." She goes, "Thank you, thank you." "You look so real for a drag queen." She looked at him [now Gugi takes on an exaggerated Spanish accent], "I'm not a drag queen! Do you think I don't know what you boys do in that back room, hee-hee-hee-hoo-hoo-hoo, boys." After that, I said, "That's my name. That's it."

The first time Dean did drag in Key West, someone asked what her name was, and she came up with "Milla," thinking "measly muscles," because he didn't have any. Roger would never use "Inga" in Sweden, but it works here since she's billed as the "Swedish Bombshell." R.V. started as "Vivian Redbush," became "Vivian Redbush Beaumont," then "V.R. Beaumont." One night a drunken friend called him "R.V. Bush-mont," and the R.V. stuck, although the Bushmont didn't. When Mat-thew entered his first lip-synch contest, after being inspired by Priscilla, he chose the name "Enema Squirts." They refused to announce it, so he had to come up with something different at the spur of the moment. Obviously he tries hard to be repulsive and in-your-face. He had cut his head shaving and felt the scab, and he had to go to the bathroom because he was nervous and all done up in his leather corset, so "Sca-bola Feces" he became.

To a different extent for the different girls, the use of drag names symbolizes the creation of a separate personality. "Sushi is different than Gary," says Sushi. In fact, Gary says, Greg (his former partner of seven years) and Sushi did not get along. Even David, who became a drag queen late in life, describes David as "an entirely different person" from Margo, although "now they are coming together more and more." He says he's a Gemini so there are two sides, but he's always been shy and introverted. "Since doing the drag, a lot of Margo has taken over. . . . I am far more verbal and outgoing as David than I ever was before." Timothy, too, is shy and describes himself as introverted. "I can't even go order a slice of pizza." Given his stage presence, we thought he would talk our ears off when we interviewed him, but then we realized that that was R.V. and this was Timothy. "That's a whole different person up there. Different personality," he says. A local gay man who is friends with R.V. says, "If I see Tim out somewhere, I'll say, 'Hi, Tim.' To me it's almost two people even though I know they're the same person; it's two different personalities, two different personas." When a professional photographer shot all the girls and hung the photos in the bar, Tim complimented her by saying she had caught him as both R.V. and himself.

Roger also takes on a different style. "As Inga I can do things I could never do as Roger, I would never do." In an interview Roger tells the reporter that his friends don't much like Inga, who is aggressive. He thinks Inga might be therapeutic, allowing him to express a darker side of his own personality.[5] Kevin says, "Kylie is me," but admits that "Kylie is more expressive . . . when I'm dressed as Kylie, I know that I can get away with so much more. Doesn't mean that I want to do it all the time." In another context he tells us, "No one calls me Kevin anymore; sometimes I worry that Kevin is gone." Desiray, Gugi's drag daughter who joined the show after Gugi and Inga left, describes being able to "go out there and do anything because it's a totally different person. Joel can't do it, but Desiray can." Dean describes keeping Dean and Milla separate because he understood that not being able to live apart from your image—he mentions Boy George here—leads to drugs and breakdown. "That's why there's Dean and Milla. For a while there wasn't." Milla "became a therapist" for him and a "healer." But at another time, Dean complains about being tired of the monster he had created, meaning the celebrity of Milla.

Gugi at first says that there isn't a difference, that "it's what's in me. It's all those years of being in myself. The pain and everything else. The fear of not being in control of my love or not feeling—it's coming out. That's, Gugi is what is on the inside of Rov." Later he adds, "But now, I can't separate Gugi and Rov." But he seems to contradict that:

"Actually, sometimes Gugi overwhelms Rov." Then he seems to notice this: "But in turn, how can I, because it's me." In fact, Gugi seems to act in ways that Rov never would: she's aggressive and sexual, while Rov is shy and sweet. Lady V describes having to work at keeping his identity. "One thing I like about Matthew," he says, "is he doesn't lose his identity with Scabby. When he takes it off, he becomes Matthew. But when he gets dressed, he becomes Scabby. . . . I mean, I've had to really work hard at separating." But now, he says, "it's just putting on a uniform."

The notions of both separation and fluidity are expressed in the language the drag queens use in talking to and about one another. The way they use names and pronouns follows no clear pattern. Or rather, they almost always use their drag names, with certain exceptions. Sushi says he barely even knows their real names, and when we gave them the book prospectus to read at a drag queen meeting, Roger commented how odd it was to see a list of boys' names. Matthew's parents don't know he is a drag queen—they think he's a bartender—and one day his mother called the bar and asked for Matthew and someone said, "No Matthew works here."

Sushi is "Sushi" to almost everyone except her former partner, and Kevin (Kylie), her best friend, and in turn Sushi is the only one who ever calls Kylie "Kevin." Sushi says she doesn't know when Kylie calls her Sushi and when Gary. Kylie says, "I consciously have to remember to call her Gary." Nevertheless, when they moved in together, their answering machine message instructed callers to push one number for Sushi or Gary and another for Kylie or Kevin. Gugi always wants to be called Gugi, while Roger dislikes being called Inga unless he is in drag. David says that as many people call him David as Margo, and he doesn't care. "If I ever retire from drag and people continue to call me Margo, it's quite all right with me!"[6] So there are different preferences among them. But unlike transgender activists, who like to be addressed in the gender of presentation, the drag queens slip easily and unnoticed out of their usual use of the female gender. For example, when we asked Sushi about how he got Kylie to come to Key West, he said: "I begged her and begged her, come on down. He was tired, I could tell he was tired of his life there." Talking about the use of drag versus real names, Sushi says, "I call him Milla; I don't call her Dean." Kevin says he has to remember to call "her" Gary and then adds, "A lot of people don't even know his name is Gary." At a drag queen meeting, when they talk about Musty Chiffon, a visiting drag queen, Matthew says, "I mean, just get to know him, because he really is sweet. She's not interfering with what we're doing at all." R.V. drives his mother nuts because she never knows when he says his "girlfriend" whether he's talking about a real girl or a guy. Verta asks Dean if he minds when she refers to them as "guys," and he says no, but Sushi says, "You should say 'girls,'" but then admits, "Well, sometimes I say 'guys' to girls."

Others outside the drag queen circle have the same trouble with pronouns. One of our focus group members, who had first met Sushi in her capacity as seamstress, said of their first meeting, "As far as I was concerned, she was just another gay man. He was just another gay man. She, he." A young straight woman said of Desiray, "She is so pretty; I'm jealous of him."

What it means to be a drag queen is different for the various girls, although it is possible to see some basic categories. For some, being a drag queen has to do with being in some sense *transgendered*. Jim Gilleran, the bar owner, gets at this when he says, "This is their identity, and you find yourself going 'she' even when the person's out of drag—like Sushi is a good example." Roger describes Sushi as looking "like a thin Japanese girl." Even Kylie, who first met Gary as a boy, commented in surprise once on a newspaper photo of Sushi, "She looks like a man!" A young lesbian couple who attended one of the shows describes Sushi as an "exception" to their notion that the drag queens are basically men, one saying, "His body just plays the part. . . . I mean I heard without the makeup on the streets, you would think that was just a woman without makeup"; and the other saying, "He's got a good face." A straight woman in her forties thinks that for Sushi, being a drag queen is "almost a role thing. You can tell, I'm not sure she/he knows where it starts and where it stops." Sushi describes himself as "some place in between" a woman and a man. Once he even said to us, "I'm not gay; I'm a drag queen." "I've always been a drag queen," he says another time.

In fact, Sushi's sense of being in between male and female led him to think about becoming a woman for a while. He lived as a woman for about a year and a half, as did Milla. When he was younger, he thought, "'Oh my god, I look like such a woman, maybe I am a woman,' and it sort of confused me." But, he says, "I know I'm a drag queen; I finally realized that. I'm a gay man who puts on women's clothing and looks good." Now, he says: "That's who I am . . . there aren't that many people like me. And if I shut down and quit and say, 'I'm a boy,' and start working out and building muscles [which he did at one point in his life—he points to the vestiges of that body in his still-toned arms] and lying to myself about who I am, then I won't be happy." Yet Kylie says Sushi "has a struggle . . . whether she should be a woman or a man. She looks so odd as a man, you know, not odd but so very distinctive."

That struggle came to the fore in the spring of 2001, when Sushi saw a television show about transgendered people in America. Over dinner she tells us about this transformative experience: "I was home alone because all of my other roommates were working and stuff like that. For some reason, by the end of it, I was crying my eyes out. . . . And I finally realized, oh my god, I'm not a drag queen. I'm a closeted transsexual-transgendered person. And I've been harping and hooting and tooting my horn for years now about being a drag queen—an openly out drag queen. And here I finally realize, I'm not a drag queen. I'm a closeted transgendered person." We ask about the difference. "A drag queen is someone like Kylie who never has ever thought about cutting her dick off. Ever. I think about it once a day, sometimes more." She says she really wants to do it but never will, partly because "it's a religious thing. . . . I was born this way," and partly because "I've been a drag queen for so long, and my whole persona—I don't want to try to change my whole personality again into Susie." We remind Sushi that she told us about her discovery that she was a drag queen, not a woman-wannabe. "But now I'm realizing that it's not that I realized I was a drag queen; I learned how to become a drag queen," Sushi explains.

Shortly after this revelation, Sushi went away for the summer to sew costumes for a theatrical production in North Carolina. He grew a goatee, which is hard to imagine. But then he began to do drag. When Verta asked Kylie whether there were gay bars on the Outer Banks where Sushi was working, Kylie replied, "There are streets, aren't there?"

Gugi, too, has a sense of himself as transgendered in some ways. He talks about the femininity in himself and says, "What I've always wanted was to be a woman." Making the link to sexual identity, he adds, "I don't know if it is because I wanted to be a woman or because I was attracted to men that I preferred to be a woman. . . . Out of drag, I feel like I'm acting. In drag, I feel like myself." The other girls tell us that they worried about Gugi when she went through a phase of never getting out of drag, going out in public all the time as a woman. "That means you've lost your identity," they say, making a distinction between being a drag queen and being on the move toward becoming a transsexual. Gugi herself seems to admit this. "It's just that certain things, I got too extreme with. . . . I started going to the straight side of town. In drag." And in fact Gugi hasn't ruled out becoming a woman.

He says he doesn't want to be a titty queen, but, "Yeah, to be honest, I would love [getting breasts]. But it's a process." He likes the idea of not having to wear as much makeup. For two months he did take hormones that he got from his best friend, a transgendered person. "I'm like, OK, like a week after she gave me the shot, I'm feeling all this weird feeling here." He points to his chest. "She's like, 'No, you're not.' I'm like, 'Yes, I am.' She goes, 'No, you're not. You're not supposed to feel it for three months from now.'" He grew breasts and his skin got softer. But he stopped because "it wasn't the right time. I did it for the wrong reasons. I did it to get away from my dad's death and the breakup with my ex–bastard husband."

Dean (Milla) says, "I love being a guy," but as an adolescent, going through problems at home and getting involved in drugs, being sent to what he calls "kiddie jail" and drug treatment, "I decided that I wanted to be a woman." Not just because he liked women's clothes, but because "I didn't like *me*." He got hormones from a counselor he was seeing with his mother by telling the counselor that he would get them from the drag queens on the street if not from him. He took them for a year and grew breasts. He would go out dressed as a woman and "just have the *men fall over,* all over me, and with no clue, no clue." He loved it: "It was so away from everything." For a while he thought that he really had to be a woman, and he was seriously considering sex-reassignment surgery. But then, "I started to love myself. I pulled away from that whole effeminate side . . . and I became a man." Now, he says, "I'm so pleased with my penis and my body." With his newly hairy legs, he feels sexy, like a man. Matthew (Scabby) says of his new look, "I saw her yesterday, I said, 'You know what, bitch, if I didn't know you so well, I'd fuck you.'"

Others never thought of themselves as between genders or as women. David (Margo) thinks that Sushi must have "thought of changing or at least getting tits" and knows that Milla has. But, he says, "I don't want to be a woman. I don't understand why anyone would want to do it." If he's in the backroom bar, he doesn't want anyone calling him Margo. There he's a man looking for a man.

For others of the drag queens, dressing as a woman is fundamentally *theatrical.* Matthew has been involved in theater since elementary school and always loved it. He wanted to go to the Rhode Island School of Design, but his parents insisted that he go to Brown University instead, because that's what his father and grandfather had done. He hated it and left after one semester. He worked with Digital Orgasm, a mixed group of men and women, doing what he describes as "performance art" as a dominatrix. They did "a simulated, futuristic cyber-fetish kind of sex shop. So instead of actually having intercourse on-stage, I kinda like beat the guys up with whips and stuff. Shoot grinder sparks in their face. Wrap them in cellophane, stick mag lights up their asses, spin them around on a chain. But it's all fake, it's all simulated, it's not real.

"I loved creating personas," he says. Distinguishing himself from the other drag queens, he says he doesn't do what they do, that is, create one character only; he fashions many. Dean is offended. "What the fuck are you talking about?" Matthew answers, "You are Milla." "I'm Milla, but when I do my fucking performance, do you guys not see me go from one personality to the other?" Although for Dean being a drag queen is more profound, he also identifies as a performer. He, too, was in theater groups from a young age. What he loves is being able to use his feelings, to evoke the pain and anger and love that audience members have felt in their own lives and to express what he is feeling.

Like Dean, Gugi experiences drag as both expressing his transgendered nature and as theatrical. Growing up as a child in Chicago, he performed in church and school plays. He went to the Palestine Christian Temple, a Pentecostal church, and he sang in a school choir until his voice changed. He says, "It just comes to me naturally." He, like Matthew, was artistic. He painted backdrops for photographers, learning from a neighbor of his sister. His first job was for OshKosh, and he did the cover for *Chicago* magazine. He later did faux finishes for houses and then learned flower arrangement. But he feels that he has found his destiny, to be a performer. "I want to be loved by everyone. I refuse not to. Then I think I'm fully invested in this. It's just part of my destiny. That's why"—he sighs—"I'm like a, how can I explain this? I fit in everywhere, basically. That's one of the talents I think I have."

R.V. did drag for the first time as a professional performer at Disney World. "I was an evil stepsister for the Cinderellabration for New Year's Eve." At thirteen he had been in professional summer stock theater, which he connects automatically with having sex with other boys. He had auditioned for community theater when he was eleven or twelve. His mother thought he wouldn't make it and he would get it out of his system, but he won a spot. Two days after he graduated from high school, he took off to Orlando, unwilling to stop smoking marijuana and live by the rules of his family home. Although he is clearly close to and proud of his mother, he describes his home life as dysfunctional and sees the stage as a way that he could create his own little world. He worked for Disney for fourteen years. There he met drag queens who took him to the Parliament House in Orlando, where he started doing drag. He thought it was really fun and learned to host shows from watching other drag queens. Perhaps that is why he likes "to take the younger girls that want experience onstage and never get a chance. . . . It's that motherly thing inside."

He eventually lost his job at Disney for swearing at a child, so he drove north, running out of gas in Providence, Rhode Island, where he met Scabby's brother, also a drag queen (but a "pretty one"). Eventually he began to perform in the winter in Key West and the summer in Provincetown, but he decided to stay in Key West for the summer of 1999. He defines himself as an entertainer: "I'm an actor in a dress." He loves "the old roar of the crowd and smell of the grease paint . . . the audience appreciation." But he also identifies as a drag queen.

Roger (Inga) has been in the theater since he was ten, and he loves performing. For him it was a natural transition from *Romeo and Juliet* and the *Inferno* to Marilyn Monroe and Madonna impersonations. In contrast to some of the other girls, he says, "I never had a need to dress as a girl or wanted to have a sex change." Drag, he says, is an act, not a lifestyle. He worked making costumes for theaters in Gothenburg and Stockholm to support himself when he began doing drag with a group called Sugar and Babes in Sweden. He was accepted into and began classes at a school of performing arts, but he didn't really like being back in school, so he came to the United States to work as a drag queen instead. "I would not trade it, even if some nights it's hard, doing the show, being paid to do it, but I would not trade it for anything. . . . It's fun. It's a game." Matthew agrees. After the death of a lover, the sense of humor that had always been part of Matthew's life as the class clown disappeared, until he came to Key West to do drag. "And now happiness just keeps pouring out," he says, adding in true Scabola fashion, "like this big oozing pimple."

Some of the other girls came to drag as part of their work and continue to see it as primarily a *job*. David (Margo) had no use for drag when he was growing up: "I thought it was a bunch of silly faggots doing whatever." He was fifty-nine when he first dressed in drag, and he did it reluctantly. He had had a number of successful careers in professional and managerial positions, working as an interior decorator in New York; a guest house manager in St. Thomas; a teacher, school administrator, political activist, and real estate manager back in New York. When he reached the top, he left: "I think I was bored and I'd accomplished what I'd wanted to accomplish." In 1992 he packed up everything in the city and moved to Key West because a friend said he'd love it there. He got a job at the desk of a guest house, and for Fantasy Fest, the wild Mardi Gras–like Halloween celebration, all the employees had to dress in drag. He told the owners, "I'm almost sixty years old. I've never done drag. I'm not interested in drag. I won't do drag."

Finally he gave in. He shaved off the beard he had sported for thirty-five years, put on a boa-trimmed French-cut leotard, donned a wig and high heels. "And the funny thing is when I got dressed and I came out, it was, it became very natural. . . . And I'd never done that since when you're five years old and you put on your mother's high heels and walk around the house." After Fantasy Fest, photographs went up at the guest house, and one day two lesbians staying there saw them and suggested that he get back in drag and come to a tea dance. So he went out, bought a yard of black fabric, wrapped it into a skirt, and went. Sushi, Milla, and Kylie were doing a show at the tea dance at the Atlantic Shores, another gay bar, and Sushi asked Margo whether she did numbers. She said no, but Sushi suggested she bring a CD and perform the next week. "So of course the next Sunday I came back and did a number." He started appearing occasionally with the girls, got fired from his day job for being rude to a guest, and the rest is history. He says he doesn't try to look like a woman: "I'm just a man in a dress."

But if it's work, David loves it. "It's fun!" he writes in *Celebrate!* "One becomes the center of attention and flaunts the feminine side of the psyche. Like a woman, one has cigarettes lighted, drinks bought and even gifts presented. Just last week a young man gave me a beautiful tennis bracelet. They may not be diamonds, but . . . like drag, it's all illusion anyway."[7] Telling his story in his column, he thanks the guest house owners and Sushi "for opening a whole new door and a whole new world for me."[8] In conversation he says, "I don't think that any job I've ever had I've enjoyed as much. I mean, there are days when I say, 'Oh my god, I really don't want to do this.' [The others present at the planning session at the pool express agreement.] But somehow the minute you start making up, that first, once you get the foundation on, you might as well go all the way." Sushi says, "It's that first cocktail." David agrees, but adds, "And *then* you get into it. I'm having more fun that I've ever had!" Sushi suggests that it wears thin after ten years, but Roger insists that he wouldn't do it if he didn't like it. "Nobody's forcing you to do it." At the same time, Roger admits that "it's work, getting into drag. That's my job. And if I don't get money for it, why should I put myself in this corset, why should I walk around in these high heels for four hours killing my feet?" But in the end, "I love what I'm doing, otherwise I wouldn't do it."

Gugi, too, first did drag as part of his job, however much it now means something more fundamental to him. When he first came to

Key West, he, like David, worked in a guest house, then he got a job where his then-lover worked, One Saloon, the leather bar (now the backroom bar, where men go for sexual encounters, at 801). The entire staff had to dress in drag to raise money. Echoing David, Gugi says, "I didn't want to do it!" Also like David, he didn't like drag queens. He, like other gay men, thought there was "something wrong with them," while now he believes that "they're more the stronger person than the regular gay fellow." At that time he had hair to his shoulders, so he thought he'd just tease his hair and put on a little tight dress.

> I walk into the bar and people look at me and just keep on talking. People that I knew, since I got into town. I was like, "Hello, it's me, Rov." I'm like, "What, do I look bad?" They're like, "No, you look so real. . . . We're going to take you to Rick's or Sloppy Joe's [straight bars]; no one's gonna tell the difference." I'm like, "Well, thank you," but in my head I'm like, "Yeah, right, motherfucker. The lights are low, you've had too many cocktails, you don't know what the hell you're talking about."

And then he performed. Alanis Morissette's "You Oughta Know."

> The first time I did it, I was looking at the ceiling. I started getting comfortable about halfway through the number. I finally looked down, I'm looking at the audience, I'm just standing there like, "What do I do?" . . . The second time around, I was like, "I'm gonna go for this, I'm gonna take it." Tore it up! Tore it up! It was like, bam! After that, people started asking me to do benefits left and right.

For Kevin (Kylie) it really is "just a job." He says that it isn't always fun, that sometimes he thinks, "God, maybe I would rather be working at Ralph's," the grocery store where he put in eleven years. "It gets to be, it can be just as tedious at times." But he does remember the first time he saw a flyer with his name on it. "I was a little bit excited," he says, obviously an understatement.

Audience members are curious about why the drag queens do what they do and come up with explanations that, interestingly, mirror those that the girls themselves offer. A gay male couple from New York who have become friendly with the girls say, "They're people just like anybody else and that just happens to be their profession." Two straight couples assume that it's just a job—one of the women thinks probably a bad one. One of the men, touching on the theatrical motivation and comparing them to women who become strippers or porn stars, wonders if they wanted to break into show business and couldn't do it any other way. A lesbian from New York disagrees, saying, "I think it's a choice. . . . There are so many things on earth that they could be doing, that for a man to go as far as to dress up as a woman, there's a leap. I think something happens." Her lover agrees with her: "I think that [it] is something very important to them." This prompts one of the straight women in the focus group to talk about the friend of a friend who is a male-to-female transsexual and wants to stay married to her wife, despite the fact that she identifies as straight.

A local gay man, comparing the girls to more traditional female impersonators, says, "It's less of a job and more fun"; they put "a lot more of their own self into it and their own feelings and they enjoy what they're doing." A young straight woman who lives in Key West and considers the girls her friends offers a psychological explanation: "I think that the reason why anybody is doing this is because there's something missing and this is filling one of those empty spots within them." A gay male physician from Boston loves drag because "it seems to me a pure expression of self. . . . They get to project exactly what they want to be." "I think there's an acceptance that they get when they're onstage that they don't necessarily get when they're offstage," says a woman photographer who has come to know them rather well. A gay male lawyer who lives in Key West emphasizes the different motivations: "For some of the performers, it's an employment of last resort. For some of the performers, it's their pattern. For some of them, it's a temporary thing between other things. For some of them, it's who they are."

Clearly being a drag queen has different meanings and different levels of importance in the girls' lives, although the lines between transgenderal, theatrical, and occupational reasons are not clear-cut. But even for those who came to the life and continue to see it as primarily a job, there's a kind of identity involved in being a drag queen. Mama, part of the 801 family, captures this when she remembers her attitude the first time she dressed in drag in São Paulo, Brazil, in 1967: "If I don't like it, I will be gay but not a drag queen." All of the 801 Girls are drag queens, and that has a profound impact on how they live their lives, how they relate to other people, and how they see the world.

☆ ☆ ☆

Watching the transformation that takes place in the dressing room, and listening to the girls' accounts of their gender and sexuality as boys, it's easy to see in concrete terms how unstable the categories of "masculine" and "feminine" really are. The rigidity of the categories in mainstream culture is reflected in the confusion of boys like Sushi, who thought that his sartorial desires meant that he wanted to be a woman. Or in Sushi's objection to being called "sweet": "It's the men inside of us. Most men don't like to be called sweet or cute." "Drag queen" emerges as a kind of third-gender category in a society that insists that there are only two. One gay male audience member captured this when he said he didn't think of them as either men or women, but as "their own thing. I feel like a drag queen is completely different." In that sense, drag queens are like others who fall between or bridge or challenge the division between masculine and feminine. As other scholars have suggested in considering the butch-fem bar culture of the 1950s or the "female masculinity" of women who look like men on a permanent or temporary basis or transgendered prostitutes in Brazil, such "in-betweens" are not about aping the other side of the divide.[9] Rather, these are people who create their own authentic genders, and those constructions are important in helping us to think in a complex way about what makes a man a man and what makes a woman a woman.

SECTION II
"TAKE ME OR LEAVE ME"

At ten o'clock, every night of the year, the girls who are performing go down to the sidewalk in front of the bar to hustle up an audience. Until quarter to eleven, they smoke, drink, chat with friends passing by, call out to strangers, hand out flyers, and invite everyone on the street to come up to see the show. As Kylie instructed us when we joined them on the street in drag, "Tell them it's upstairs, at eleven, never a cover." This is the most public part of their performance, for the 801 is on Duval Street, the main drag that runs fourteen blocks through the heart of Old Town, Key West, from the Gulf of Mexico to the Atlantic Ocean. Everyone walks, bicycles, takes a pedicab, or drives down Duval. Tourist families, groups of gay men, lesbian couples, locals—everyone goes by the 801 Girls at some point. Straight tourists who might never think of going to a drag show gawk, or hurry past brushing aside the flyer, or pretend they don't notice the girls towering over everyone else in their five-inch heels. But most of them are intrigued, and many stop, have their pictures taken with the girls, and come back for the show. These forty-five minutes on the sidewalk—being who they are, eliciting both interest and hostility, taking part in the life of the community—are symbolic of the girls' public role in Key West. "Take me or leave me," they seem to say, echoing the words of one of their favorite numbers, the lesbian duet from the hit show *Rent*, in which a woman who has turned both male and female heads on the streets since puberty demands that she be taken for what she is. In this section we consider the drag queens' activities, interactions, and relationships outside the cabaret.

FIVE

THE CONCH REPUBLIC

Key West is known locally as the "Conch Republic," the "Rock" (as in "I need to get off the Rock"), or, simply, "Paradise." All of these names come down to the same thing: Key West is a small tropical island, only about one-and-a-half miles wide and four-and-a-half miles long, closer to Cuba (90 miles) than Miami (154 miles), and it seems to have little to do with the rest of the United States. It is even the subject of a recent (three-volume, yet!) University of Chicago dissertation in anthropology.[1] As the city in the continental United States lying the farthest south, Key West sports not only the "Southernmost Point" and "Southernmost House," but the "Southernmost Pharmacy," "Southernmost Motel," "Southernmost Air Conditioning and Refrigeration," "Southernmost Gastroenterology Consultants," and even "Southernmost Church of God in Christ Prayer Room." And there's a drag queen, LaLa Belle, with a talk show called—you guessed it—*The Southernmost Queen of Talk.*

The weather is wonderful all winter, and in the summer the heat is mitigated by the trade winds, the brief afternoon downpours, the bright blue sky, and the blooming of the royal poinciana trees. As an address delivered at the dedication of the new city hall in 1876 put it, Key West's "uniform temperature" equals "that of Italy or the South of France," so that "the least clothing is most comfortable, and only just so much needed as modesty demands, with nothing of winter but the name," meriting the city the title "poor man's Paradise."[2] There are even Key Westers who decide to vacation in Key West: "Why not? The weather is perfect. . . . We have everything here."[3]

Key West is tenuously attached to the mainland by a narrow strip of road, practically at sea level, strung across a series of smaller and larger islands. As an article in *National Geographic* put it, the Florida Keys are "like a cheap, ugly watch chain, with a magnificent gold piece on the end, ticking to its own time."[4] Culturally, the connection is also

pretty tenuous: hence Key West's proud status as the "Conch Republic."
("Conch," the tough animal that lives inside a beautiful shell, is the local
name for people born in Key West.) In 1982 the mayor proclaimed Key
West's secession from the Union, declared war on the United States
(as an act of aggression, a city commissioner hit a navy officer with a
loaf of stale Cuban bread), immediately surrendered, and appealed for
a billion dollars in foreign aid from the United Nations.[5] This colorful
event came in response to a roadblock set up across the only way onto
the keys by the Drug Enforcement Administration. Since the early
1970s, Key West had been a haven for marijuana smugglers, and by
the early 1980s, so much cocaine was entering through the city that
the federal government branded it the "Drug Smuggling Capital of
America." But the Border Patrol operating by the Last Chance Saloon
just south of Florida City claimed to be looking for illegal aliens, not
drugs. As agents stopped and searched every car coming off the keys,
they created a massive traffic jam that scared away tourists and
prompted objections that the government was treating the keys as if
they were a foreign country. When all administrative and legal strategies failed to halt the annoying roadblock, a coalition of city officials,
chamber of commerce types, and various local activists and personalities launched the secession, to great fanfare. Eventually the roadblock
disappeared, quietly dismantled under cover of darkness.

But the Conch Republic lives on. Entrepreneurs sell Conch Republic
currency, stamps, and flags, and Conch Republic anthems, foods,
flowers, birds, and a national holiday have proliferated. The Conch
Republic, as "the world's first Fifth World country," even has a foreign
policy: "The Mitigation of World Tension through the Exercise of Humor."[6] Beginning in March 1999, a flourishing business in Conch Republic marriage licenses for same-sex couples led to a series of highly
publicized weddings, some onstage at the 801. The secretary general
of the Conch Republic announced that since the Republic exists as a
"Sovereign State of Mind" if not a sovereign nation, it has the right to
license same-sex marriage.[7]

The serious playfulness of the Conch Republic secession is characteristic of life in Key West. And flying or driving into Paradise, one does
seem to have left the country. Brown-outs are common enough that
there's little reason to reset the clocks; dogs are welcome in restaurants
and grocery stores and bars, including the Green Parrot ("The first and
last bar on Route 1"), where laid-back Key West dogs wander in past
a sign reading "No pets allowed, by the order of the health department."
Roosters and chickens, not to mention the ever-present cats, including
six-toed descendants of the Hemingway menagerie, wander the streets;

the roosters crow all day and night, ignoring their conventional role of heralding the dawn. One December a man showed up on Duval Street walking a dog, on top of whom balanced a cat, on top of whom teetered a mouse. In Key West you expect the unexpected. As an advertisement for a local tourist attraction puts it, "Once you've been to Ripley's Believe It or Not, the rest of Key West looks normal."

Legend has it that Key West got its name from a fierce battle between the Seminole and Calusa Indians that left the beaches littered with bones, prompting Spanish explorers in the sixteenth century to call it "Cayo Hueso," or "Island of Bones," a name later corrupted into "Key West." In the eighteenth century, Spanish settlers on the island made a living fishing, and pirates and shipwreckers found Key West a perfect spot for their nefarious activities. Florida shifted from Spanish to English hands in 1763, but Key West remained a possession of Spain until 1822, when the Spanish owner sold it to John Simonton, an American businessman with a good eye for potentially valuable property. That same year England ceded Florida to the United States. Prompted by Simonton, the government established a naval base at Key West, dubbed the "Gibraltar of the Gulf."

In the 1830s, populated by Spaniards, American southerners and New Englanders, Cuban cigar makers, English people from the Bahamas, Jewish merchants, and African American laborers and spongers, Key West was already a cosmopolitan community with a reputation for unconventionality. The census of 1840 recorded the population as consisting of 516 whites, 76 "colored," and 96 slaves.[8] The diary of a young lawyer who moved to Key West in 1828 describes a rowdy environment: "The greater part of the persons who call themselves householders are drunken and vagabond sailors who build themselves palmetto huts on the keys and are usually drunk from the time of their arrival to their departure, or all their money is gone." "There was a dance at the house tonight. . . . They kept the fiddle going until near two this morning." "There was a great quantity of wine and other liquor drunk and the usual consequences ensued."[9] These descriptions, with the exception of the vagabond sailors and the fiddle, could apply to a night at the 801. Likewise, an anonymous sketch of the city from that same time, with a little modernizing of the language, could also describe Key West today:

> The island was originally settled by persons from almost every country and speaking almost every variety of languages. They brought with them habits, manners, views and feelings, formed in different schools and in many instances totally dissimilar and contradictory. . . . [I]n

consequence of there being no court or modes of legal restraint, they had no rules of conduct for their guide, except such as their own views of what would conduce to the attainment of their own wishes afforded.[10]

The sense of independence from the rest of the country is not surprising, given the relatively recent physical link to the mainland. When the only way to get there was by boat, Cubans and Bahamians were more likely to arrive than people from the U.S. mainland. In the 1870s, thanks to Cuban expertise, Key West was the cigar-making capital of the world and the most prosperous city in Florida. Not until 1912, with the completion of the Overseas Railroad, could people get to Key West by land. As an early history of Key West put it, "That there could be a city of 22,000 population on an island in the Gulf, without a railroad, or a wagon road connecting it to the country of which it politically forms a part, is the best evidence of the commercial importance of Key West."[11] The devastating hurricane of 1935 washed the railroad out to sea. Three years later the Overseas Highway took its place.

This link opened Key West up to tourism, the mainstay of the island's economy, along with fishing, the navy, and (unofficially) drugs. But the Great Depression had already hit hard, and Key West suffered a reversal of fortune. Bankrupt and desperate, the town turned to Washington, and the Federal Emergency Relief Administration came to the rescue.[12] Gussied up with FERA funds, Key West resolutely went after the tourist dollar, and despite persistent complaints these days that there are too many tourists, the city in truth can't do without them. Key West along with Tahoe and Hawaii's big island are the only three communities in the United States entirely dependent on tourism.[13] Yet the influx of tourists, as *USA Today* put it, threatens "the very things that make the continental USA's southernmost island so popular: quirky charm, a laid-back pace and crystal clear waters."[14] When the beaches closed during the summer of 1999 because of unacceptable water quality, the debate about how many tourists are too many rose to a fevered pitch.[15] "If it's tourist season, why can't we shoot them?" ask bumper stickers also popular in Maui.[16]

Key West remains a flamboyant mixture of cultures. In accord with its history, it shelters not only vibrant Cuban and Bahamian enclaves, but also artistic, hippie, and gay communities. And it touts its tolerance. This is not, of course, absolute, but it is pretty refreshing for those of us who have to live off the Rock. Early in its history, Key West, according to the 1876 address at city hall, diverged from standard American practices of segregation, at least in death: "The friends of the Northman and the Southerner, the negro slave and his Caucasian master, the wealthy and the poor of all religious denominations, content with the rites of Christian burial, laid the bodies of their dead side by side."[17] If live residents in the city today tend to live in gentrified or Cuban or African American neighborhoods, it is nevertheless true that ethnic neighborhoods have survived in an extremely expensive town and that there is a lot more mixing than is characteristic in other American cities and towns. The memoir of a gay man who first came to Key West in 1959 reports the absence of antigay sentiment, noting that every black, white, and Cuban family had a relative who "got drunk and acted crazy."[18] Charles Kuralt describes Key West as "the greatest of all the end-of-the-road towns." The city, he says, is "full of dreamers, drifters and dropouts, spongers and idlers and barflies, writers and fishermen, islanders from the Caribbean and gays from the big cities, painters and pensioners, treasure hunters, real estate speculators, smugglers, run-aways, old Conchs and young lovers. The residents are all elaborately tolerant of one another, and that is where the style comes in."[19] Spreading the word about Key West's famed tolerance, in an effort to spread the tolerance as well, local resident J. T. Thompson launched a campaign to distribute thousands of free bumper stickers proclaiming: "We invite everyone around the world to share the 'Official Philosophy of Key West, Florida' and to *Spread the word. The truth is that we are all ONE HUMAN FAMILY.*"[20]

Many of the diverse populations that make up the one human family have a long history in Key West. The artists and writers sent to save Key West from the depression lent to the city, already a favorite haunt of Ernest Hemingway and Tennessee Williams, a reputation as an artistic and literary haven. In the 1960s hippies looking for the good life discovered Key West and contributed to the island one of its featured rituals, the celebration of the sunset. Every night crowds gather at Mallory Square (and now also at the Hilton on the waterfront) to watch the sun go down in a blaze of color and to enjoy a wide range of eccentric performers, including tightrope walkers, fire breathers, human statues, costumed dogs, and trained house cats who jump through fiery hoops. When the sun disappears beneath the horizon, everyone claps, and then they head home, or to the multitude of restaurants and bars that cater to every taste.

Duval Street is sometimes divided between "Lower Duval," where the most famous straight bars such as the Hog's Breath Saloon and Sloppy Joe's are located, and "Upper Duval," home of galleries, restaurants, and gay bars. As one gay male tourist who came to the 801 show put it, "You have . . . gay people up at this end and straight people down there. We have a hard time going down there at night. Down at that end of the street. It's really scary." A humorous piece in *Celebrate!* proclaimed the 700 block of Duval (Upper Duval) 33.4 percent gay in the morning and 92.6 percent gay at night while the 300 block would have rated a zero except that Bobbie Nesbitt, a well-known gay singer who performs at that end of Duval, was spotted going to work.[21]

One block off Upper Duval, on the ocean, is Atlantic Shores, a gay motel and clothing-optional pool and bar. The gay bar on Duval closest to the Atlantic is La Terraza di Martí, known as La Te Da, once *the* gay guest house and restaurant, where, according to local lore, newly arrived guests were greeted in their rooms with a line of coke and a houseboy placed at their disposal. La Te Da has had its ups and downs but now offers, in addition to Alice's award-winning restaurant, the venerable Crystal Room, a restored venue for drag shows and other entertainment. It is there that crowds flock to see the incredible talents of Mr. Randy Roberts and Christopher Peterson, who do impersonations of icons such as Cher, Barbra Streisand, and Mae West, singing in their own voices. Closest to the straight end of town is Diva's, a dance bar that also features drag shows. In between is a growing gay complex consisting of the 801 (the "girl bar"); One Saloon, a backroom bar behind the downstairs of 801; Bourbon Street (the "boy bar"), with its male strippers dancing on the bar; the New Orleans guest house, complete with garden and pool; Magnolia's Café; and Pizza Joe's, a late-night eatery. Yet audience members at the 801 are divided about whether the cabaret itself is a gay space. Two gay men who come twice a year on vacation describe weekend crowds as "annoying, because . . . the straight people infiltrate and it goes beyond the comfort level." Several lesbian couples, on the other hand, say they came because they feel comfortable in gay bars.

The gay presence in Key West grew in the 1970s, when gay guest houses, restaurants, bars, and snorkeling boats proliferated. There were two gay bars—the Monster and Delmonico's—and a horse-drawn carriage that took patrons from one to the other. (On Lower Duval, both are now straight tourist bars.) The Key West Business Guild, formed in 1978, is a gay "chamber of commerce" that has done a lot to advertise Key West as a gay tourist destination. Despite its reputation for "bubba politics," corruption, and control by the Conchs, Key West has had a gay mayor and a woman mayor. The International Conference of Gay and Lesbian Criminal Justice Professionals ranked the Key West Police Department second best in the nation for "being out of the closet and behind the badge."[22]

The city has a strong gay feel, and people are as likely to assume someone is gay or lesbian as straight. When our friends Carla and Don stayed at our house, our (straight female) property manager kept saying to Carla on the phone, "I hope you girls are having a good time." Tongue firmly in cheek, *Celebrate!* proclaimed that, within two percentage points of potential error, Key West is 91.5 percent gay.[23] The *Key West Citizen* put it this way: "You know you're from Key West when 1) A man walks down the street in full leather regalia and crotchless chaps and you don't even notice, 2) If it's 60 degrees, you break out the fur coat and space heaters, 3) Your hairdresser is straight, your plumber is gay, the woman who delivers your mail is into S&M and your Mary Kay rep is a guy in drag."[24] This is a place where lesbians and gay men tend to feel comfortable. Upper Duval, after about eleven at night, feels like a gay public space. A lesbian couple from Orlando describe it as "more gay than straight, and if you come here, then people know that that's what they're getting into." A gay man who moved to Key West from Massachusetts says, "This place does open up a lot of people, and I think a lot of straight men from where I came from would be a little more understanding down here." A straight female Key West resident loves the fact that "you can do everything you want. Nobody judges you."

It's not perfect, of course. There are gay bashings, one in 1999 right on Duval Street in front of the Epoch, a once-gay club that reportedly (this is in dispute) suddenly announced in March 1998 that "fags" were no longer welcome and that all the women there would now be real in order to attract straight spring breakers. "Apparently no one ever told these kids that Key West is a diverse community that prides itself on that fact," wrote David (Margo).[25] In November 2000 Destiny, then one of the 801 Girls, was attacked on the street by three teenage boys shouting antigay slogans. Then, as the *Key West Citizen* reported it, the "Case of Alleged Beating of Drag Queen Takes Bizarre Twist" when the three young men involved accused Destiny of first confronting them and then their attorney challenged Destiny's credibility by dragging in her arrest record.[26] (Destiny is introduced in the show as "the three-time felon from Texas"; according to the other girls, Destiny's mother, a sex worker, put her in pornographic films as a child, and Destiny was convicted just after turning eighteen for having sex with a boy under the age of consent.)

In other incidents, one year at Fantasy Fest, the outrageous celebration at Halloween, two men pulled rolling crosses up Duval Street while two women companions handed out literature proclaiming that homosexuals are doomed to burn in hell.[27] David lambasted the newly opened Duval Street Denny's in late 1999 for allowing a group of kids to harass the 801 Girls when they went to get a bite to eat after the show.[28] And in winter 2001 two lesbian tourists from England complained in *Celebrate!* about a sunset performer telling homophobic jokes, and in the next issue a white gay male couple reported that someone at a local restaurant where they were eating with their young African American child called the police to investigate whether they had kidnapped the boy.[29] But nevertheless most would agree with David, who writes that "Key West is a unique and caring community with people who have an overabundance of love and compassion. Sure, Key West has some faults, but name me a place that doesn't."[30]

It is Key West's reputation as a gay-friendly town, along with the weather, that prompted most of the girls to move there. Both Matthew (Scabby) and Mama were in terrible car crashes and came both for the gay ambience and the warm weather that keeps their formerly broken bones from aching. David, who had lived on St. Thomas, also came for the weather, island life, and gay community. Gugi came at the invitation of two gay male friends celebrating their anniversary. "So I get to Miami, and it's like, 'Feel that humidity!' . . . I take a small plane flight from Miami to Key West. When the door opened, it was like something hit me. I knew I belonged here. I just knew it; I belong here. I have to come here."

Not all of the drag queens set out for Key West directly. Roger (Inga) was thinking of going to visit someone in Spain when a friend in Key West said, "Why not try to go down to Key West instead of Spain?" So he packed two suitcases, one of drag clothes and one of boy clothes, and he thought, "I'll give it a try and see." Sushi was thinking of going to design school in Miami, and when that fell through, his boyfriend Greg suggested they try Key West. "I had always wanted to come here," says Greg. "And I'm always up for a good trip," adds Sushi. All Greg knew was Jimmy Buffett, and Sushi had never heard of the place. But they sold everything they owned and drove across country.

Likewise, at seventeen Dean (Milla) just wanted to leave home, bought a bus ticket to Memphis, but someone said, as he tells it:

> "Hey, Key West, it's real gay down there."
> "Where's Key West?"
> "It's in Florida."
> "Oh well, I don't have to go too far, and how much is the bus ticket?"

So he traded in his ticket to Memphis, and although he has left several times, he always comes back.

Key West is not only to some extent a gay mecca: it is also a drag queen mecca. Bar owner Jim Gilleran estimates that there are about a hundred drag queens in Key West, if only about fifteen who perform professionally. David says he sometimes thinks "that there are more drag queens per capita in Key West than anywhere on the planet!"[31] And in truth one does meet drag queens everywhere. At Key West Aloe, a local gay business, Verta received advice about makeup from a gay male employee who does drag. When Leila went to get back issues of the local gay/lesbian newspaper, the receptionist, Bobby, on hearing about our project, introduced himself as "Hellen Bed, Queen Mother XI." When the news came out that a Hooters restaurant was to open in Key West, a local man wrote to the CEO of Hooters of America proposing the hiring of drag queens on the wait staff.[32] Drag queens show up at the most improbable places. For National Earth Day in 1997, for example, La Te Da hosted a "Mother Earth Drag Contest."[33] At the first-ever Cuban American Festival in the autumn of 1999, Sushi, Gugi, and Scabola were welcomed into the conga line, "once more proving," as David put it, "that Key West is the true home of accepted diversity."[34] Drag queens are so common that they don't always attract a lot of attention. As Roger puts it, "Where else can Sushi go out being Sushi and looking like a small Japanese girl without people bothering her?" Sushi herself asserts proudly, "If it wasn't for the drag queens, the gay community wouldn't be here."[35]

Key West is a town of about twenty-eight thousand inhabitants, but at seasonal peaks, up to eighty thousand people converge on the tiny island. Anyone who has lived or visited there for any length of time laments the pace of growth, seemingly unabated despite laws designed to curtail building. Yet even the construction of a few four- or five-story condominiums along the ocean (called to a halt in the 1980s), the development of gated communities (Truman Annex on some of the site of the naval base, the Golf Course on Stock Island, and Roosevelt Annex on the last undeveloped land on the island), the appearance of new hotels and time-share resorts such as the Hilton and Hyatt, and the increase in the number of cruise ships that dock there have not fundamentally changed the character of Key West. According to *USA Today*, "Amid the time-shares and T-shirt shops, a trace of Key West's quirkiness remains."[36]

The biggest concern of many residents is the skyrocketing cost of housing. The tourist industry creates so many low-level service jobs that Key West has one of the lowest unemployment rates in the country, but people in those jobs can't afford to live there, as Barbara Ehrenreich has so eloquently described in her book *Nickel and Dimed: On (Not) Getting by in America*.[37] A strange-bedfellows alliance of hotel owners, advocates of affordable housing, and people wanting quiet in their neighborhoods backed the passage of an ordinance banning transient rentals of anything other than licensed guest house rooms. The idea was that if people could no longer rent their houses on a weekly basis, tourists would have to stay in hotels, houses would be cheaper to buy or to rent on a long-term basis, and noisy renters would be pushed out of residential areas. Challenges to the law persist, but its passage, despite fierce opposition from many different quarters, speaks to the economic dilemma of many local people. The drag queens, for example, survive on their nightly tips (from under $20 to almost $200) and salaries ($50 a night for generally three nights a week; one night they work only for tips). It may be Paradise, but it isn't always an easy life.

As all of this suggests, Key West is a unique and quirky place, but at the same time it shares some common history with gay meccas such as Cherry Grove, Provincetown, and San Francisco.[38] All began with artistic/bohemian communities that proved welcoming to gay men and lesbians. In all, gay or gay-friendly establishments and institutions played a critical role in creating gay communities. Yet despite the reputation as gay havens, class and ethnic and political tensions raised challenges to tolerance, as straight residents sometimes resisted their community's notoriety. And in all, drag lies at the heart of the community's culture. Key West proudly asserts its difference and independence from the rest of the country—and place does shape gay life there in profound ways—yet that tenuous physical connection to the mainland assures that what happens is part of the story of life in the United States.

When the girls come out on Duval Street, they confront both a gay/lesbian community and the curious, sometimes hostile, gaze of outsiders to that community.

SIX

ON THE STREET

From the outside, the 801 is a pretty unprepossessing place. It's on the corner of Duval and Petronia, across from the entryway into Bahama Village, the heart of the black community. It's a small two-story pink stucco and frame building with white iron sunburst-design bars on the windows downstairs. Generally the windows on the first floor are thrown open to the sidewalk. People, mostly men, sit around the downstairs bar or at a counter that runs along the Duval Street side of the bar. There's an awning over the sidewalk outside these windows. The girls perch their drinks in plastic cups on the windowsill just inside the bars. They stroll along the sidewalk or simply stand and hand out brightly colored flyers that advertise the show.

If their height and appearance alone don't, the juxtaposition of their clothing, makeup, and wigs with their clearly male voices attracts attention, both positive and negative. "Are you in the show?" a curious young female bystander asks Margo in her sequined dress and white wig. "Would I be dressed like this if I weren't?" replies David in his smoky New York–accented voice. One night a German couple stopped to ask what makes someone gay. It turned out that the woman wanted to know if she could be a lesbian that night. Sometimes men proposition the drag queens. One night a man asked Kylie, when she was handing out flyers, "Do you do anything else other than the show?" and when Kylie asked what he meant, finally said he wanted Kylie "to suck his dick." Another time a man with his nine- or ten-year-old son came up to Kylie thinking she was a woman. "And then I said, 'It's a free show,' and a look came across his face, 'It's not a hooker; it's a man.' But I thought it serves him right—what is he doing cruising women with his son?" Mostly people are friendly, but we've seen groups of young men staring at the girls from across the street, looking as if they wanted to kill them. Sometimes we're afraid for them.

Gugi, Kylie, Sushi, and Milla on the street (photo by the authors)

Most people take the flyers the girls hand out, although some refuse. Scabby complains one day about the "rude people" on the street. "Very obnoxious and heterosexual and rude. And every time I would hand them a flyer, they would drop it on the ground. Don't take it if you're gonna drop it." Two young lesbian audience members who went to the show during spring break commented that they watched male college students walking on the other side of the street and "laughing and being like 'whoo-wee,' you know, obnoxious." "They don't know what to do but to make fun," the women say. "You know, if they don't make fun, there must be something wrong with them." Another lesbian couple commented that people cross the street to avoid the girls, "and they'll whisper, like, 'Oh, look at that!'" A straight woman in her sixties, a professional photographer who had once been married to a very big-name movie star and who began doing photographs of the girls, describes talking to them on the street one night when "some guy kind of approached me and somebody stood between me and that person, and I was very touched by that actually." Sometimes people yell things at them, especially from moving cars, and even throw things. Scabby says no one's ever said anything really bad to him, but "I get a lot of weird looks." R.V. says he's fearful sometimes, especially because they're so close to the street. "I've had a couple of times bottle caps whizzed at me from a car and you hear 'faggot' from a car." He wrote a letter to the editor of *Celebrate!* complaining about "this horrible, vile hatred" he hears as he barks the show on Duval.[1] Sushi says he is afraid when people call him a "faggot" on the street.

But the girls are not just passive objects while they advertise the show. They yell to people they know and to strangers alike, calling most everyone "sweetheart" or "darling," which takes care of the fact that they often don't remember people's names or even if they've talked with them before. "Hey, dykes!" Inga is likely to shout as we ride our bicycles up to the bar. They comment on attractive men who come by, saying "Hey, baby!" or simply "Ooooh." Scabby wags his tongue at a handsome man and says, "Anytime, baby!" A taxi driver who regularly drops Dean off at the bar told us on the way to the airport once that he was driving by one night and only when Milla called out, "Hi, darling!" did he realize what it was that Dean did. It's this kind of banter on the street that got Matthew to Key West and into the show. He and a lover had come on a vacation, and the very first night they were walking down the street, both with shaved heads wearing black Armani suits, one in a pink and the other a chartreuse shirt. Sushi was in front of Bourbon Street, where she was then performing, "and she started calling us, 'Hey, Versace boys!'—just snapping her fingers. And she's got her legs up all over us. And that's how I met her."

Sometimes the girls really take the time to talk people into coming to the show. Scabby says, "I always try to talk to people on the street, not just [hand them a flyer and] say 'here.' I always say, 'Where are you from,' or 'Love that dress,' or, you know, just stupid small talk." Lady V describes such a typical conversation:

The girls mingle with the crowd on the street (photo by the authors)

Lady V: Have you seen a female impersonation show before?
Passerby: Well, no.
Lady V: Well, you should come up and experience it.
Passerby: Well, we've always wanted to do it, but we've never been anywhere . . .
Lady V: Well, you are now. So, experience it. Even if you only experience it once. Go see what it's about.

We'd spent a lot of time observing the girls on the street, but it wasn't until we joined them in drag that we really understood what happens there. We had quite different reactions that seem to mirror both sides of the experience. Verta felt vulnerable because a kind of sleazy man sporting a cross and a tattoo, whom she couldn't identify as either gay or straight, was staring at her in an ominous way, and she was afraid he would come up and touch her. Because people do touch the drag queens all the time, in ways they never would anyone else, and the girls, in turn, grope them back. If a man they know comes by, they might fondle his crotch. Sushi once put his hands on both of our pubic areas, announcing coyly, "It's a service." One young lesbian audience member describes grabbing Milla's breasts, thinking they were real, because "I wanted to feel what implants felt like."

David says that when they're in drag, men treat them as if they are women and touch them in certain ways. "They'll touch the ass. They may run their fingers over the breast. It's the butt and the thighs and the legs. Running the hand up and down the legs and the knee and the thigh. . . . And they want to stroke your hair." A gay male audience member who has dressed in drag himself for parties comments, "I noticed that when I was in drag, people were more comfortable with coming up to me and being touchy and feely and not meaning anything by it." He and his lover think this is because women can get away with touching and being touched and this privilege extends to men in drag. The girls to some extent provoke the physical interaction, as David says, by coming off as "sluts" on the street. "I mean, we're not good girls. I mean, I think we try to not be good girls." They dress mostly in "prostitute drag" in contrast to the glamorous gowns that female impersonators choose. R.V. says, "We look like a bunch of hookers down here." And in fact that's just how they behave while they're hustling for the show.

But as their boldness in grabbing people suggests, it's not all vulnerability on the street. In contrast to Verta, Leila felt powerful disguised as a man dressing as a woman. She felt freed to say and do things she wouldn't ordinarily, and she enjoyed the in-your-face nature of the performance in front of straight tourists. Despite her fear, Verta also started to act like a drag queen. A male friend came up to see us, and Verta began squeezing his butt, something she would never have done out of drag. Like Gugi and R.V. and Kylie, Jinxie and Blackeé took on lives of their own and shed Leila's and Verta's inhibitions (or good sense, depending on how one looks at it).

Watching the girls on the street deepens the impression that drag queens are not at all feminine. The freedom to call out to passersby and the sexually provocative manner and talk are, in fact, profoundly masculine in the sense, ironically, that female prostitutes are masculine. Or, more accurately, as we've already suggested, drag queens are neither feminine nor masculine in any conventional sense. They are, in fact, simply drag-queenish.

These forty-five minutes on the street are incredibly important for business. At one drag queen meeting, Sushi spent a long time emphasizing how important. The girls had been running off here and there— going over to Bourbon Street or down the street to meet friends or attend to personal business—and Sushi made clear that she wanted only one person to leave at a time. "If you need to leave the street, the sidewalk, for a drink, or to go to the bathroom, you wait until the other person is back. OK? . . . You say, 'It's my turn to go to the bathroom.' Or 'It's my turn to go get a drink.' So no going across the street; you stand in front of there, you know, flyer the people. You know? You

Gugi (photo by the authors)

swing on the pole. You act like a slut." Amidst a lot of joking around
about all of this, Kylie supports what Sushi is saying: "Well, it's got to
be under control at least. I mean, half the time I look around and I'm
alone." They all laugh. "Where did everyone go?" Sushi emphasizes,
"Your job is to be on the street; it's just like part of your job is to have
a one-and-a-half-hour show."

It is part of the job that they sometimes love and sometimes hate.

Scabby says that at first he loved it, that it was his favorite thing to do. "I couldn't wait to get to the club to paint a face and get on the street and start harassing people. I loved it." In July he tells us, "During season I love it, too. But off-season I can't stand it." Yet they realize how central a part of the job it is. One day Scabby was passing out flyers when a straight couple walked by, and he attempted to hand one to the woman. She wouldn't take it, but her husband did and stopped right there to read it. Scabby struck up a conversation, seeing that the man really wanted to go see the show but his wife was resisting because it was in a gay bar. "And I said, 'Girl, what's the matter? You got a problem with gay people?' She said, 'No, I have gay friends.' I said, 'What is it, you got a problem with drag queens?' She said, 'No, I know drag queens.' I said, 'Why don't you come in? . . . Girl, we're not gonna steal your husband.'" The man went on in and she left, then came back to try to get him to leave. But he wouldn't. "Anyway, they sat right up front and it got to her. And at the end of the night, she said, 'I had the best time, thank you for convincing me to come up.' I said, 'I didn't convince you; you did it yourself.'"

The vast majority of people come to the show for the first time precisely because they see the girls on the street. Two straight couples at the show "had seen a couple of the girls out on the street the night before" and had even posed for a picture with them. Straight people especially, says a straight male regular, "come because the girls are barking on the street. . . . Without that on the street, you wouldn't see as many straight people up here as you normally would." A bisexual man, who works for the bar, agrees: "The straight people . . . they're coming back from dinner back there in town, and all of a sudden there's these wild, crazy, lunatic gay people in dresses out there just mucking it up, grabbing people, and doing all this crazy stuff and they're like, 'Hey, let's go up there. This is something we can tell the people back in Iowa.'" A straight woman part-time resident ends up bringing visitors from her home state of Ohio to the show because "they know Key West has that gay element and so they're walking—you can't miss it when you're walking up and down Duval. So the curiosity kills them. They want to go."

A lesbian physician from Paris, now living in New York, saw "this beautiful woman in a very nice sexy dress" and wanted to come in because "the fact of knowing these are men is pretty attracting, interesting." Another Parisian woman, but straight, who now lives in Key West and attends the shows regularly describes seeing the girls on the street for the first time: "I was looking at the clothes and, you know, [I thought] it can't be a woman." A local gay Latino man who has become a regular came the first time because "Sushi dragged me in from off the street." "We were pulled in practically by the drag queens," say a gay male couple visiting on vacation. A lesbian couple from Orlando says simply, "We saw him standing outside."

So the people walking by on Duval may avert their eyes or let themselves be toyed with by the drag queens, but lots of them end up at the cabaret, at least for a little while. In the tradition of what Esther Newton calls "street impersonators," their performances on the street extend the shows to a larger audience.[2] But before we follow the girls back upstairs, where they retouch their makeup before the show begins, let's move off Duval Street for a moment, where the girls' public performances of gender and sexuality are played out in a number of different venues.

SEVEN

A PLATE OF FOOD AND
A DRAG SHOW

This is how David describes benefits in Key West: "You stand in line, you get a plate of food, and then you sit down and watch a drag show." And in fact drag queens in general, and the 801 Girls in particular, are central to both fund-raising and the life of the gay and lesbian community. So frequent are benefits in Key West that the gay bars got together in June 1997 and decided to meet regularly to schedule events so that they wouldn't compete with each other for the same audience.[1] D.D.T., an organizer and emcee of the Queen Mother Pageant, one of the biggest events of the year, writes that "it always blows me away that this community, where it seems there is at least a benefit a week for some worthy cause or another, always pulls together and gives and gives."[2] Says the executive director of AIDS Help, "I can't say enough about the drag entertainers in this town. For years they've been at the forefront of fundraising efforts in Key West."[3] Not only do the 801 Girls participate in numerous benefits, but they periodically contribute their tips from a special number to AIDS organizations. R.V. and the late Miss Q, an outrageous and political drag queen from London who performed in Key West in the winter and Provincetown in the summer and who herself had AIDS, began the practice, and they raised more than $27,000 in five years. When Milla's best friend died of AIDS, she began performing the Braids' version of "Bohemian Rhapsody" and donating the tips in his honor. "That's what the drag community has done through the years," says R.V. "When the AIDS epidemic came up, it was the drag queens who got together to start raising money and all that for causes and that. . . . We are like the wrapping, I think, and the bow on the whole thing 'cause we are the ones that go out and are able to convey it without ACT UP or anything like that."

And it is not just AIDS organizations that benefit from the plate of food and the drag shows. Fund-raisers cover the gamut of local causes. Of course, the public performances of the 801 Girls beyond the walls

Scabby at the Annual Breast Cancer Benefit (photo by James Dillon O'Rourke)

and sidewalk of the cabaret not only raise funds; they also get publicity for the bar. And they embody the ambivalent status of the drag queens as both celebrities central to the life of gay/lesbian Key West but in other ways living on the margins. Perhaps the best place to begin in considering the girls' role in the civic life of Key West is with New Year's Eve.

The turn of the millennium (if we put aside arguments that the real date was 2001) was the third year in a row that gay Key West welcomed the New Year with Sushi descending at the stroke of midnight in a giant papier-mâché red high-heeled slipper suspended over the street in front of the Bourbon Street bar. At the other end of Duval Street, a straight crowd gathers at Sloppy Joe's to watch the lowering of an eight-foot-tall conch shell. In 2001 one could also choose to go either to the Schooner Wharf Bar to see a woman dressed as a pirate wench fall from the sky or, off the main drag, to observe a huge tennis ball come down from the top of the 3-Legged Dog art gallery. For New Year's 1999, the festivities started out with Sushi dancing in the street, blocked off to traffic, in what she called a "circle of life." Kylie announced over a loudspeaker from the balcony of Bourbon Street, and the other girls threw beads and waved and displayed themselves from the second floor of 801 as well. A local cameraman filmed the lowering of the shoe, put it on digital feed on the Internet, and CBS, CNN, the BBC, and the Associated Press picked it up. Jim Gilleran got a call at two in the morning from someone in Texas who heard about it on National Public Radio, wanting to know if he knew the person in the shoe. "Someone living in the middle of nowhere . . . and they were talking about the shoe," Jimmy tells the girls at their drag queen meeting. "The shoe is the only one of its kind in the world," Jimmy tells the *Key West Citizen.*[4]

This was followed up the next year with coverage of Sushi in the shoe as part of CNN's focus on millennium celebrations around the world. It was even wilder than usual. The streets were mobbed, and Sushi egged on men to drop their pants and women to show their breasts. *Celebrate!* reminded readers that "just one-third of a century ago in the streets of New York—and other major American cities—men who wore high heels became the target of hatred, including hatred by the police. Now as we head out of the 1900s, we celebrate that the high heel has become not only a symbol of our freedom but one Key West high heel has gained more and more national focus."[5]

The next big event of the year is Mardi Gras, sponsored by Bourbon Street Pub. On Fat Tuesday the girls participate in the two big events, the tossing of beads from the balcony of New Orleans House and the sidewalk parade down the odd-numbered side of Duval and back up the even-numbered side, with stops at every bar along the way. In 1998 Sushi and Kylie stopped to use the ladies' room at Sloppy Joe's and got kicked out by the bouncer. David, in his weekly column in *Celebrate!,* reported the incident and asked, "Can you imagine the reaction had the girls used the men's room?" adding, "Come on Sloppy, lighten up one night a year."[6]

Saint Patrick's Day is a big holiday in a drinking town, and in 2001

Sushi in the shoe, New Year's Eve (photo by James Dillon O'Rourke)

the gay bars joined together to offer an alternative to the traditional Pub Crawl from bar to bar. *Celebrate!*, Bourbon/801, Diva's, La Te Da, and Atlantic Shores sponsored "Think and Drink Pink." "We got tired of the color green for St. Patrick's Day . . . we got tired of hearing that gay groups couldn't march in the parades in New York and elsewhere . . . sooooooo we are doing something gay and festive."[7] For $10, participants got a T-shirt, pink fedora, parasol, and free drink at all the gay bars. The *Key West Citizen* devoted its front page to the event, provoking a spate of complaints about "flamboyant behavior" (read: men in dresses) and the violation of "family values," much to the chagrin of *Celebrate!*[8]

In April 1998, as part of the Annual Conch Republic Independence Celebration, the first annual Ripley's Believe It or Not! Great Conch Republic Drag Race took place on the "Duval Street Dragway." No cars here: contestants in full drag with at least three-inch heels ran thirty yards down Duval Street to raise money for the Metropolitan Community Church's Heart-to-Heart community outreach program. In true camp fashion, the grand champion was determined not by running fastest (there were trophies for the first three who finished) but by bribing the judges. Spectators and business sponsors could contribute money to buy the title for their favorite girl. The contestant who complained the most won a special award for the Bitchiest Queen. *Celebrate!* reported that a straight couple from Kenosha, Wisconsin, "surveyed the festivities in total disbelief, as their two toddlers . . . were carefully tucked out of view of the drag queens." The woman "rather cautiously remarked: 'I cannot believe my eyes. We just got out of church and we walked into this. Key West has some pretty weird people, but it is kind of fun, isn't it?'" Shortly after talking with the *Celebrate!* reporter, she began snapping photos of her children with Queen Mother XIV, LaLa Belle, a prominent Key West personage.[9] The race gets bigger every year. "There's nothing like the sound of stomping heels and puffin' stuffed chests, along with the smell of cheap hairspray and cologne to drive a crowd wild!"[10]

After the Drag Race comes the Bed Race, a fund-raiser for AIDS Help. The local gay bars organize teams to push decorated bed floats down Duval Street. In 1997 a columnist in *Celebrate!* reported that "the Bourbon Street girls pulled down their own stage-curtains to canopy their creation. Is that Scarlet O'Hara or what?"[11] The next year the 801 entry, "Cleopatra, Queen of Denial," won. Matthew designed a huge barge that carried Sushi as the Egyptian queen and Jim Gilleran as Little Caesar (of "Pizza, Pizza" fame). Matthew portrayed Anubis, the god of the dead; Milla, Kylie, and Raven, another drag queen, were Daughters of Isis;

Margo and Ice, a drag queen then performing occasionally at 801, served as ladies-in-waiting; and standard-bearers and slaves completed the entourage. Sushi designed the costumes.

And then comes Queen Mother, the Monday after Mother's Day. Each year since 1982, drag queens (actually the first year the Queen Mother was a woman, and women are still eligible) have competed for the title and the responsibility of appearing at a host of fund-raisers throughout the year. At the beginning of the 1999 festivities, held at Atlantic Shores, one of the emcees explained the origins of the contest: "The whole idea was to raise money for different charities in town and give awareness to the gay community in general and our friends out there who are gay friendly in town." The contest actually started with a bar owner from California, who modeled it on the imperial court concept so popular in the West.[12] The causes supported include both gay/lesbian and general community groups and services such as AIDS Help, the Hospice and Visiting Nurse Association, Helpline, Metropolitan Community Church, the Leukemia Society, Wildlife Rescue of the Florida Keys, and the local animal shelter. In 1997 Queen Mother XIII, Charlena D. Sugarbaker, raised $238,000. Before stepping down at the end of her reign, she advised her successor, "Keep the wig teased and ready to go at any time, because it's a job!"[13] Queen Mother XVI, Krystal Klear, in addition to the fund-raisers, took on the writing of a column, "Listen to Your Mother," published in *Celebrate!* Just the pageant itself raised over $11,000 for the Hospice and Visiting Nurse Association of the Florida Keys in 2000.[14]

In a spoof of beauty pageants, contestants of all ages and sizes compete on appearance, poise, originality, talent, and responses to questions from the judges. The answers in this last category are as silly and insipid as at the Miss America Pageant. One contestant at the 1999 contest, asked whom out of anyone in the world she would invite to dinner and what she would serve, says the Pope and, after a long pause, names two friends, and she'd make turkey and pour champagne. Another, queried about what question she would ask anyone in the world, says she'd ask Monica Lewinsky why she kept the dress and why she stirred up all the shit over what was sure to have been a small thing. There are judges, and at the end of the evening the outgoing Queen Mother performs (she, unlike the other girls, whose tips go to AIDS, gets to keep what she is offered), takes a last walk down the runway, and then crowns the new Queen Mother. There is also an award for Miss Congeniality.

It's a major event, and the 801 Girls come out in force, sometimes as contestants (R.V. was Queen Mother XVII; Mama Crass, who was then in the 801 lineup, was Queen Mother XVIII), sometimes as audience members. As observers, they come sometimes in drag, sometimes out. This is where Sushi, decked out in boy drag and his pink feather-wrapped bun, sat demurely with her boyfriend Greg's arm draped around her. Gugi, Margo, and Scabby were there in drag. Another 801 performer, John "Ma" Evans, is one of the organizers and emcees of Queen Mother, and he shamelessly promotes the 801 show. Ma's co-emcee at the 1999 event called for a round of applause for her: "Don't you love Ma Evans? Don't you love to hate Ma Evans? God knows, she is one of the best persons I've ever met in my life. And she's also one of the nastiest." She does have a reputation for being bitchy, but she is also the organizer supreme of the gay and lesbian community. Local author June Keith calls her "a tireless and brilliant party maker, fund-raiser, and ultimate diva of drag."[15] And she organizes more than big events. One year the drag queens were planning a Christmas dinner, but, "as the minds of drag queens sometimes work," they forgot that they had to shop in advance. According to David, "Ma showed up with all the fixings for a full holiday feast. Ma has shown himself to be a guardian angel to many in Key West."[16]

Memorial Day, when the "stream of tourists is lightening up and the humidity is coming in full force," is cause for a celebration known as the Survivors' Party, although increasingly there is no real end to the tourist season.[17] This is Ma Evans's baby and has been since 1975. Described by *Celebrate!* as an evening of "entertainment, food and frolic," the event raises money and gives locals the chance to celebrate surviving the onslaught of tourists. As of 1997, the parties had raised over $232,000 for local groups, including the usual AIDS and gay groups as well as the American Red Cross. Drag queens, including the 801 Girls, join a wide variety of other entertainers. John "Ma" works at combining drag performers with singers, actors, jugglers—three-ring-circus style. He's spectacularly successful, and his approach brings drag to people who might never choose to go to a drag show.

After Memorial Day comes PrideFest, which, not surprisingly, is a golden opportunity for the 801 Girls. Unlike in some other cities, where drag queens have met with disapproval from at least some sections of the gay, lesbian, bisexual, and transgendered movement, in Key West they are absolutely central. Several of the girls have won the title of Miss PrideFest, Milla in 1997, Gugi in 1999, and Desiray in 2000. "Are you man enough to wear high heels and a wig?" asks the flyer. "Spiked heels are being sharpened, fingernails are being painted to a high gloss, and girdles and panty hose are getting stretched to new limits," *Celebrate!* announces.[18] At PrideFest '98 the paper described the girls as "a

Margo, Milla, Inga, Sushi, Scabby, and Kylie at Pride '98 (photo by Peter Arnow)

half-dozen local lovelies clad in rainbow tones." Calling themselves the Pride Girls, they did a rousing rendition of "We Are Family" at the kickoff rally.[19] Matthew designed (and Dean and Sushi helped him build) a float, and Sushi, as usual, created costumes for the bar's entry in the PrideFest parade. According to the society editor BellaDonna's column, "It was called Pride Island and it starred SUSHI, of course, sitting on top of a volcano that exploded confetti all over everybody. It had a waterfall and all kinds of smoke and about a hundred scantily clad natives."[20] As a troupe, the girls won a community service award that year for their many contributions. As the "girl bar," 801 hosted the Miss PrideFest contest, while Bourbon Street was the site of the Mr. PrideFest competition. David concludes, "The gay community sees Bourbon Street and 801, and they are basically the same organization, being in the forefront of all gay activity taking place here."

Summer is slow, but the drag queens sometimes show up for the community picnic on the Fourth of July, a holiday that also features the Miss Firecracker Pageant. They decorate the 801 lavishly, even filling the downstairs bar with sand for the beach party theme. In 1998 the girls put on a carnival at 801 to raise money for their sets. They create their own event during Bikers Week, which follows Womenfest during the worst weather of the year, in September. During Bikers Week the town is overrun with Harley-Davidson owners. Rather than cede the streets to these most masculine of men, Sushi one year got the idea to lead the girls down Duval to the bars where the bikers hang out. There they engage in "seat sniffing," a bold and now traditional ritual that the bikers (thankfully) appreciate. Milla describes the event: "We create a parade out of this where every fucking drag queen is wandering down Duval Street, we're all dressed up in drag, and we are going into a straight venue. And we literally sniff seats, hang out with all the Harley-Davidsons, all the bikers." Jim Gilleran says people were very nervous the first time they did it, but "the girls, the men, the drag queens, everybody has been very well accepted, and it's one of the most popular events for Bikers Week." Says Inga, "It's a bridge between two totally different things. And it's fun." It is, of course, also confrontational. As Sushi puts it, "We're going down to Sloppy Joe's to mess with the bikers."

And then comes the biggest event of the season, Fantasy Fest, an international celebration around Halloween that draws tens of thousands of tourists from all over the world. Beginning in August, candidates for Fantasy Fest King and Queen (not sorted by either sex or gender) compete by seeing who can raise the most money for AIDS Help. It's by far the most important fund-raiser for AIDS: in 1996 the royal race raised $134,000 and over $36,000 came from just the sale of beads; in 1998 the take was $164,000.[21] Contestants throw parties, sponsor car washes, organize $100-a-plate dinners, and have drag lingerie fashion show and drag queen dog and car washes—do whatever they can to fill the coffers. The one in each category who raises the most money receives a crown, a cape, and a ring, and then the new King and Queen reign for the year. The first drag Queen of Fantasy Fest was LaLa Belle, crowned in 1997, the same year that she was both Queen Mother and Southernmost Queen. (It's easy to lose track of the drag queen contests in Key West!) More recently, LaLa, as L.A., served as King, while the Bitch Sisters, in drag, shared the honors as Queen. No wonder that, when the elected King of Fantasy Fest in 1998, Jerome Covington, an African American physician, appeared in drag at several events, *Celebrate!* published a tongue-in-cheek report that the "once homophobic Coors family, newly recruited to their gay friendly awareness that lesbians prefer Coors over Bud," was demanding an investigation to determine if Covington was suffering from "sexual identity disorder."[22]

Fantasy Fest includes the Key West Business Guild's Headdress Ball, the premier gay and lesbian event, held in the garden of New Orleans House in 1998, 1999, and 2000; a street fair on Duval; a march from the cemetery, in the center of Old Town; a street party at 801; and the centerpiece, the spectacular parade on Saturday night, filled with floats that inch along the parade route, down streets filled with people in the most elaborate and creative costumes and in various stages of undress (although in 2000 the police cracked down on nudity or the display of "simulated genitals," arresting over thirty people, including a man sporting a four-foot penis hat on his head!). The 801 Girls play a big part in the festivities. They entertain at fund-raisers leading up to Fantasy Fest, and for the events of the weeklong celebration, they go all out. They sponsor a Bal Masque Carnival, throw beads during the street festival to those who respond to the call to "Show your dick" or "Show your tits," and serve free hamburgers and hot dogs at a drag queen barbecue at the boy bar on Sunday night when the week winds down.

They also began, in 1998, to stage a lavish special production for the Bal Masque Carnival. That year they spent $12,000, contributed by Jim Gilleran, Budweiser, and the gay business guild, on spectacular sets designed by Matthew and splendid costumes created by Sushi for "Return to Oz" in the newly opened garden behind the gay guest house next to Bourbon Street. Sushi, of course, played Dorothy, Inga was Glenda the Good Witch, Scabby the Wicked Witch, Milla (with funnel breasts) the "Sin Woman," Kylie the Cowardly Lion, Mama the Scarecrow, and Ma Evans the Wizard. Here's the way a local drag queen describes the production:

> The costuming, the choreography, everything was right on the money, and they mixed everything together and they had a different, how can I phrase it, class of audience. They had straight, gay, bi, tri, everything and they all got along. They did the show very well and drew it all together, and I give them a lot of credit for that. Sets, makeup, everything was right down like professional theater. It was almost like doing a movie. They're very professional at what they do and that made a lot of money that went to the [gay and lesbian] community center, and they donate their time, money, and effort. I give them a lot of credit on that. Not many people do that.

An expensive production by 801 standards, "Return to Oz" was a fund-raiser for the new Key West Gay and Lesbian Community Center. The girls won Best Performance by a Group in the annual Hissy Awards that year, sponsored by the No Name Drag Players, an amateur group.

A tough act to follow, but in 1999 they put on the "Rocky Bourbon Horror Show," an "even more warped version of the warp-timed" original that had been so important to so many of them growing up.[23] Again, the casting was perfect: Sushi as Magenta; Milla as Dr. Frank-N-Furter, "the sweet bisexual transsexual from Transylvania"; Scabola as Riff Raff; Gugi as Columbia; Margo as the Criminologist; R.V. as Dr. Everett V. Scott; and Kylie as Janet Weiss. According to *Celebrate!*, the "hit number of the evening was the Busby Berkeley inspired water ballet in which the dancers, outfitted in gold lame tuxes, . . . floated in kaleidoscopic formations" and shot plumes of water into the air from giant water guns in the New Orleans House pool.[24] The 2000 production of "Alice in Wonderland," featuring Kylie as Alice, also included a water ballet in the pool and the water guns hidden in the tails of mice costumes, but the most enthralling number was Sushi changing from a caterpillar to a butterfly to the song "I'm Changing," from *Dream Girls.*

Dean thinks that their central presence in Fantasy Fest 1998 did them a lot of good.

> I don't think that there's one person in this town that does not know me, and can not have something good to say about all of us. Have some sort of respect for us now. I was so pleased with that because I do believe that we did get a lot of respect that we didn't have from the community. With all that talk about the drugs and alcohol, I believe that Fantasy Fest and all the work we put into it, regardless of whether there were drugs and alcohol involved in it, we put all of our heart and love into it. We took on incredible responsibility.

Kylie makes the same point: "It's ever changing and evolving, what we're doing. We were never asked to do anything, you know, like a year or two years ago. Each year that goes by, we seem to get more and more opportunities."

It's not long after Fantasy Fest that the winter season begins in earnest. David comments in his column, "I can't wait until season is in full swing and we all begin complaining how busy we are and how tired we are."[25] John "Ma" Productions (his production company) puts on "Red Ribbon Christmas" the first Saturday in December to raise money for AIDS Help. At one point John "Ma" also organized a "Wish for the Holidays" at La Te Da to raise money and collect toys for children, but there was so much going on that he concentrated on Red Ribbon Christmas.

There's hardly an event in Key West that doesn't involve drag queens. Or if that is an exaggeration, certainly there's not one in the gay and lesbian community that doesn't. The girls are celebrities. Yet it is not by any means a simple status, for they also sometimes describe themselves as outcasts. David describes Margo's appearance at the Caribbean Music Festival in the heart of Bahama Village in May 1999: "Now I'd like to mention that Margo was a bit apprehensive since in many cases drag queens and 'sissy boys' are not the most popular form of entertainment in the Caribbean. Margo figured she would either get a decent reception or be torn limb from limb and thrown to the wolves."[26] In fact, the crowd went wild, but clearly the anxiety was not unwarranted.

"Freaks, we're still considered that," says Dean. "On the street, how they stop to look at me . . . they see the freak thing. . . . Some are just looking at freaks," Roger tells us. David says that people who know he writes a column for *Celebrate!* begin to understand that "drag queens are not these drugged-up, drunk, you know, freaks running around the streets." Lady V describes sitting at a bar looking like a man and having someone ask him what he does. "I either say one of two things. Depending on whether I want to talk to this person or if I want to blow them off. If I want to get to know them a little better, I tell them I'm a hairdresser. If I want to blow them off, I tell them I'm a drag queen." If he tells them about his night job, "the reaction on their faces is shock, amazement." Gay men, he says, want to be with men. "But see, the thing is that drag queens over a period of history, they're snappy, da-da-da-da, they're a lot of fun to watch, but they're really miserable to people. . . . Fags idolize it, but they don't want to get involved in it." Then—news editor of *Celebrate!* Eric Selby reported in an article entitled "In Defense of Drag Queens" that gay men kept asking him to stop featuring drag queens, that one complained that "they give us a bad reputation."[27] Yet Kylie distinguishes Key West from other places where drag queens have to put up with dirty looks from gay men: "I can't believe how much they love drag queens here. It's bizarre."

At the same time, they sometimes talk about themselves as if they *are* freaks. Dean once described to us a fan with whom he had become very friendly who confessed he was a serial killer and another man he wanted "to spend his life with" who had twenty-one personalities, eight of whom Dean had met. "And I'm a drag queen," he adds needlessly, as if he indeed belongs in a category with criminals and people with multiple personalities.

Like other celebrities, the girls have to deal with people who think they know them because they've seen them perform. Roger expresses particular dislike for people who grab him and expect him to be their friend. "I have to take time with them as Inga. . . . But . . . Roger has a lot of personal problems and I want to deal with them in my way."

Dean says, "People will come into town and they'll be like, 'I want you to meet somebody,' and then they'll be like, 'Milla!' And I'll have to pretend like I know them well." "They invite us to the parties to work and entertain, but nobody wants to sit down and get to know us. It's lonely." Fans do in fact invite them out to dinner, singly or in groups. One time when we went with Dean to Seven Fish, a popular local restaurant, he was the object of a great deal of adoring attention, but at the same time a group of gay men at the next table (our New York friend Josh described them as looking as if they came from Atlanta, although he's never been there) rolled their eyes at Dean's tasteful eye makeup and polished nails.

The ambivalence expressed in this combination of celebrity and hostility carries over into the personal lives of the drag queens. If the story of the 801 Girls' centrality in community life mirrors the adulation they sometimes receive on the sidewalk in front of the bar, the more negative, or at least more ambivalent, side of that experience is reflected in their descriptions of more personal relationships. As Sushi puts it in choosing to perform a powerful song by the Jody Grind, "One Man's Trash Is Another Man's Treasure."

EIGHT

"THE HERO WOULD BE YOU"

One of their best group numbers, "If You Could Read My Mind," by Stars on 54, compares their lives to a pulp novel. And when the plot gets to the part where the heroine's heart is broken, "the hero would be you," they tell the audience. And in fact their intimate relationships do seem to involve more than their share of heartache.

A big source of the heartache is the lack of interest on the part of the masculine gay men whom they tend to desire in being with a drag queen. "I go out to seduce masculine men," Dean (Milla) tells us. "The men I love to be with, they're very masculine, heterosexual we'll say, whatever, or just coming out or bisexual, whatever that is. But that masculine something, the feminine part, that vixen, that little, goes out to get ahold of this masculine—it's something I'm not supposed to be able to attain." Around the pool of the house where David is house-sitting one day, we tell David (Margo), Sushi, and Roger (Inga) that audience members often ask us if they sleep with one another.

> David: We don't sleep with each other. That I know of. I certainly haven't slept with any of them.
> [All of these responses in unison:]
> Roger: I would never be attracted by a drag queen.
> Sushi: Yeah, I wouldn't be attracted.
> David: I would never be attracted to a drag queen.
> Roger: We're attracted to boys.
> Sushi: I like masculine men.
> David: Yeah, exactly.

Roger tells a story about a boyfriend back in Sweden who was very macho, although he was a dancer, and after they had been together a couple of months, the boyfriend started to do drag.

> Roger: And I had a hard time dealing with, that my boyfriend wanted to be a drag queen. But it was too late because I was al-

ready in love with him as a person. . . . But if I were to know
from the beginning that somebody was a drag queen, I would
not—

Sushi and David: No.

Sushi: I don't like feminine boys, though. It just doesn't do anything to me.

David: Yeah, I like masculine men. I'm a man who loves men!

More than once we talked to them about the lesbian feminist ideal and
sometimes practice of loving and sleeping with your friends, but the
idea of being erotically attracted to someone like them in gender style
seemed incomprehensible.[1]

In his column for *Celebrate!* David asks, "Why is it that so many
guys will not go out with a drag queen?"[2] Another time he tells of a
bartender at Diva's who insulted one of the 801 Girls who was walking
by: "It seems that, although he has worked in drag bars on the island
for years, he does not like drag queens and will go out of his way to
say disparaging things about them."[3] R.V. says that one of the reasons
he performs the song "What Makes a Man a Man?"—recounting the
lonely life of a drag queen—is to "let them know that most of us are
without boyfriends because people really have a stigma against it." Like
Lady V, he says he often hides what he does. "Miss Q says no one is
going to fuck a drag queen on vacation. That's true, you just got to
hide what—someone says, 'What do you do for a living?' 'I work in a
bar.' And then afterward, all of a sudden, 'I'm a drag queen! Ha-ha!' "
We wonder what gay men fear. "I don't understand. I don't know,"
R.V. says. "That's the weirdest thing. I don't know what is wrong. They
think I'm going to be effeminate or something. Most drag queens I
know are more manly in the bedroom than anyone else." David would
agree. "I don't know whether men don't want to go to bed with drag
queens because they think we're possibly more feminine than we are."

R.V. sometimes talks in the shows about the problem of finding men.
"When tourists are on vacation, no one wants to have sex with a drag
queen. Never, ever. I can't get the tide to take me out in this town."
So he dedicates a song "to all of those who look at us and go, 'They're
freaks.' Though they don't realize that they walk by us in the day and
we're the most gorgeous boys there on the streets." He tells the gay
entertainment guide in an interview that men come on to him when
he performs. "It's difficult to have a partner. It takes patience and trust."
He describes his romantic life as variable and his romances as serial.
"I have a roll of paper wedding dresses."[4]

Sushi says, "Gay guys aren't attracted to drag queens. Most gay men are not attracted to drag queens. You get these straight, bisexual boys, all the ones I've had." Ricky, Matthew's (Scabby's) boyfriend who works for AIDS Help, tells us in the summer of 1999 that he's "surprised at the animosity that a lot of gay men hold toward drag queens. I mean, gay men can be like really rude and really mean." A straight man who is good friends with the drag queens tells us a story about a gay friend who picked up a very attractive young man at R.V.'s Christmas party:

"[The young man] says, 'Well, listen, I'd like to stop by my house and dress up. Change.' And he did. And he came out in full drag. . . . [The friend] had taken this exquisitely handsome young man and now he saw the shape of a female body walking in the shadow in front of him and he was completely turned off. I mean it was like he couldn't wait—"

His wife interrupts: "Until the date ended."

He continues: "I mean, he was trying to get away at that point. He didn't even know how to gracefully do it. He didn't realize to himself that, well yes, they look wonderful up there, but I don't want to be with one of those. . . . I'm going, you know, he was a handsome young boy, the one that he had met. But in drag, it was like—"

His wife again: "He wasn't interested anymore."

He finishes, quoting his friend: "Yeah. I want a man."

It seems to be important to the drag queens that they win over gay men who don't like them. Sushi describes meeting leather men and "Bears" (gay men who embrace such aspects of traditional masculinity as large bodies and hairiness and outdoor activities), commenting, "They hated drag queens. They didn't even talk to me." But, as his creativity in instituting the seat sniffing suggests, he kept at it. "And it took awhile for them to even accept me and acknowledge me." Dean tells us with a certain amount of triumph that "it worked, I won," having gotten a gay man who said he didn't like drag queens to express interest in him. "He and I have a lot of stuff in common. Except for this whole thing about drag. 'I don't like drag queens, blah, blah.' 'Oh really, you're gonna like this one.' So I worked on it."

On the other hand, there are other gay men who are especially attracted to drag queens, but these can be problematic for the girls as well. David explains:

A lot of men who are attracted to drag queens want to go to bed with a drag queen. And some drag queens will do it. I won't. I mean, I find that [he makes a disgusted noise]. I find it disgusting, but that's only my opinion. I mean there is no way that I am going to get into bed in drag with anybody.

We compare this to going to bed in our work clothes, although it really isn't the same thing at all. David continues:

> I had a guy a couple of weeks ago, month ago, first he walks up to me and said, "What color panties are you wearing?" And I said, "I'm not wearing panties." And he said, "I am." And I thought, "Oh god, here we go! Here we go!"

Verta asks, "Was he in men's clothes?" David responds:

> Here we go! Men's clothes. And he said, "I want to go to bed with you. Will you wear panties?" And I said, "I don't wear panties. I'm not going to wear panties. And I'm not going to go to bed with you, with or without panties."

There are also straight men attracted to drag queens. Gugi describes going to straight bars in drag when he was depressed over his father's death. Men would approach him and he'd say, "Thank you very much, but I'm a man." "They'd go, 'Oh my god.' Then five minutes later, they'd come back with, 'You're so beautiful.' I'm like, 'Thank you. That means I'm doing my job well.'"

We ask Gugi if any of them didn't care that he's a man. "Um, yeah, most of them. . . . Let me put it this way. I was bringing a straight man home with me almost every night last year." In contrast to what people tend to think about men who identify as straight but have sexual relations with men—that they take the insertive role in sex—the drag queens insist that this is not the case. Straight and bisexual men, they say, almost always want to enclose, rather than insert, a penis. Sushi says she's a top, and was in her relationship with Greg. Finding this out—like reading about the fact that the "real men" who have sex with transvestite males in Mexico City and with transgendered prostitutes in Salvador, Brazil, sometimes reverse roles with their partners—makes us question the historical assumption that the part men played in sex acts was tightly tied to one's gender of presentation.[5]

The only one of the girls who has recently been in a long-term relationship is Sushi. Some of the others have been through a lot of boyfriends since we've known them, and some never mention anyone special at all. Relationships aren't easy, given the way they live: the hours, the drinking, the drugs. Lady V says, "I never had a lover. Never a lover. That's one of the things in my life that I wished I'd had." Sushi tells us that Kylie has never had a serious relationship, that he's never lived with any of his boyfriends. "But he has a lot of advice." Sushi laughs. "He knows it all. And he's never, I don't think he's ever opened his heart to another person." Kylie says he worries about losing his looks before he finds a satisfying relationship. "I have very high standards," he says; it's hard for him to trust people, but he then adds, "Well, less nowadays, I'm getting more desperate." Sounding a bit like the teenage girls he imitates so well, he says, "Yeah, I have deep relationships with my friends. However, these ones are so obsessed with relationships, once they get someone, I'm pushed to the side. . . . I think that if I could find someone that I was as close to as Sushi and had that kind of relationship with and be sexually attracted to them, then that would be a really good lover for me."

David's columns in *Celebrate!* chart the fleeting nature of some of their relationships. In January 1998 he congratulates Milla on her "new live-in Stuart" and R.V., "who has connected with Michael and is happier than she's been in ages."[6] Then he reports that Inga is in a snit because her bonding with Skunk—"an up and down union," David says—wasn't mentioned.[7] By the summer of that year, when Dean and Matthew came to dinner at our house for the first time, Dean was with Skunk (Joey), who had just broken up with Roger and later went back to him. All the girls were angry with Dean for starting up with Joey while Roger was still hurting. Matthew was having trouble with Brian, a very sweet but confused young man whose parents had both just died, leaving him with an inheritance that he was spending far too quickly. Dean, who says that if he had ever finished high school and gone to college he would have been a therapist, analyzes the situation:

> Scabby, can we be honest? Scabs. The feeling that Scabby is having is, Scabby could probably deal with it if [Brian] was throwing himself, asking for help, asking for emotion, asking for love. And instead what he's doing is, he's saying, "I want to be with you," and then [he's] never there.

Joey, a young street punk, wasn't exactly making Dean happy, either. Dean confides:

> I've been through relationships . . . I could be really bitter. . . . But I do still have one thing, I still have my heart and my love, and I do believe that somewhere, it's out there, and I'm willing to take all these lessons—Joey is a lesson, I'm learning from this. . . . I want him to learn something too—it's like a mirror; he's going through what I once was.

If Dean identifies with Joey, David puts himself in the place of someone who had had a lot of Joeys in his life. Although he likes Joey and says that "he's cool now," he also analyzes what it means to be attracted to kids like him. "I think it has to do with self-esteem. . . . We think that we're . . . It is a very involved thing but it becomes a thing of self-worth. And this is all we deserve. We deserve people like this. . . . I mean, I've had them. I mean, my god, that's what I gravitate toward. Except most of the time just before the connection it's like, you stupid fool. Come on." He describes seeing a kid on the street a few nights before, looking at him and watching him looking back. "And I thought, yeah, I'll take him home, and now let's see, tomorrow morning it means I get up and I buy a new television, a VCR, a stereo system. I said, that's exactly what I'll have to do. Now I have to do other things tomorrow, so I'm not going to take him home and have to go out and buy everything."

Their pickups really do sometimes steal from them. The next boyfriend after Joey stole Dean's tips one night, disappointing him terribly. Such betrayals mean, as Dean says, "it's a lonely life, a lonely life." Yet they always seem to have hope.

> "I found a guy that I like a lot," says Matthew.
>
> "You like him, girl," Dean says encouragingly, then adds, "He's attractive, he's sweet, he's older than eighteen, and he has a better head on his shoulders."
>
> Matthew continues: "The only thing I want is, they have to come home at night. All I ask is that you come home at night, you fall asleep with me at night."

At another time, Dean says he's put away thoughts of becoming a titty queen: "No, I'm gonna be a man. And I'm gonna have a relationship with a wonderful manly man."

Some of the drag queens have had good relationships in the past. Matthew tells of meeting the first big love of his life, Michael. At the time, living in Providence, Matthew was hanging around with a boy prostitute, "because I always hung around with the degenerates and the weird people that nobody would hang around because I found them more interesting." So one night they were sitting in the park, drinking beer and smoking a joint, and the friend went over to talk to a man who kept driving by in a little red Toyota. Then the friend walked back to Matthew and said, "He don't want me; he wants you." Matthew was mortified, but it turned out the guy wasn't a john. He just thought Matthew was cute and wanted to meet him.

> He took me out for a beer; we smoked some pot. And then we went to another park which overlooks the city. . . . It's got this huge statue, granite statue of Roger Williams; it's massive and he's got his hand

out like this. And if you crawl up the statue, you can go sit in his hand. And then you can overlook the city skyline. I never knew that you could climb up there. And he took me out there the first night I met him.

We ask if they had sex. "No!!! [said with exaggerated horror] I didn't have sex with him—we dated for like almost three weeks before we had sex." We get off on other subjects, then back to Michael. "I'm sure you two can relate to this. Do you ever find that one person and you know that you're gonna be together forever? Michael was that person."

They dated for two years before they moved in together. They had been buying and selling antiques, and then they decided to open their own store with money Matthew inherited from his grandfather.

I was on cloud nine. I had a beautiful home filled with beautiful antiques. I had the man of my dreams in my life and in my bed. And I had money that I was getting every month. Didn't have to work if I didn't want to. And I decided, you know, I want to open my own business. . . . I want to be independent. And everything was fine.

And then the day after they opened their shop, Matthew came home to find a note from Michael's sister saying that she had taken him to the emergency room. He had been sick, and Matthew had been afraid it was AIDS. The other girls insist that it was, but Matthew told *Celebrate!* that it was liver cancer and us that it was a hereditary disease that destroyed his liver and kidneys.[8] For the next year and a half, Michael was in and out of the hospital. At the end, his family kept Matthew from seeing him.

They wouldn't let me go in. I had to go in and get a lawyer and fight them just so I could go in and see him. They allowed me in for fifteen minutes the day before he died. They wouldn't even leave the room. They stood there over me like I was gonna, like, unplug him or something. Which I would have if I had been left alone. I would have unplugged him because he did not want to be put on any machines. . . . I went to the hospital, I got to spend fifteen minutes with him. . . . And then finally getting to be able to see him, I was like relieved.

He decided to go to the beach the next day, and before he left, a friend called to see how Michael was doing.

And I said, "I didn't call. I'm going to the beach. I just wanna, you know, relax." She says, "I've got three-way call, let me call." So she puts me on hold, she calls the hospital, and the nurse said, and I remember it like it was yesterday, "He expired this morning at seven fifteen." . . . Expired. They said he expired. They didn't even say he had passed on. He expired.

Already hooked on coke, which they had starting smoking together so Michael could stay off morphine, Matthew lost the business, their house, the furniture, everything. He just didn't care anymore. It was a long time before he was able to pull himself together.

Although David says he never had a long-term live-in relationship, he has written poignantly about two different men in his columns. When he was twenty-two, he became lovers with Frank, a fifty-year-old man with whom he worked at W&J Sloane Home Furnishings in New York. "At the time I was in my mid-twenties and attracted to older men with gray hair and blue eyes," he writes.[9] Frank, David tells us, was "beautiful, looked exactly like William Holden, when William Holden was really good-looking." Frank was in a long-term relationship but it had become platonic, so Frank and David became "boyfriends." They went out for drinks or dinner and started to vacation in St. Thomas together. "We had what I considered and still do an absolutely perfect relationship." When David decided to move to St. Thomas, they continued to get together when Frank came down. Then Frank stopped traveling much and they drifted apart, although they stayed in touch. David admits that he really wanted Frank to remember him as he had been in his twenties. "I remember calling him when I reached fifty and saying, 'Do you remember all those times years ago, when . . . I wanted to "play" and you just wanted to go to sleep?' I understand!" When Frank died at the age of eighty-three in January 1999, David wrote his sister a letter: "Your brother was quite a man. . . . [He] was the important relationship in my life and I treasure having had him as a mentor, a friend and a lover."

And now that David understands just wanting to go to sleep, he—following in a well-established tradition of age-differentiated relationships in the history of male same-sex sexuality—hangs out with those who still want to play. While recovering from his surgery for bladder cancer in the autumn of 1998, he wrote about a nineteen-year-old lover with whom he had spent three "sometimes great, oftimes stormy" years. "Tall, reed-thin, tanned and with a head of tousled sun-bleached hair . . . and a face that would cause a chorus of angels to gasp in admiration and jealousy, he has no conception of how truly beautiful he is." Shortly after their relationship began, the boy left to be a Deadhead in New Orleans, and David wrote of his pain. "I resist laundering our bed quilt;

the scent of his body and the fragrance of his cologne, Patchouli, linger and they are among the very few things I have left. . . . He left twenty days ago and at times it feels like twenty minutes. Just a few minutes before he left, I snapped a few photographs of him. . . . In the picture he is wearing baggy trousers and a sweatshirt. . . . I can vividly remember the body underneath."

He came back, and when they finally parted, David says that there was no great drama. Like so many of the young men the drag queens find attractive, he was bisexual. David tells us, describing the boy's relationships with women, "I've become very liberal in my—as I get older. I mean, twenty years ago I would have been, like, 'I'll fucking kill you.'" Eventually the boy left him for another drag queen and then went home to Louisiana, where he started living with a woman.

David continues to write in his columns about young men with whom he has usually brief relationships. In August 1998 he announced a new relationship with Yancy, "proving it is never too late to have sparks fly. He is just a tad bit younger than I (by 38 years!)."[10] That was at the three-week mark, and two issues later it was over. In one issue David wrote movingly about getting older. The day comes, he writes, when you look in the mirror and wonder, "Who IS that? The face and body are familiar and it does resemble you, but it isn't the face that you see in your mind." He remembers past days of looking at a guy on the street and striking up a conversation. "Now, when you turn around to look at a guy, all you see is the retreating rear of the man you wish like hell would turn around and glance back at you, but he never does. And you continue walking, maybe turning around one more time with hope for what never happens."[11]

But these are past stories, and they aren't really about being a drag queen. The more relevant one is the story of Sushi and Greg, who were together for about seven years. Sushi says he has an odd habit of falling for bisexual adopted sons of preachers, and that is what Greg is. Greg describes the first time he saw Gary:

> He was [at the club in Portland where Sushi worked as a drag waitress] and he was with a friend. From about three-quarters from behind I saw somebody, he didn't have a wig on. [To Sushi] Your hair was short, actually, but you had makeup on. I never really saw the face, but I will never forget that one-point-five second of seeing this person from twenty feet away in a crowd. Didn't see him again, but I never forgot that moment. I don't know why, it was just one of those things.

About a year later, Greg was going to get married and asked a friend who knew Sushi to invite him to the party after the wedding. Sushi doesn't remember being invited, but if he was, he didn't show up. Six months after the wedding, Greg's wife went out of town and Greg went down to the club to meet Sushi.

> Sushi: I noticed him staring at me.
>
> Greg: So I hung out that night and drove him home. Gave me a kiss on the cheek. Freaked me out. . . . We set up a first date. . . .
>
> Sushi: I was all, who's this guy?
>
> Greg: Just another cute straight boy you could score with. So we set up a date and I came over. You were sick. But I came over and he opened the front door and it was the first time I'd seen him in boy clothes. And that was it.
>
> Sushi: I'd dyed my hair. Purple.
>
> Greg: That moment it was over, it was done. I knew within thirty seconds that I was through. My life was ruined, it was horrifying, it was this really bad feeling.
>
> Verta: Because when you saw him you thought he was so adorable.
>
> Greg: Yeah, as a boy. I just knew it was done. And then I had a good time. I'd spend a couple of hours there, but then I was miserable for the next few months.
>
> Verta: So you had sex? [We seem always to assume that they do it right away . . .]
>
> Greg: No, we didn't have sex until . . .
>
> Sushi: Three weeks later. Right before I found out that he was married. I didn't know he was married.

At another time, when we talked to Sushi alone, he described the beginning rather differently, sounding far less uninterested. He had sworn off men, having been hurt badly several times. "And I met Greg. And instantly fell in love. . . . Met the man that I knew was my soul mate." He tells about kicking Greg out of the house when he found out he was married, a confession that followed on the heels of Sushi telling of having been a prostitute.

> And then [Greg] kept on calling. He said, "You're the one, I know you're the one. I can't believe I've fallen in love with a drag queen prostitute." . . . Yeah, he had been lying to himself for so long. And he just couldn't believe how I lived my life so freely, so openly.

Then one day during the Christmas holidays, they got a phone call saying that Greg had won a $3,000 shopping spree in a drawing Sushi had entered in both of their names. Sushi got in drag, a limousine came and picked them up, and they shopped at all the fanciest stores in town. "But that's when I realized, wow, this is my soul mate. This never happens."

Greg had dated men before, but this time was different. Things at home became unbearable, and he finally told his wife he wanted a divorce. His life was pretty complicated—his father was a Baptist minister, and Greg was helping to raise a son from a previous relationship with a woman who had since become a lesbian. Meanwhile Sushi was crushed when he found out that Greg was married, so he started to date other people. His friends told him to get out (as his drag queen friends constantly did).

> Greg: I really fell in love with Gary, I didn't fall in love with Sushi. We've never—
> Sushi: Sushi doesn't get along with Greg.
> Greg: Sushi and Greg don't get along. I've never had sex with her in drag, I wouldn't. Wouldn't even consider it. I like women, that's the deal; drag queens don't work sexually for me. Yeah, it was when I saw him as Gary, it was just like over.

Yet Greg says he loves being involved with a drag queen, loves going out with Sushi in drag. "I definitely think there is a sexual, bisexual, thing going on with a man that dresses as a woman." Besides, he loves being with someone who draws a lot of attention to himself. They eventually moved in together and then ran off to Key West. Greg, who was working as a graphic designer and had leased a warehouse that he had subdivided into co-op apartments, sold it all, introduced Sushi to his parents the day before they left, and drove a 1957 trailer across country to a new life. He found a job as a bartender at Bourbon Street and freelanced in graphic design.

Needless to say, it wasn't an easy relationship. Sushi slept around as Sushi. Greg says he prefers sex with women, although he was in love with Gary, and he continued to sleep with women. But it's the men he slept with that hurt Sushi the most. And not just any men. For a while Greg was having sex with Milla, and that was a betrayal, from both sides, that really hurt. The other drag queens hold it against both Greg and Milla. David said, while Sushi and Greg were still together, "Sushi needs a little more strength to leave Greg, which is what she wants to do." David thinks they were probably very much in love at one point, and he recognizes that Greg gave up a lot to be with Sushi. "But Greg is a philanderer." Sushi also plays around, "But it isn't a serious thing. But when Sushi finds out that Greg has slept with so many people she knows. It's not like you sleep with a tourist and they leave, you know, to go back to Boston the next day. These are people Sushi will talk to the next day." Sushi "said the other night in the dressing room that she will work with Milla, you know, she still loves Milla, but she cannot respect Milla anymore. And I totally understand it."

Sushi tells us, "Everybody else knew except for me. But you know, I don't blame Milla; I don't blame the boyfriend. I just hate when people lie to me. Because . . . he sleeps with women; I sleep with other men. But I know that he's a good man." He confides that he almost missed one of their drag queen meetings because he and Greg had stayed up all night drinking and "bonding." "That was the first time we had stayed up that long and got drunk together. Just drunk. I mean, sorry-ass drunk, falling around the apartment, laughing, rolling around the floor, cuddling." And about Milla, Sushi says, "I had Milla crying on my shoulder the other night. And I'm like, 'Girl, I love you. Don't worry about it; it was just sex.'" Another time she says she'll never forgive Milla, but she loves her anyway. "She's like ice cream or cigarettes: you know they're no good for you, but you love them anyway."

The one who really had a hard time with Greg was Kylie, who after all has such a deep and complex relationship with Sushi. Sushi tells a story about Kylie begging him to stay in L.A. with him. "L.A. is not home," Sushi says he told Kylie. "I love ya. . . . I said, 'Well, I have . . . my plane leaves in an hour; you need to take me to the airport. He goes, 'Take the bus.' He made me take the bus to the airport!" One night in the dressing room, they were all talking about a married man someone was interested in and Sushi said, "Greg was married when I met him, and he's the best thing that ever happened to me." Kylie rolled his eyes and said, in a voice dripping in sarcasm, "Yeah, that's what you were telling me last night, right?" One day at the beach, Kylie tells us, "She really should dump him." "But," Leila asks, "Sushi really loves him, doesn't she?"

> Kylie: I don't know. She talks about the time, always the time has something, some special meaning to her. But what always comes to mind is that song, the Culture Club song, about time, something about time won't give you time and time makes lovers feel like they have something real. You know, they've got nothing but time.

And that did, in fact, turn out to be the case. Finally, over Thanksgiving 1999, they broke up. "It was a long time in coming, and Greg finally had the courage to say the word," Sushi told us. With what looked like great haste, Greg moved in with a woman and made plans to marry her. "At least he's not sleeping with all my friends," said Sushi. In June 2001 David began to name "The Hunk of the Week" in his column and the first was—Greg.[12] All along it had been easy to think of Greg—as well as so many of their stories—when the girls do "If You Could Read My Mind."

☆   ☆   ☆

The 801 Girls are something of an institution in Key West, which is, after all, both cosmopolitan and a small town. Although it is their shows that make them known, their performances are not just within the walls of the cabaret. From their hustling on Duval Street to their centrality in the creative and funky fund-raisers that are so typical of the Conch Republic, they have an impact on their community. In a culture in which the mass media create celebrities, they are both a familiar and a different kind of celebrity: glamorous, fantasy-dependent, good for business, but also self-created, accessible, revered and marginal at the same time.[13] In their public presence and in their relationships, both casual and intimate, they regularly cross what we tend to think of as the firm lines of gender and sexuality; they earn both admiration and hostility; they embody in so many ways ambiguity and ambivalence and in-betweenness. "Take Me or Leave Me" is a bold assertion of drag-queenness. Some they encounter do leave them. But more take them by following them up the stairs for an eventful evening. And what happens on the stage, and in the audience, has its own kind of impact, even beyond the Rock.

SECTION III
"LIFE IS A CABARET"

Or, perhaps more to the point here, the cabaret is both life and about life. It's life, or part of life, for the drag queens, because they work hard at putting on the shows. Despite the fact that they lip-synch rather than sing, they are professional performers who plan the shows, rehearse, make or put together their costumes, advertise, perform as a group every night of the year, and do it all for not very much money. And it's about life because the shows in multiple ways question societal understandings of gender and sexuality. The songs the drag queens choose to perform, the meanings they give to the words and music, their gestures and intonation, the costumes they wear, the way they move their bodies, their talk, their exchanges with the audience—every aspect of the show has meaning, sometimes obvious and sometimes hidden.

Now we finally meet the girls as they present themselves onstage: Margo, world-weary and a little disdainful, doing classic numbers such as Peggy Lee's "Big Spender"; Scabola, comedic and outrageous, performing songs such as "Wedding Bell Blues" in a torn wedding dress with blackened buck teeth and thick glasses; Sushi, svelte, elegant, gorgeous, an incredibly talented dancer who learned her moves watching Hollywood films on television and could pass as a woman on a Las Vegas stage; Milla, who describes herself as "omnisexual," beautiful and sometimes vulnerable and sometimes angry, who ranges from a creditable Erykah Badu to Alanis Morissette; Kylie Jean Lucille, "the California dream," who swings herself up and dances on the rafters and on Saturday nights strips naked at the end of the show, juxtaposing a well-hung man's body to a woman's made-up face and long blond hair; Inga, "the Swedish bombshell," voluptuous and sexy, who moves between comic routines such as "Barbie Girl" and classic female impersonation; Gugi, the Puerto Rican spitfire, seductive and aggressive, sometimes putting on a fake thick accent; and

R.V., moving from Bette Midler to "What Makes a Man a Man?"—during which she transforms herself into Timothy. As the show proceeds from group numbers to individual performances to various forms of audience participation, the standard categories of male and female, straight, bisexual, and gay, are continually brought into question. This section considers that process.

NINE

"SHE WORKS HARD FOR THE MONEY"

Onstage the girls make it all look easy. They sometimes even say that there isn't much to what they do, especially comparing themselves to Key West performers such as Randy Roberts and Christopher Peterson, both of whom sing rather than lip-synch as they impersonate stars from Carol Channing to Barbra Streisand. But the 801 show is deceptive, for a lot of hard work and talent go into every evening. And in fact audience members tell us this is the best show in town. A gay physician visiting from New England reports that his brother and sister-in-law, who live in Key West, told him that he and his lover had to go to 801 because "it's the only entertainment worth seeing in Key West." Even more extravagantly, a gay hairstylist from Philadelphia insisted that it was "the best live drag show that I've ever seen," and his lover, the assistant to a state senator, agreed: "It was definitely the best."

So how did it come about? Once upon a time, the 801 was a local hangout, a "Cheers" kind of place where everyone knows your name. The 801 opened in 1987, "bringing a touch of Provincetown, Mass., flair to the island of Key West" as *Celebrate!* put it.[1] At one time the upstairs was a piano bar where the audience would belt out show tunes. A number of different drag queens performed in the upstairs space, including R.V. and her sidekick Miss Q. But the regular cabaret was the creation of Sushi, who got his foot in the door when he first moved to Key West and was cleaning Bourbon Street after hours. He really didn't want to do drag, he says, because he had just come out of his years as a drag waitress in Oregon, yet "after two months, I started hinting around that they should have a drag show" at Bourbon Street. Joe Schroeder, who owns Bourbon Street and co-owns 801 with Jim Gilleran, "hated drag queens, despised everything that they were, stood for." (One night at a benefit, Joe told us he doesn't hate drag queens; he's scared of them. Sushi responded, "Who's the first drag queen you loved?" batting her eyes at him.) Sushi describes Joey as "the straightest gay man I've ever known" and Jimmy as "the gayest straight man I ever met." But Joey finally gave in, and after six months of cleaning the floors, Sushi got one night a week.

Sushi called Milla and another drag queen, and they advertised "Drag Your Friends to Friday." The girls bartended in drag, and it turned out to be the busiest night of the week. Even though Milla was a disaster as a bartender. "She'd sell one drink and then talk, and say, 'I need to go get a cigarette,'" Sushi reports. Milla herself says, "I'm the *worst* bartender—I always want to sit down and talk to everybody." At first they just tended bar (Milla nominally), but then Jimmy suggested that Sushi do a number. "I started starring in a number behind the bar at the end of my shift as I'm going up to the stage, and it just got crazy. It was packed, packed, packed." They moved to doing two shows a week, on Fridays and Sundays, and Sushi quit cleaning. He called Kylie, talking him into coming to Key West, and Kylie took over the cleaning job. Then Joe Schroeder and Jim Gilleran bought 801, where R.V. was doing shows, and Jimmy told Sushi, "There you go. I bought you a club with a stage, a real stage—do whatever you want to do with it." Sushi says Jimmy put him in charge because he was the first drag queen at Bourbon Street and they felt loyal to him. "Because I kept it going on. I wasn't a flighty drag queen that ran out of town. I always showed up on time and did my job." So, he says, "that's when this all happened."

The first time we ever saw Sushi was a Sunday night in the summer of 1997 at Bourbon Street. Verta's twenty-one-year-old nephew, Jason, a devout southern Baptist from Tennessee, was visiting with his friend Sarah, who expressed interest in seeing a drag show. At that time we were going to La Te Da to see Vogue, an African American drag queen who has been performing for a long time and is a local celebrity in her own right. We called around to see where there would be a show and ended up at Bourbon Street. At least, we thought, Sarah, a beautiful young blond, wouldn't get harassed there by men trying to pick her up, as had been happening all over Key West. In fact, the minute we walked in the door, a very drunk gay man from Nashville proposed to her, promising to give her everything she wanted if she would provide cover and have his babies. That and the pornographic videos playing over the bar proved to be too much for Jason, but like a good sport he watched us win a free drink when Sushi asked for the couple that had been together the longest. That we were lesbians (among very few in the bar) was so predictable that Sushi also brought up the male couple who had been together the next-longest. It was a political commentary on gay relationships. We were taken by the sexual energy in the bar, albeit male sexual energy, and when we later heard the bar called the "boy bar" by the drag queens, there was no question in our minds what they meant.

Now the Bourbon Street complex has something for everyone. The three-part ads in *Celebrate!* proclaim their specialties: "Key West's premier video bar," a reference to the pornographic videos, and "DANCERS," meaning the male strippers on the bar, at Bourbon Street; the backroom Saloon One, "where the real men go to have fun"; and "The Finest Shows in Key West, Seven Nights a Week! The Best Show in Town! Never Has So Much Talent Tottered on Such High Heels!"—obviously the pitch for 801.

"The Best Show in Town" continues to be Sushi's responsibility as house queen, a role the other girls acknowledge. "She is our house queen. She is the boss. She's in charge of the drag mafia," R.V. says in introducing Sushi at the show. Originally Jimmy paid the girls individually, but then Sushi insisted that she be paid as an independent contractor ("Gook Productions") who would, in turn, pay the other girls. At first she paid them on Saturday nights, "after we were drunk," then they started having regular Monday afternoon drag queen meetings, where they plan their schedules and receive their pay. When we first stopped into the show and got hooked, Sushi invited us to come to a meeting. "That's when we get paid, so everyone shows up."

Sushi runs the weekly meetings, negotiates with the owners, supervises the performance schedule, deals with problems, and hands out the cash. She tells us that she learned a lot from house queens on the West Coast, where the concept is more familiar, but she also ran up against some abusive house queens there and swore never to be like them. And in fact she is very consultative and even-handed, to say nothing of playful. Here's a typical start: the girls are all sitting around the bar in the cabaret, and Justin, a bar employee, shows up in a Captain Morgan (of Captain Morgan rum) pirate costume, an advertising gimmick. They are merciless:

Kylie: What are you doing up here? What are you doing up here? This is our meeting. Hello!
Milla: Love that, where'd you get that?
Ma: Are you Captain Morgan?
Kylie: What is that for? Oh, Captain Morgan! [laughter]
Margo: You look like a refugee washerwoman. [laughter]
Kylie: It's Aunt Jemima-ish, the way you're wearing it.

Milla [quietly, to us]: They just love to make an ass out of him.
Kylie: If he knows he looks so stupid, then he shouldn't do it. [He
    laughs.] But he's doing it, so—
Sushi: Let's start the meeting.

At this meeting, as at others, they talked about money, the weekly
schedule, publicity, money again, spats and complaints, the division
of labor, the need to be out on the street, and our book. After they talk
things over and work out the schedule, Sushi pays them one by one,
they repay each other for money they've borrowed, and then they take
off, sometimes to go to the grocery store together or to get something
to eat.

There's a lot of campy play involved in the meetings. At one meeting,
when it was time for Sushi to pay everyone, he announced that he was
going to his office. He picked up his papers, went to the front of the
bar by the stage, and sat down at one of the tables. He then proceeded
to call them up one by one, instructing them to knock on one of the
tables so that he could call out "Come in!" They sat down across the
table from him and he shelled out the cash. They rolled their eyes and
laughed, but they all went along.

When the show first started, there wasn't much organization. "We
were sort of messed up," Sushi says. "We didn't have a schedule; we
didn't really have any real shows. It was just sort of, 'We got a stage,
whoo, let's have fun.' We were all excited. Then I realized that we need
to sit down and organize this whole thing." What they did was to divide
up the shows, so that each night a different girl would be in charge.
In the spring of 2000, Sushi told us that he was assigning all the girls
rankings, based on seniority and how hard they work, and that each
would have to listen to the girls higher in the pecking order. At that
point Sushi was number one, Kylie two, R.V. three, Scabby and Ma
Evans were in competition for four and five, and Destiny and Desiray
for six and seven. (Milla had left town for a while, Margo was ill, and
Inga and Gugi had gone to Diva's.)

It's a little hard to figure out what really makes a drag queen a "house
girl" or an "801 Girl": Her own stool in the dressing room? Or a regular
weekly show? Margo says "there isn't a drag queen in town who
wouldn't kill to be an 801 or a Bourbon Street Girl." The lineup was
pretty constant during the period on which we concentrated: Monday,
"Milla's Martini Madness"; Tuesday, Margo's "Stonewall: The Legend";
Wednesday, at first Scabola Feces' ("She's Not Right!") "Politically Incorrect," then "Between Good and Evil"; Thursday, "The Inga Show,"
then "A Night in Havana with Gugi Gomez"; Friday, Sushi's "Broadway

Backstage"; Saturday, Kylie's "Girlie Show" ("A Naughty, Nasty Nympho Full of Sex & Seduction!"); and Sunday, R.V.'s "Return to Paradise." The girl in charge of the show generally, but not always, serves as the mistress of ceremonies, and she determines who will perform, makes a program of numbers for the evening, and makes sure that there is someone to take charge of the music. But they all have particular strengths and weaknesses, so the division of labor is flexible. And Jim Gilleran keeps a hand in, not only determining how many girls Sushi can afford to pay but influencing who gets a show and commenting occasionally on the lineup. When La Te Da closed down and Ma Evans lost his job, Jimmy hired him for an early show at 801. As Arlene Goldblatz, she and Margo did a show called "Two Tickets to Toledo," a warm-up for the regular show. They performed at nine, and a lot of the audience stuck around for the start of the eleven o'clock show.

Sushi's role as negotiator, his democratic style, yet his responsibility as leader are all evident in one conversation about asking for a raise and making a slight change in the way they were paid. Here he tangles with Kylie, his best friend:

Sushi: We got a two hundred–dollar raise per night, which is really good. I wish. [laughter]

Kylie: You could have seriously believed it.

Sushi: But that is something we need to talk about this week, because—

Milla: Want to talk about it today at the meeting? [laughter] Why not right now?

Sushi: What I'm thinking is, since we get a hundred dollars a night—

Kylie: You better wait for Inga, she'll have a flip, she'll flip.

Sushi: I talked to her last night about it. Monday, Tuesday, Wednesday, Thursday, we just get paid a hundred dollars a show, which I think is too cheap. So, I think that, I think the girl who gets, the girl who's hosting, it's her show, should get seventy-five dollars and then there should be two other girls who get fifty dollars. So basically I think that's fair.

Kylie interrupts: What about on the weekends, too; I think the girl who hosts should get seventy-five dollars as well.

Sushi [ignoring this]: So that's actually asking for a seventy-five-dollar raise a night, per night. Is that agreeable with everybody, do you guys want me to ask for more?

[They all talk at once.]

Kylie: Go ahead and ask for it, but I don't think you'll get it.

Milla: I think you should start there.

Kylie: I don't think you're going to get it, but ask for it. Start there.

Milla: I think you should start there.

Kylie: And twenty-five dollars on Fridays and Saturdays.

Sushi: Well, Fridays and Saturdays it's because we have so many girls.

Kylie: Look, don't give the girl who hosts on any night twenty-five dollars extra if you're not going to do it *every* night. [He chuckles.]

Sushi: Uh, you're Saturday night, if you don't want to pay four girls, uh—

Kylie: Oh, OK, I see where we're going with this now.

Sushi: I think two hundred dollars per show—

Kylie interrupts: If I don't like it, then one of the other girls can leave? [Everyone laughs.]

Sushi: If you don't like it, then one of the other girls can leave.

Kylie: All right.

Sushi: Unless you don't want to do Kylie's Saturday night, and I can put you Thursday—

Kylie interrupts again: Oh, I can leave, even better! I see, OK. [more laughter]

Sushi: I can put you on Wednesday—

Kylie interrupts once again: OK, I see where you're going, go ahead.

Sushi [finishing his sentence]: . . . if you want—

Kylie: I'll think about it.

Sushi still finishing: . . . the Kylie sex show could be on Wednesday.

Kylie: A Wednesday, no less.

Needless to say, Kylie's show remained on Saturday. This wasn't an angry exchange, but it wasn't entirely playful, either.

Sushi has responsibility not only for paying the girls but for disciplining them when there are problems. It isn't an easy job. At one meeting he addresses R.V.: "We came to your show last night: you did the opening and a number, then you talked for fifteen minutes, then someone did a number, then you talked another ten minutes. And all it sounded like was 'da da da da da da da' [this said in a monotone], no inflection, no highs and lows." R.V. starts laughing and puts his head down on the bar. "I'm serious," says Sushi. "I know," says R.V., "I had a bad day."

David reported in one of his columns that a drag queen who had been appearing regularly at 801 had been going around town saying that Milla fired her. "Now girl, let's get this story straight," he added.

> If a girl doesn't show up for work for two weeks, then comes in for one night (which happened to be Milla's show) and then doesn't show up for work again, nor call, nor give anybody any indication of what her plans are, and she has not been fired by anyone but spreads rumors to that effect, that girl has a problem. By the way, neither Milla, nor Kylie, nor Margo nor any girl but the House Queen, and that is Sushi, has the authority to dismiss anyone.[2]

If a girl doesn't show up for work, she can be suspended, and if she's late, she gets docked. Other kinds of behavior can lead to being suspended or even fired. Sushi is firm about this: "Backstage, I do not want to hear, and if you do say, 'I'm going to leave,' you will be suspended; anybody who walks out the door during the show, freaks out, leaves, will be suspended for a whole week, no questions asked." Milla gets suspended regularly for being late and other infractions, and even Kylie was out for two weeks when he became infuriated over the bar owners' response to citations issued by the Alcohol, Tobacco and Firearms investigators. (Details on that shortly.) More than once Sushi had to ban Mama from the bar when she caused trouble in the dressing room. Once Mama got into a fight with Inga; another time she got drunk and Super-glued the zipper on Ma Evans's boots. Sometimes we would hear that she had been banned from the dressing room forever, but before long she'd be back.

Despite the undeniable existence of the fabled drag queen bitchiness, Sushi seems to inspire a great deal of respect from the other girls. At one point Sushi held back money from the salary of Desiray, who joined the 801 Girls late in 1999, so that she would be able to pay the rent when it came due. "That's why she's house queen—she's our mother," Desiray told us. That is not to say that he is never challenged. Dean (Milla) confided his ambition to do Sushi's job. "I know I could take care of the group much better. I know that, I know that as far as promoting us, I could promote us much, much better. But in a way I'm lazy and I let her do it and she wants the responsibility but yet she doesn't want the responsibility." In the summer of 2001, when Sushi took a "leave" to go to North Carolina to make costumes for a theatrical production, Kylie took over. He didn't like it, but the show seemed to run smoothly.

In addition to their regular shows, holidays and special occasions mean extra work. Several times a year (Christmas, the Fourth of July, Fantasy Fest) they decorate the bar inside and out. As we have seen, they perform a special extravaganza during Fantasy Fest, and during the 2000–1 season they put enormous amounts of energy into a production called "Va Va Voom." Performed three nights a week before the regular show, with a cover charge of $10, it was a moneymaker. Conceived and directed by Ron Marriott, the revue featured Sushi, R.V., Desiray, Scabola, and Kylie. It combined "the styles of Las Vegas and Cirque du Soleil," involving spectacular costumes they sewed themselves and elaborate dance routines, which the girls complained bitterly to us about having to learn.[3] The show utilized the special talents and styles of the girls. Scabby did her signature "Wedding Bell Blues," but this time dressed as Monica Lewinsky, so that the refrain, "Come on and marry me, Bill," took on new meaning as she changed from an elegant dress into one with a sperm design splashed across the front and clutched a photograph of Bill Clinton. Dressed as Miss Corn and Miss Carrot, Scabby and Kylie descended on R.V. in a purple beet costume and twirled her around to "Turn the Beat Around." It was a fabulous show.

They have a very complex division of labor. Sushi works out a lot of the concepts for the shows and designs and makes most of the costumes, Roger (Inga) did the choreography for group numbers and continues to help out even since moving to Diva's, David (Margo) takes flyers around to the guest houses, Kylie washes the wigs and Milla styles them, and Matthew (Scabby) creates the sets. But they all help with most aspects. Kylie does choreography and sews under Sushi's direction, Sushi did most of the choreography for the *Rocky Horror* show and just farmed out the water ballet to Roger, and Milla sews and helps with the sets. There's really a lot of talent involved. Kylie says of Matthew, "Scabola needs to be reined in 'cause if you let her go, she'll just work and build and do all this stuff, and before you know it, it's this humongous thing. She's one of those types that can get very out of control. It's so typical of an artist. She's an artist." Scabby claims to work more hours than anyone else. Asked what Milla does, he says, "Nothing. She sleeps and drinks and performs. . . . She helps me once in a while. . . . But she'll show, I'll go in at eleven, and she'll say, 'I'll meet you down there in a little while.' Then she shows up at four o'clock. And she'll work for like two or three hours." About Margo, he says (always the clown), "Takes her all day just to get up the stairs. She has to get there at about eleven, too, so she can get up the stairs by five."

Scabby as Monica Lewinsky, in "Va Va Voom" (photo by James Dillon O'Rourke)

So there's a lot of work they do during the week, learning new num-bers, sewing, creating new backdrops, rehearsing. How long it takes them to learn the words to songs and perfect their moves differs from girl to girl. Gugi says, "It just comes to me naturally. I don't sit down, choreograph anything that I do. I have an uncanny ability to remember songs. Just play it and I know them and I just do them." Sushi says

Milla can learn the words in ten minutes, but "it takes me days. Days, hours. I don't have too many brain cells left," which he blames on too many years of doing drugs.

During the shows someone has to take charge of the music, someone has to work the lights, and someone has to serve as emcee. After Roger left to work at Diva's, he told a reporter that one of the things he liked was not having to think about doing the sound, lights, fixing the stage, and dealing with the "bitching and fighting" in the dressing room.[4] The girls aren't all equally good at everything they have to do, although Sushi urges them all to work on their weak points. Milla's is the music (she can't seem to learn how to work the equipment), and Inga's was talking, not surprisingly, since English is not her mother tongue. During the "Inga Show," Inga might say hello but then someone else would do all the announcing, and that's true to a much lesser extent for some of the other girls. At one meeting Sushi reinforced Inga's efforts: "And I do want to make one good point: Inga did talk on the microphone a couple of times [they all applaud]. I'm very impressed with that." (Milla pipes up: "I did music this weekend; I did my best.") Kylie feels strongly that if "it's your show, you should really host the whole thing all by yourself because it's a rapport with the audience. It's like you're telling a story to them and the way you tell it, you make it a whole different show. It's the way I would tell it. It's your personality, and it's not so much what they necessarily do onstage during the numbers, but it's the mood of the show that you set by hosting it."

Sometimes the girls—Kylie, Sushi, and R.V.—who are good at both talking and doing the music complain that it's too much. "I'm sick of it. I want to sit back there during a show and not do a fucking thing," says Kylie. Sushi, aiming at Milla, says, "What I want is, when there's a situation like that, I can depend on a person who's been working here over a year, that should know the system, that gets paid as one of *the* premier house stars, I want to be able to say, 'Go do that,' and you be able to feel like, instead of, like, 'Oh my god! I can't do it!'" Kylie is more direct: "Learn the music!" Milla says she can, promises to learn, and then admits, "I freak out! I freak out!"

Sushi as house queen runs the show, but Jim Gilleran's genius at publicity also has a great deal to do with the success of the cabaret. He's a pretty unlikely person to be running a gay bar because he's straight and a recovering alcoholic, but he says that it's both a "long-term investment to put my kids through college" and a business he really enjoys. Although he hasn't had a drink in eighteen years, he still likes "being out at three o'clock in the morning, seeing people have fun." BellaDonna, a drag queen who writes a column for *Celebrate!*, calls him "that cute, cuddly straight boy . . . who is always all over the 801 Bourbon complex and who seems to work 36 hours a day."[5] Dean describes 801 as Jimmy's "baby" (despite the fact that he actually has children) and his "dream." "He can finally create all that he's ever thought of; he's, he's the best promoter I've ever met in my life, and I've met promoters." Kylie, too, says, "He is a master of publicity," that he knows how to do "something that is going to catch the attention of everybody." Gugi calls Jimmy "the whole engine to the whole thing." He is the one who pushes community involvement because it's good for business. Gugi doesn't think "the girls would actually go out of their way to get up early after a glorious night of frolicking to do a bed race on their own."

Perhaps the best—certainly the most fun—publicity for the bar is the "Street Bus Named Desire," a small tour bus whose engine died at the end of Route 1. Beautifully if garishly painted by a local artist, supplied with neon lights and curtains à la Sushi, outfitted with a stereo system and bar with blender, and driven by Jim Gilleran himself, Desire transports revelers to 801 from the weekly tea dance or whatever special events might be taking place at Atlantic Shores. The music blares, the drag queens perform, the drinks flow freely, and riders are instructed to be sure not to keep their arms and legs inside the bus and not to sit quietly. "It's another way of annoying the tourists and locals alike," says Jimmy. "We'll be driving around town letting our presence be known, providing free transportation to all those naive enough or intoxicated enough to board." Desire carried a crowd to the local movie theater for the opening of *Star Wars: Episode I—The Phantom Menace* in May 1999. The drag queens dressed as the characters, transformed the entire complex into a *Star Wars* set, and combined a show with the trip to see the movie. "When we at 801 and Bourbon Street see an opportunity to celebrate life together we do it," Jimmy tells the paper.[6] There is in fact something about jumping aboard the bus that makes it hard to stop laughing. As *Celebrate!* put it, welcoming Desire, "You are a delightful addition to this wonderfully zany place."[7] Occasionally the bus serves a more serious purpose, as when it delivers voters to the polls on election day.[8]

Jimmy says modestly that 801 is a good investment. The drag queens believe that 801 makes more money than Bourbon Street and that Joe Schroeder can't take it. "They told us that they wanted the boy bar," Dean says, "they always wanted the boy bar, but the drag queens were the ones that were making the money. Once we got 801, they just kind of shipped us over there." David says that Joe Schroeder denies he kicked the drag queens out of Bourbon Street but that he clearly wanted

The "Street Bus Named Desire" (photo by the authors)

the male strippers, and "you can't do both at the same time because you get two different crowds in." Yet Bourbon Street keeps bringing the girls back for occasional appearances. First the plan was for a drag show called "Main Event" after the Sunday tea dance at the Atlantic Shores; then just a few of the girls started doing "Hot Spots," individual numbers scattered throughout the evening, on Sunday night. But none of them really likes performing over there; it's clear that it feels like alien space. The audience, as Matthew says, "is more worried about picking up a boy than they are watching a drag show." One night Milla tore off her wig, walked off the stage, grabbed her stuff, and was out the door, back to 801. At one drag queen meeting, Sushi comments, "I don't want to work over there, take their shit." Then she screams at the top of her lungs, "Fuck you!" And goes on, "How many girls want to work across the street? For fifty bucks, how many girls will work across the street?" Inga and Gugi say yes, Inga adding, "I don't want to, but I'll do it," but then she changes her mind. Kylie says she wouldn't. Milla won't bother anymore but says R.V. will. "I don't think they'll have her," replies Sushi. Kylie suggests, "Tell them the truth, tell them that none of the girls want to work over there, but Gugi's willing because she needs the money."

The drag shows do bring in patrons, and although the girls don't complain too much about the pay, they aren't exactly getting rich performing. They generally get a salary of $50 a night, but they aren't paid for every night they work. At the end of 1998, Sushi was getting just $100 for the shows on Mondays through Thursdays, which meant that only two girls could get salary. Milla and Kylie made the most, $300 a week in salary; R.V. and Margo made $200, and the rest less. Sushi makes a percentage over what the others earn and gets a cut of the bar take when she does "Hot Spots" at Bourbon Street. Some nights if they perform, they work "on the bucket," which means they get tips but no salary. Or they can, although this is usually reserved for guest drag queens who just happen to stop in, perform "off the bucket," for tips they receive individually for a number. Early on they were likely to tell the audience they worked only for tips, which was true for some of them on any particular night. Jimmy complained about that at a drag queen meeting in June 1998, but they wouldn't back down. He also reported that people didn't like too-vigorous solicitation for tips. But that doesn't stop them: they are shameless in calling for tips. Inga and Gugi passed along to Desiray a particular style, which generally works: she looks disgusted and gives the finger when someone gives her a dollar and stands there demanding more until finally the person refuses to shell out any more bills. Or she snatches a man's wallet and riffles through it looking for cash.

One night Kylie, who was not on the schedule, came to Scabby's show to do a guest spot. Scabby took away the bucket and explained to the crowd: "She works with us all the time, but tonight she's just doing a special guest spot, and what she's going to do is, she's gonna do a number and you're gonna have to tip her on your own, put it in her tits or twat, her twing twing—wherever you can find a place to put it. That's her money. She's not sharing the bucket with us tonight, OK? Do we get a clue, do we understand?" A male audience member shouts out, "She don't get paid!" and Scabby responds, "She don't get paid, right, honey. She don't get paid. God, you should go on *Jeopardy*, Mary!"

As this makes clear, they pool their tips, a practice that started when they first began doing group numbers and realized that people were reluctant to come up and give one of them money while they were performing a choreographed routine. Pooling also allowed them to go around in the bar with the tip bucket to get money from those who would never come up and tip them onstage. Although at first the girls who tended to get lots of tips worried that they would be subsidizing the others, after a couple of months they realized that they all made more money on average.

How much they make varies dramatically from night to night, depending on how many girls are in the show as well as the season and night of the week, which affect the size and composition of the crowd. They have made as little as under $20 and as much as nearly $200. Sometimes when there are a lot of people in the bar, they don't make as much as when there is a smaller but more devoted crowd. Scabby says they make $400 or $500 a week, but David, who keeps track, says some weeks it's $125 and others $400. He can't imagine how he lived on the low figure and wonders how he spends all of the high end, but in general it's enough to pay his rent, phone bill, and food. Before Kylie moved in with Sushi, David and Kylie both had rooms in the same building, with a shared bath for three tenants, and they each paid $600 a month. David gets some social security, has already spent all the money he will ever inherit, and is debt-free, except for his medical bills. Kylie will get a pension from his grocery store job when he turns fifty-five. None of the others has this much financial security. R.V. took a day job for a while as a hotel clerk; Sushi makes money on the side as a costume designer, seamstress, and interior decorator; and the others live more or less hand-to-mouth. Roger, at twenty-five, worried about the future: "I'm not old, but I should start to think. Milla's over thirty, Scabby's over thirty. . . . I don't want to be another Milla or Scabby. But it's just six years from now. Sometimes the better me starts to think about that and I should invest and I should do that. But I have a good time." Gugi relies "on a higher power that I know is not going to let me down. I've got to have somebody watching over me because anytime I get stressed out over the money situation, it'll come to me."

Just to put the drag queens' salaries in perspective, and to show how meaningful, in unintended ways, the designations "girl bar" and "boy bar" are, consider the male strippers at Bourbon Street. They dance on the bar in skimpy underwear and toy with the customers and make $150 a night in salary.

The girls occasionally perform at other places both in Key West and out of town, and they generally make better money that way. Several of them have performed on a gay sunset cruise ship and at different restaurants around town. Sushi, Kylie, and Milla went to New Orleans one year and did drag in a Chinese restaurant. Milla, Scabby, R.V., and Gugi flew to North Carolina to perform at a big furniture trade show and got $300 for one night and all their expenses paid. Inga did two songs in Miami and earned $130. In the summer of 1999, Milla and Scabby went to Provincetown, Providence, Boston, and Washington and made $675 a night for two twenty-minute shows. When Inga left 801, she went to Diva's, down the street, where she made $75 a night for two numbers. Later Milla briefly joined her, then Gugi.

At the start of 1999, Jimmy gave the girls a bonus. Sushi announced it at their meeting, making clear the complex dynamics between Jimmy and Sushi and Sushi and the other girls:

> Sushi: Yeah, we did get a bonus, I'm trying to figure out how I'm going to do it. He [Jimmy] wanted to take us all out to dinner, I said, "I don't think they're going to like that," so I said to him, uh, "Either we go on a shopping spree or you give us cash." And I sat down with him and we figured it out. I'll tell you today how much you're going to get . . . we're either going to go on a shopping spree, which I think would be fun [there's a lot of background talk at this point], it depends on how long you've been here, but each girl will get a different amount.
> Margo: Five dollars, fifteen dollars. [laughter]
> Sushi: Like a hundred bucks. [Lots of talk.] So do you girls want to go on a shopping spree or do you just want the cash?
> Inga: Cash.

Occasionally the possibility of making extra money for selling sexual services comes their way, although this is not something they seek out or appreciate. Unlike the street queens they resemble in so many ways, they are not engaged in prostitution, although some have had adventures with earning money from men for sexual encounters. Kylie tells of charging a man $100 to let him wear lipstick and perform fellatio on him. Another time a man came up to him on the street and asked, "Do you do anything else other than the show?"

> Kylie: And I said, "What do you mean?" And he was so afraid to say it, like I was a hooker decoy out there. And he finally came around and said it. And I said, "I don't know." I said, "I don't know, maybe if you come to the show, after the show I might feel like doing it." He said, "Well, I have 140 dollars." I said, "Well, that's not gonna be enough" 'cause I thought, if I'm gonna do it, I want to make it worth my while. So he stuck it out and I just kind of ignored him. . . . He said he wanted me to suck his dick and he wanted to know how much. And I didn't know how much I should really charge for that. So I

> turned to Sushi and I said, "How much? He wants me to suck
> his dick—how much should I charge him?" Sushi was drunk,
> "Uhh, two hundred dollars." So he said OK. Then I said, "I
> need the money first," and I also found out where he was stay-
> ing and I told Sushi so if he did murder me, at least he would
> go to jail.
> Verta: So you went over there?
> Kylie: Well, he only had a hundred dollars on him, so I thought
> I'd just take the risk, and I gave Sushi the money and went to
> his place, and it turned out that's not what he wanted to do at
> all. He wanted to wear my panties and suck my dick.

The experience was less than exciting for Kylie, who agreed to meet the
man again but clearly didn't think it was a great way to make money.

Another kind of compensation comes in the form of free drinks
when they perform and half-price drinks when they aren't working.
"I've never seen a drinking town like this in my life, even New Orleans
wasn't this much," says Kylie. Some of them are drunk every night they
perform; others are more moderate. David describes sticking to three
drinks a night, one in the dressing room ("Always!"), the others on the
street or during the show. One night someone in the audience sent up
shots of Jägermeister and Goldschlager, and just to prove he could do
it, he downed five double shots. "And I made up my mind that I had
not been that drunk in forty-five years, and there was going to be another forty-five years before I did it again." But most of the rest of the
girls are drunk far more frequently than that. R.V., that same night,
was so drunk she threw up in a trash can on the way on stage, wiped
her mouth, and went on. "*That* is a showgirl," says David admiringly.

Drugs are available most everywhere in Key West. Cocaine is the
drug of choice in the drag world. It's cheap in the Conch Republic—
$20 a bag at the end of the 1990s, compared to $60 in Provincetown.
The dealers know that at the end of the show, when the girls go out
on the town, they have a lot of money in tips. Dealers are also willing
to extend credit and collect after payday on Monday. Some of the girls
spend so much on drugs—five or six bags a day—that they never manage to save anything. Sometimes they cut way down or quit altogether.

Many of them are in and out—but mostly out—of recovery. After
his lover Michael died, Matthew's mother and best friend Annie broke
into his apartment and dragged him off to a rehabilitation clinic, where
he got off coke during a three-month stay. Dean was hospitalized twice
when he was a teenager, the first time after a fight with his father and
the second time for alcohol and drugs. And then for years he would

go away from and come back to his addictions. "Mostly drugs and alcohol have been my vacations," he tells us. And for him, drugs and drag "go hand in hand." R.V. went into treatment for his alcohol and drug addiction when he was twenty-five and working for Disney in Orlando. He was in a residential facility for a month and then did a twelve-step program. That was when he first came out to his parents, and afterward he stayed clean and sober for six years. Now he describes himself as a "practicing alcoholic." At one point he told us he controlled his drinking by waiting until nine or ten o'clock at night to have his first drink, since once he starts, he keeps going, but that seemed to be just a phase or, perhaps, wishful thinking. Sushi periodically goes to AA meetings, but mostly he drinks a lot.

At the time we were recording the shows, they were quite open about alcohol and drugs. Of course it is a bar. One night Milla announces, "We need your money. These queens have very expensive habits." Sushi, another night, tells the audience, "Everybody keeps on asking me, 'How do you stay so thin?' I say, 'Honey, you drink like two pints of alcohol, you get up onstage, you run around in drag for the last fifteen years, and you'll be thin, too.'" At another show Sushi says she loves Judy Garland: "She was such an alcoholic. My kind of girl." R.V., who calls herself "the booze bag herself" one night, talks about performing "A Spoonful of Sugar" with coke but says he can't do it at the 801 because "this is a drug-free zone," and then he snorts with laughter. On New Year's Day 1999, R.V. asks if the audience ever thought they'd make it so close to the year 2000 and adds, "I didn't. I didn't. I thought I'd be dead from alcohol poisoning by now. But not yet." After a long pause, he calls out, "Give me a cocktail!" R.V. regularly demands a drink when "there's too much blood in my alcohol system!"

Drug and alcohol use may be, as David says, "one of the pitfalls of any part of the entertainment business." Kylie started doing coke because he was nervous onstage, but later he backed off when he connected his anxiety attacks to drug use. When Roger first came to Key West, he didn't do drugs at all and rarely drank. Then, through his boyfriend Joey, he began to use coke and drink more. The other drag queens worried about him, seeing a lack of growth in Inga onstage. "She's gotten lazy, and I think, once again, here we go, drugs. Drugs and alcohol can destroy," says Milla, who ought to know. Yet David recognizes that Roger can stop, distinguishing him from some of the other drag queens. (David worries, in a motherly sort of way, about the younger girls, who have their whole lives ahead of them.) Occasionally Roger would tell us that he had lightened up or quit altogether, and he does indeed seem to be in control of himself. Dean says it is possible to do drag without drugs, but he also contradicts himself. "It becomes part of the job. You gotta have a pencil to write, right?" "Every time I get away, I don't want to do drugs . . . and then suddenly you gotta go back and you go back into it and it happens all over again."

In the late summer of 1999, the 801 ran afoul of the Bureau of Alcohol, Tobacco and Firearms. In what came to seem like prescience, David in March of that year had made a crack at a drag queen meeting about hoping our focus group members wouldn't be from the ATF. And then ATF agents did come to town and issue citations to all of the bars in the Bourbon Street complex. The 801 was cited for drug use on the premises, employee drug use, employee assistance in drug transactions, underage drinking, lewd and lascivious behavior, and, what outraged Kylie, "unnatural acts." As a result, the drug dealers had to leave, the employees were no longer supposed to use any drugs at the bar, and they had to make a lot of changes in the shows.

It is a hard life, and there's no question that they dream of something bigger and better. Especially being discovered and becoming famous. They can see that Randy Roberts, who performs during the season at La Te Da, has made it to the top of the profession, but as the *Key West Citizen* reported, "One senses neither professional jealousy, nor personal resentment, from the more working-class queens at the 801."[9] Kevin Truehart (Lady V), when he was performing at 801, had ambitions of getting back to doing the one-man show he performed in Provincetown and becoming a nationally known female impersonator. He had even thought about the publicity: "If I were to do a talk show, I would want to do a classy one," like *Oprah*. R.V. tells the South Florida gay entertainment guide of having been on television, in a documentary, and featured in Leila's book *A Desired Past*.[10] Matthew hoped his sets would be discovered during Fantasy Fest and he could move on to become a big-time set designer. When Dean was the subject of a documentary for LTV (London television), he felt it was time to move on, and he set his sights on London or Tokyo. They know that making it means leaving Key West, as hard as the thought of that tends to be. In the summer of 1998, David told us that "Milla was the one who had the greatest potential to get out of Key West." The next summer, when Dean and Matthew took off for points north, Dean harbored high hopes that it would lead to something. "I'll always be back," he told us. "I could have a house here and there. I just want what you have." Then he fell in love with nineteen-year-old Jared and left in March 2000 for Providence in hopes that they could make their relationship work outside the drag queen world.

We worried that they had the same kind of dreams about what this book would do for them. Kylie, at least, seemed to take to the idea that it wasn't likely to make them rich and famous but would give them a kind of immortality. Sushi was so excited when he heard that Verta had quoted him in a talk at Harvard that he called his mother to tell her. Once, when Dean asked us when the book would be finished, he moaned, "I'll be dead by then!" The others comforted him with the notion that he could be "the late Milla." Another time, at a drag queen meeting, he exclaimed with both exuberance and self-mockery, "We're going to be in classrooms all around the world! History class! No more George Washington, no more Albert Einstein, you'll be learning from us. Yes, I'll be lecturing at Brown University. We'll be on *Oprah*. 'So what's it like to have been a coked-up hooker, Milla?' [They all laugh in appreciation.] 'I loved every minute of it.'"

They do, indeed, work hard for the money, learning the songs and routines, rehearsing, making and setting up and taking down the sets, promoting the show, meeting and planning, drinking and ingesting and surviving, staying up, performing. Finally, it's time to see what all this hard work produces every evening upstairs at the 801.

PERFORMING PROTEST

From behind the red velvet curtain, as "Key West Welcomes You" finishes in the background, comes the voice of R.V. Beaumont:

Good evening, ladies and gentlemen, and welcome to 801 Bourbon Upstairs Cabaret Lounge! It's Sunday night and it's the 801 All-Star Revue, starring, from Orlando, P-town, and London, R.V. Beaumont! From Providence, Boston, and Fire Island, Scabola Feces! From Chicago, Illinois, Gugi Gomez! And from Dallas, Texas, Destiny! Sit back, relax with your favorite cocktail, the show's just about ready to begin. And now, ladies and gentlemen, please help me welcome to the stage, your emcee and hostess tonight—she's known from every campground all the way up and down the eastern seaboard as the Divine Miss M.—give it up for R.V. Beaumont! Make some noise!

The crowd cheers and claps, the disembodied voice of R.V. calls for more, and finally, when the volume really picks up, R.V. in her blond Bette wig and silver-sequined short dress, comes onstage and performs "I'm Beautiful." Or on Monday night it might be Milla doing Alanis Morissette's "You Oughta Know," on Friday "All That Jazz" by Sushi, or Saturday night a group performance of "Free Your Mind." Sometime after the first number, the emcee for the evening gives some version of the three rules: "First of all, where are you? You're in a bar! What do you do in a bar? [Audience members shout out, "Drink!"] Yeah, you drink a lot. The more you drink, the better we look! Second rule, you need to make a lot of noise because contrary to popular belief, drag queens do not work on drugs and alcohol. [The audience shouts its disbelief.] We work on noise!" In another version Scabby adds, " 'Cause that's what we like, foot stomping, hand clapping, screaming, ranting and raving, like you're having the best orgasm you've ever had in your life." Then: "Our third rule: Tipping is not a city in China! All the girls here pool their tips; they put everything in there [points to the tip bucket] and split it up at the end of the night. The more noise you make, the better we work for you. The more money you give us, the better we will work for you. And drink a lot of booze because my boss likes that!" Or, as R.V. is wont to say, "It costs a lot to look this cheap. So if we make you laugh, scream, cry, whatever, it's worth a buck, a five, a ten, a twenty, a fifty, a hundred, we take travelers' checks, I'll swipe credit cards through my ass and do the pin numbers on my nipples." Kylie has a slightly different way to put this: "If you like what you see, if we do something to titillate you, make you smile or laugh or cry or run out of here in total embarrassment, feel free to throw some money in the bucket. And if you're in back and you're afraid, the girls will be periodically coming around, giving you the opportunity for humiliation and love." Once Milla added her rule, number four: "If you don't like the show, there's an escalator right there. If it's not turned on, just tell me, I'll help you down the stairs."

After the rules, another song. Before each number, the emcee or another one of the girls in the case of those who don't much like to talk, introduces the performer and works up the audience. "You know her as the Sex Goddess. Welcome the talents of the tall, lanky, sultry girl. Let's bring to the stage the ever-so-talented, the ever-so-voluptuous, the diva of the group, let's hear it for the Amazonian goddess herself, Milla!" Or: "At the present time, let's bring to the stage the raw fish herself, the sexiest of sexies, right out of the ocean, give it up for Sushi! Noise!" Or: "Now keep that applause rolling and welcome to the stage the fabulous talents of our Chicago Chicano, ladies and gentlemen, my daughter, the one who's getting plump, thank god for that, give it up for Gugi Gomez! Make some noise!"

For Margo, there are many variations of age jokes, including this one from Ma Evans: "Who else could I get to do these favorite songs of mine but of course the lady who did them first originally, and of course, I know I wasn't supposed to say this but I have to, ladies and gentlemen, these songs were first performed in Arabic by the one and only Margo, and this was when they were building the great pyramid. Ladies and gentlemen, put your hands together for the fabulous, talented, one and only, she's sassy, Miss Margo!" Scabby, too, gets a special introduction. At one show she did Eartha Kitt's "Where Is My Man?" for our friend David. Kylie made David, embarrassed to death, come up front. "Our next performer is kind of, how would you describe our next performer, David? Let's let David describe her. 'Fantastic.' Well, that goes without saying. She's a bit odd. Stand back. So get back if your heart's weak. Let's hear it for Scabola Feces!" R.V. likes to introduce herself: "Please welcome to the stage, direct from P-town, London, Orlando, and every trailer park known to man, she's the recreational vehicle herself, seats eight comfortably from coast to coast, she's fabulous, she's wonderful, ladies and gentlemen, give it up for the fabulous talents of me, make some noise!"

Collectively they portray great diversity. Gugi, who is Puerto Rican, presents herself as Cuban, although she is sometimes introduced as a "wetback." In her show "A Night in Havana," she puts on a thick and obviously fake accent, asking audience members, "Watcha matter, you can't understand my English?" Her outfits include Carmen Miranda, complete with fruit hat, and a Cuban costume. Sushi plays on her Japanese heritage, sometimes speaking a little Japanese or Thai, sometimes dressing in a Japanese-style dress and using a wood-and-paper umbrella for a prop. She calls herself a "gook" and R.V. might introduce her that way: "She's the house queen, she is our boss, ladies and gentlemen, and she's a gook, but we don't care about that because we still love her!" Milla, whom Sushi sometimes introduces as a "soul sister" or "a black woman trapped in a faggot's body," does what is called "cross-ethnicking" by portraying an African American woman, wearing outfits made from African-style cloth, sporting head cloths, and talking like a tough black woman.[1] After a while she began to add giant breasts and buttocks. Audience members refer to her as "the light-skinned African American one." David, in his column, refers to her as a "six-foot six-inch drag queen who thinks she's black!"[2] The girls also portray— and talk about—"white trash." Destiny, introduced as "a long tall drink of water from Texas," specializes in numbers such as "Harper Valley P.T.A.," the song about the sassy mother with the too-short skirts who unmasks the PTA hypocrites, and "Fancy," about a poor girl whose mother puts all of their meager resources into a dress that will allow the girl to sell herself. It's a moving performance for those who have heard about Destiny's mother selling her into child pornography, and the crowd often reacts enthusiastically to the class critique in such numbers.

In a typical show, if there is such a thing, the girls perform fifteen to twenty numbers, but if the crowd is enthusiastic and tipping well, they'll keep going. Each show has a particular character (from Broadway tunes on Friday to primarily sexy numbers on Saturday), and the show evolves over time. They have their own styles, and some quite a range of personae. They can be angry or tender or funny. The basics are the emcee chatter, the lip-synched individual and group numbers, the calling up to the stage of audience members in the middle of the show, and introductions at the end.

Gugi as Carmen Miranda (photo by the authors)

Milla cross-ethnicking (with R.V. and Scabby, performing "Saved") (photo by the authors)

The numbers they perform range from fairly straight female imper-sonation (Inga doing the theme song from "Flashdance," a Spice Girls medley), although they almost always break the illusion in some way, to songs that take on a special meaning because they are being per-formed by gay men in drag ("Cell Block Tango," from *Chicago*, about women who kill their husbands, ending with the refrain, "He had it coming"), to ironic performances ("Saved," from *Smokey Joe's Cafe*, about a reformed sinner who used to smoke and drink, performed in choir robes), to comic numbers (Bette Midler's "Otto Titsling" about the invention of the bra) to gay songs such as "I Think He's Gay," by Pussy Tourette, or "I Kissed a Girl," Scabby's lesbian number.

What ties together this wide variety of performances is a persistent if sometimes subtle questioning of the meaning of gender and sexuality as we normally understand them. It is in that sense that the drag queens "perform protest." Their performances fall into three categories: some (but hardly any) embrace traditional images of femininity and hetero-sexuality; some explicitly reject those images; and others transform femininity and heterosexuality into something else, what we have been calling "drag-queenness."[3] In other words, when the curtain opens, there is more than entertainment taking place onstage.

Lingering for a moment on the songs that are the heart of the show, let's consider some examples. In a few numbers, it's almost impossible to believe that these are not beautiful women dancing and singing their hearts out. When Sushi does "All That Jazz" or "Le Jazz Hot," which show off her beautiful legs and talented dancing, when Gugi or Inga impersonate Celine Dion in "My Heart Will Go On," it's just like watching a straight stage show. Sushi, you remember, learned her moves from Hollywood films, and we don't mean from Fred Astaire. Her graceful arm gestures, high kicks, and shimmies show off her long slender body. And she knows it, sometimes thanking God and her mother and father for giving her that body. Inga appears for "My Heart Will Go On" in a floor-length gold lamé ruffled coat that she holds closed. Her wig is straight and blond, and she mouths the words with a trembly vulnerable face. She doesn't move much, but partway through the song (Roger, the professional, tells us he always makes a change in the middle of a song, in order to keep the audience's interest), she throws open the coat to reveal a short shimmery dress. Inga does this song totally "straight." Gugi does the same number wearing an elegant gown. She says when she sings it she thinks about her father, who died not too long ago.

These are the kind of female impersonation numbers that come to most people's minds when they think of drag. There is no critique of conventional ideas of femininity, although such numbers reveal the social basis of femininity and masculinity by showing that men can attain the feminine ideal. Despite the fact that these performances appear to pay homage to feminine beauty, the fact that straight men find the drag queens sexy complicates heterosexuality. But these are not typical of their performances.

A more common type of song rejects or mocks traditional femininity and heterosexuality. This is Scabby's specialty. The Fifth Dimension's version of "Wedding Bell Blues" is a perfect example. In a ripped-up wedding dress, Coke-bottle glasses, and a mouthful of fake rotten buck teeth, and gripping what looks like a silk dogwood tree in a cement flower pot, Scabby laments her rotten treatment by Bill and then grabs an attractive man from the audience, hugging and clutching him and begging him to marry her. Scabby also specializes in Karen Carpenter medleys, in which she is likely to spew water over the audience in a simulation of the bulimic vomiting that killed Carpenter. (They tend to push the limits of good taste.) Mama Crass, introduced as "three hundred pounds of love and laughter," performs Mama Cass while

Sushi dancing (photos by the authors)

eating a ham sandwich, ending by choking and keeling over in reference to the false rumor that that is how the artist died. Crowned Queen
Mother XVIII in 2001, Mama Crass took to doing numbers dressed
as Cher—mocking her thinness—or performing "Dance: Ten; Looks:
Three" from *A Chorus Line,* flashing her (real men's) breasts at the appropriate time. Or Scabby does Liza Minnelli's "Ring Them Bells,"
a ballad about a single New York over-the-hill woman who travels

Inga, "My Heart Will Go On" (photo by the authors)

around the world looking for a man to marry, only to meet her next-door neighbor in Dubrovnik. But Scabby does this as a hunchback (with the same buck teeth as in "Wedding Bell Blues"), wearing a bright green wig, a pink velvet short dress, and white go-go boots. She grabs a rope hanging from the rafters (to "ring them bells") and then swings across the stage and out across the audience. The crowd goes wild.

Scabby, "Wedding Bell Blues" (photo by the authors)

With such performances, Scabby mocks the prescribed striving for marriage and beauty.

Inga's comic side also relies on her juxtapositioning of female beauty and defiance of conventional femininity. On occasion she will tear open her dress during a "straight" number to reveal three remarkably real-looking rubber breasts. Or she performs "It's a Gas" following another

Inga with three breasts (photo by the authors)

song. As the music starts up, Inga grabs a beer bottle from a table down front and takes a swig, and as she returns the bottle to the audience member, the music is interrupted by a loud belch. Inga covers her mouth, looks embarrassed, but this keeps up. At one point, as she leans over, the gas comes out the other end. During this number, Inga also grabs the crotches of men in the audience, then sniffs her hand and makes a face as though she smells something foul and wipes her hand

R.V., "When You're Good to Mama" (photo by the authors)

disgustedly on her dress. The crowd loves the image of the Swedish bombshell burping, farting, and repulsed by men's odors.

R.V.'s impersonation of a prostitute merges deviant female heterosexuality with male homosexuality. In "The Oldest Profession," from the Broadway show *The Life*, R.V.-as-hooker totals up how many tricks she's turned and is horrified to count "fifteen thou-ow-ow-sand men," playing on the legendary promiscuity of some gay men. In "When

You're Good to Mama," from *Chicago*, R.V.-as-madam—sometimes in curlers and head scarf, cigarette dangling from her lips, gesturing to her nonexistent vagina—teaches the lesson of reciprocity: "When you're good to Mama, Mama's good to you." R.V. also does a number, "The Pussycat Song," about my "warm, wet, bald, free pussy," which women in the audience find hugely entertaining.

The vast majority of the girls' numbers appropriate dominant gender and sexual categories and practices, neither embracing nor rejecting them, but instead using the fact that femininity and heterosexuality are being performed by gay men to make something quite different. They do this in a variety of ways, sometimes commenting directly on sexuality and gender, sometimes challenging their apparent femaleness with their actual maleness, sometimes arousing erotic responses that do not fit into the categories of heterosexuality or homosexuality, thus confusing or exploding those categories.

R.V. and Inga's joint rendition of "I Think He's Gay" portrays two women with suspicions about a man who "walks like Wilma Flintstone," wears leather pants in the hottest weather, and whose "wrist seems unattached" when he throws a ball. The stereotypes and the chorus—"Why won't he touch my snatch? I think he's gay!"—draw their humor from the fact that it is gay men dressed as women who are mouthing them. In this way, the performance makes gay identity visible. The same kind of impact can be found in Scabby's rendition of Jill Sobule's "I Kissed a Girl," which illustrates the fluidity of sexuality. With her usual garish makeup and long fake eyelashes, Scabby skips around the bar kissing women and acting embarrassed, lip-synching a song about two presumably straight women who are talking about their boyfriends and end up making love with each other.

In a number of songs, the girls could on the surface seem to be doing simple female impersonation, except that they draw attention in all sorts of ways to their maleness. Milla sometimes does a number with a dildo between her legs. Everyone knows she has a real one tucked away as she strokes the fake one or picks it up to caress it with her lips. In this way they use the cultural equation of the penis with maleness to mix up gender categories. R.V. sometimes announces that her "right ovary keeps trying to pop out." One night she went on:

> This is a lot of work, kids—it's a bitch being a drag queen. 'Cause number one, you've gotta put things you have places they shouldn't be. Then there's the foam, the corsets, the water balloons—you never know when they're gonna spurt off and soak the whole front row.

Inga, "Barbie Girl" (photo by the authors)

You seen these monsters yet [taking one out]? You know how much pressure's in one of these things? Watch out!

Or Inga might be introduced as "Inga with a pinga." One of her signature songs is "Barbie Girl," performed in a hot-pink miniskirt and jacket with "Barbie" emblazoned on the back. "You can brush my hair—undress me everywhere," she mouths. The lyrics invite the audience to imagine undressing Inga/Barbie, knowing what they would find underneath the outfit. A variety of other songs, such as Gugi's "I Was Not Supposed to Fall in Love with You," Kylie's rendition of Shania Twain's "Man! I Feel Like a Woman" or Peggy Lee's "I'm a Woman," Scabby's vampy version of Eartha Kitt's "Where Is My Man?" or Gugi's "My Discarded Man" by the same artist work because they emphasize that the performers are not in fact women but are, rather, men looking for men.

But perhaps the most powerful numbers are the sexy ones that evoke responses in audience members that cannot be characterized as heterosexual or homosexual, because it's not clear what about the drag queens—their maleness or femaleness—is the cause of the response. Sushi occasionally pulls down her dress and bra to reveal her male chest, provoking the same kind of wild audience response a real female stripper might, even though everyone has spent the day seeing male nipples on the beach and on the street. Sushi also performs "Crazy World" from *Victor/Victoria*, a song about a world "full of crazy contradictions." It's a haunting melody, and Sushi does it behind a sheer white curtain, stripping down to nothing but keeping her penis tucked between her legs as she backs off the stage. Or she keeps on her gaff but lifts up the scrim, arms held far over her head, and then lowers it again, making even more visible the contrast between her man's body and woman's face framed by (real) long hair.

Dean describes Milla as "omnisexual." "Yeah, I, Milla is a black woman, she is a Puerto Rican woman, she is a lesbian, she is a heterosexual woman, she is a gay man. She's all these things, and that's why she can seduce in one way or the other, whether it's friendship or sexually, everybody." Milla's signature numbers—Natalie Imbruglia's "Torn," the Braids' "Bohemian Rhapsody," and Bette Midler's version of "When a Man Loves a Woman"—leave the audience overwhelmed and begging for more. There's something so powerful and emotional about the way she performs, and one simply suspends all sense that she is a woman or a man. She's just Milla, a drag queen. Her characteristic gestures—legs apart, arms bent at the elbow, her big man's hands up with fingers spread, or the same stance but arms out straight from the shoulder, or one hand caressing her cheek and the other extended, or shoulders back and pelvis thrust forward and arms down and out from the sides—all combine femaleness and maleness in a way that's hard to describe. When Sushi and Milla, or Sushi and Gugi, perform "Take Me or Leave Me," the lesbian number from *Rent,* they caress each other and roll around on the floor and it's very erotic. And confusing: two

Sushi baring her chest (photo by the authors)

gay men playing lesbian lovers. (When Milla left the show, Sushi started performing with Gugi, then with Destiny or Desiray, but the erotic impact was never quite the same. When we told Sushi that, she looked shocked and said, "But she slept with my boyfriend!")

The girls also perform what might be considered gay or drag anthems: "We Are Family," "I Will Survive," "I Am What I Am," and "What Makes a Man a Man?" Despite scholars' tendency to dismiss such

Milla, "When a Man Loves a Woman" (photos by the authors)

songs as banal and clichéd because they are part of the standard drag queen repertoire—and the girls' description of "What Makes a Man a Man?" as "tired"—these numbers attract rapt attention from the audience and become an opportunity for the drag queens to make political points. Margo, who performs "I Am What I Am," tends to explain the song's importance:

Sushi and Milla, "Take Me or Leave Me" (photo by the authors)

The next song I'm going to do for you will explain to everyone who, what, and why we are. We are not taxi drivers or hotel clerks or refrigerator repair people. We are drag queens and we are proud of what we do. Whether you are gay or straight, lesbian, bisexual, trisexual, transgender, asexual, or whatever in between, be proud of who you are. Are you proud of who you are? Let me tell you, darlings,

Margo, "I Am What I Am" (photo by the authors)

we are goddamn proud of what we are and what we do!" Another time she adds, "Be proud and try to understand and accept those who may not be exactly who you are."

Rather more vulgarly, R.V. introduces his rendition of "What Makes a Man a Man?": "This song actually sums up what happens in a drag queen's life, because, number one, no one wants to have sex with a drag queen on vacation. Number two, the tide can't even take me out. Number three, the most decent piece of ass I've had was my finger stuck to the toilet paper, OK? So this is gonna tell you all about it." Despite this flippant introduction, you can tell that the plaintive song about loneliness means something to R.V. And to the audience.

Scabby began performing "I'm Not a Fucking Drag Queen," from the lesbian romantic comedy *Better than Chocolate*. It is a perfect illustration of a complex and contradictory performance that questions the meaning of gender and sexuality. In the film a male-to-female transsexual, Judy Squires, performs the number in a lesbian club, insisting that she is "in another bracket" and not a drag queen, and that refusal to recognize her as a woman stabs her through her "tender transgender

R.V., "What Makes a Man a Man?" (photo by the authors)

heart." Scabby begins in an elegant gown and shoulder-length wig, but then proceeds to strip, removing first the wig, then the dress, finally the bra. In makeup and black underwear, untucked, with his unshaved body and legs, he raises both middle fingers in hostility, then hugs his tender transgender heart. So a drag queen showing that she is a drag queen portrays a transsexual denying she is a drag queen. The performance in the film lectures the lesbians in the audience, while Scabby's rendition takes on new meaning for the mixed male and female and straight and gay audience. The words point out to them that if they think she is a freak, they might want to wonder why their "knees like castanets / are giving way." It's a powerful and confusing lesson about sex, gender, sexual desire, and identity, communicating among other things that when men dress in drag, their apparent transgression is a performance, not an essential identity.

But the songs, with all they evoke, are only a part of the show and a part of the way that the drag queens perform protest. Their talk and interaction with the audience is a crucial part of the act. The audiences,

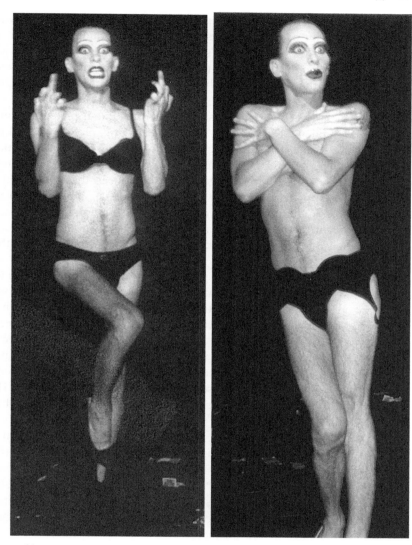

Scabby, "I'm Not a Fucking Drag Queen" (photos by the authors)

in fact, consistently name the interactive nature of the show as the thing that most separates the 801 from other drag shows that do much the same kinds of things all over the country.

The most structured part of the interactions is what they call "doing shots," and it is here that the audience, too, begins to perform. Sometime in the middle of the show, they call for audience volunteers to come up to the stage and get a free shot, usually of some kind of horrible-tasting liquor. (Jägermeister, or perhaps "Hot Sex," which was the favorite for a while.) At first they called for the couple that had been together the longest (that's how we met Sushi), or anyone with a birthday or anniversary. But then they settled on asking for a volunteer from that they call "each sexual category," meaning a straight man, gay man, straight woman, and lesbian. Sometimes a bisexual or transsexual. One night Kylie asked a man his sexual preference and the man replied, "Hard to tell. Whatever feels right." R.V. is fond of saying she's a bisexual: "Buy me something, I'll be sexual." Sometimes they find a transsexual in the audience. "My people," Sushi says, bringing Michelle, a local, up onstage. "It's a drag queen that got her dick cut off. She's got a real pussy now." Another time Kylie calls for a lesbian and says to a volunteer, "Are you a lesbian? You're more than a sex change, right? Do we have a real lesbian?" In this way they introduce the audience to the diverse genders and sexualities represented in the bar.

Looking for volunteers, the girls play on stereotypes. "Now, darlings," Margo says, "do we by any chance have a lesbian in the house? Come on. Darling, I can tell by the hair on the upper lip." Or, bringing our research assistant Betsy onstage, Margo says, "She's a lesbian. Check the shoes out." When Betsy gets her paper cup, Margo says, "You're a prissy lesbian, aren't you?" (She is.) To the audience: "She's sipping it!" Kylie taunts a straight man who's reluctant to come onstage: "Come on, chicken shit. You're supposed to show us how to be macho." He wouldn't come. "We need a straight man," Kylie announces. "I'm straight and proud of it," calls out a man in the audience. "Well get up here, bitch," Kylie responds. Kylie pours right from the bottle into the volunteers' mouths, making comparisons to fellatio. When the straight man gags, Kylie gives him grief: "God. And I bet you beg her to suck it until you come. Maybe now you understand more why she doesn't want to swallow." In this way they express antimale sentiments and critique male domination of women. There's a lot of hostility in the show directed at straight men.

Here's Kylie at a Saturday night "Girlie Show," also known as the "Sex Show." He starts with the gay man and has the audience count to three before he starts pouring:

Take it like a man. Yes. Ooh, that boyfriend of yours must have a very big load. Girl [to the straight woman], you need to lick that off his chest because I'm sure he's never had a woman lick his tits. Come on, do it. Go ahead. Go on. Right here, lick it off. Oh yeah. She acts like she's never licked a man. He was more into it than she was. She's supposed to be straight.

Kylie asks the straight woman her name, asks her how much her implants cost (never have we seen so many women with breast implants!), and pours a shot into her mouth. Then he turns to the straight man:

> Open up wide. Oh, he'll take it like a man. . . . Suck on it like it's your girlfriend's nipple. Oh yes. You swallow just like a fag! You've never sucked a dick? Oh, you have to try. You'll love it. Have a threesome with her—she'll love it too. You know what they say, two dicks are better than one.

And to the lesbian:

> Have you ever sucked a cock? I have licked a pussy. But I didn't like it too well. I know you know about pussy licking. So tilt your head back. Open wide and I'll give you all of my gushing juices inside.

In all these ways they challenge the audience members to cross sexual boundaries, if only momentarily.

One evening a woman who was to be married the next day came to the show with all the other women from the wedding party. She ended up onstage with a leather man in chaps and a bare butt, and Gugi had her put her hand over the leather pouch holding his penis. The bride-to-be's grandmother-in-law, a woman who appeared to be in her eighties, turned to us and said, "I hope my grandson doesn't know what she's doing tonight!" Another night Sushi had everyone feel the breasts of the straight woman volunteer. "It's so weird, I meet so many women and they don't care if I feel their tits. They love it."

Sometimes the girls define the categories by sex acts. At one show Sushi opened the shot segment by calling for a "pussy licker," a "cock sucker," a "pussy licker and cock sucker," "a woman who has had a baby squeezed out of her pussy" (well, that isn't a sex act), and "a man who has never sucked another man's dick." When her volunteers came onstage, she announced, "Now we have the whole world here." This is kind of a Sushi theme. At another show she raised her glass: "Here's to gay love! Oh no, here's to love. To love, baby, all across the world!" Introducing Kylie as her best friend from high school, she adds, "This is the person that . . . [t]old me that I was special and that every single one of you is special no matter if you suck a cock or lick a pussy."

After a while the girls began to position the straight man and gay man, the straight woman and lesbian, in sexual positions: the straight man on his back, the gay man sitting across his pelvis, the women lying on their backs facing each other with their legs intertwined. One night the straight man looked anxious when Desiray told him to lie down. "It doesn't have anything to do with him, does it?" he asked nervously, pointing to the gay man, in jeans and a leather harness over his bare chest. "Don't be so homophobic, girl!" Desiray chided.

On the surface, these performances might seem to make concrete and distinct the categories of sexuality and gender, but in fact the point is just the opposite. Even when the girls call attention to the existence of conventional categories by asking audience members to situate themselves individually or collectively ("How many straight people in the house? Good, keep breeding and making more homosexuals for us! How many lesbians? You know, the politically correct word for lesbian is 'vagitarian,' because you are what you eat! Good, then all the rest are beautiful homosexual men!"), the meaning of the categories is challenged. R.V. might ask the people who signal that they are straight, "When did you actually come out to your parents and tell them that you were straight?" Audience members join the performance by miming sex acts that are outside their category of gender and sexual preference. One night a very thin young woman in an incredibly short skirt and skimpy halter top came up onstage to dance with Desiray and began to strip down to her thong, acting very much like the drag queens. Desiray bent her over and pretended to have anal sex with her, then the woman turned her around to exchange the favor. In addition, there is a great deal of latitude in who fits into what category. "Who wants to be a lesbian?" asks Margo. A whole table of gay men might volunteer. A burly gay man will raise his hand and he'll say, "My name is Lisa; I'm a policewoman." Straight women also volunteer as lesbians. R.V. asks how many straight women there are in the audience and gay men scream in falsetto voices. "All you damn fags, shut up," responds R.V. One night a gay man in drag as a lesbian ("our gay man-woman," according to Kylie) came up onstage.

In other less structured interactions with the audience, too, the girls confuse the categories they lay out. Kylie will invite a lesbian to pretend to "lick my pussy. You'd have to, I don't really have one." R.V. tells the audience that they could take Kylie down to the straight part of town, "and she could be a stripper until they find out that her clitoris is larger than the average clitoris and it goes all the way back to her ass. OK? I think she's the most well hung in the group, just to let you know." Milla identifies as a lesbian onstage, taking off her wig and sticking it in her armpit. R.V. questions an audience member about whether he's a top or bottom. "It's not a hard question: you a top or a bottom?

Honey, it's back near my ass right now—it's not hard. You're a top? It's getting hard!" R.V. is also likely to readjust her tucked penis onstage or comment on the fact that her balls are falling out. But she also says, constantly, "You're making me moist," touching her crotch as though she has a vagina. Kylie uses this line, too: "I'm getting a little moist in my nonexistent vagina." Sushi brings a lesbian onstage and asks her to "feel my clitoris. It's big tonight. I was born with a big clitoris. Some people say it's a dick, but I refuse to believe that." Other times she refers to her "man-pussy" or "mangina." She tells the audience that the model Naomi Campbell, "a gorgeous woman, has a body just like mine except without the dick." And one night she tells of dreaming of Coco Chanel, who told her, "Go on, girl! Just because you have a dick, doesn't mean that you're not a woman."

Sushi's discussions with the audience about whether or not she should get breasts and the girls' fondness for getting women with breast implants to show them off also challenge the notion of biology as destiny. "Do you think I should cut my dick off?" Sushi asks. "Should I keep this little thing, darling? Do you think I should get tits?" The audience shouts, "No!" "No titties? Titties and a dick, that's fabulous, darling. It's 1999, we have computers, we have guys that run around with tits and a dick." She then calls for a woman with "fake titties" to come up onstage. "Not a single woman has fake titties? Liars!" She feels a woman's breasts and pronounces them real. "All you straight men who sleep with women, when you feel a rubber thing jiggling around with air bubbles in it, that's a fake titty," she instructs.

When audiences encourage Sushi not to change and she agrees, "OK, I'll stay the way I am and I'll be proud," people are educated about transgendered and transsexual people. So, too, are they during the performances of and banter about Baby D, an eighteen-year-old on hormones. One night Baby D, introduced by Destiny as her daughter, performed a number from the *Little Mermaid*. Ariel, the sixteen-year-old mermaid, has fallen in love with a human man and sings of her wish for legs. It was a powerful metaphor for the desire to change body parts.

Such performances and talk blur the boundaries of genitalia, and the girls also scoff at any firm dividing line between heterosexual and homosexual. Kylie will drag a woman onstage and pretend to hump her, then ask after the song if she is a lesbian. "No, I'm straight," she says. "Even after being with me?" Kylie asks in mock astonishment. To a man who claims to be straight, R.V. retorts, "You're straight to the nearest dick!" One night Kylie wanted to know if straight men knew about cock rings, so she asked if there were any straight men out there. "You're straight? Kinda? Maybe now, a little drunk, seeing drag queens, you change a little bit? When you wake up in the morning, you'll regret it, honey!" Another night Kylie asked a straight woman if she was "gonna try some pussy-licking tonight. You will, won't you? You won't pass that up? Try it, girl, you might like it." Addressing two women at another show, Kylie deadpanned, "Hello, are you lesbians? Do you want to be? Are you sure? Have you ever had a lesbian experience? They say that ninety percent of the population has had some sort of homosexual experience." R.V. asks two straight men if they want to "change." "The only difference between the heterosexual and the homosexual is a six-pack of beer, trust me." One night during Fantasy Fest, when half of Key West is in drag, the girls brought a young straight man up onstage and dressed him in drag and tried to teach him how to walk in high heels. (It was the same lesson as Leila's: "Don't walk on your heels! Walk on your toes!") Later Sushi began bringing men from the audience onstage and having them tuck in a women's bikini bottom.

On top of all this is the fact that the drag queens make sex, which is usually far more private, a very public affair. This is to some extent in keeping with the sexual openness that characterizes Key West. When the local paper, the *Key West Citizen,* moved to a seven-days-a-week publishing schedule, a bumper sticker advertising the move proclaimed, "I get it every day." The language the drag queens use about sex and their constant talk about sex acts contribute to an environment in which anything goes and nothing is shocking. Kylie asks a straight woman there with a male friend whether he licks her vagina. "He doesn't? You guys are so boring. You've got to experiment, hello! Try it tonight. I hope you guys do try oral sex tonight." They can be quite outrageous about sex. One evening Milla, whose talk can really push the limits, announced onstage, "Don't look at my ass. I know I have enough ass. It's six inches before you hit moisture, OK? Jesus. See, you have to have six inches or you ain't even gonna get in. Those little limp dicks, forget that shit." Sushi proclaims, "I've licked pussy before but, you know, I prefer cock. The last pussy I licked was my mom's when I was being born." She makes a "V" with her index and middle finger and flicks her tongue in the "V" in imitation of cunnilingus and announces, "I love to lick pussy." And one night she did lift a woman's dress, and finding no underwear underneath, gave a little lick. Kylie says, "Even I have licked a pussy. I tried it. I felt like I should at least try it before I gave it up. Contrary to popular belief, pussy does not taste bad." R.V. advises the audience one night, "Never suck someone off with a Prince Albert on his bone; it will scratch you bald. Straight people? If you don't know, a Prince Albert is when the piercing goes through the head of your dick and out. Feels great just clacking against the teeth."

R.V. sometimes tells dirty jokes. One is about a gay man who says he feels some irritation up his ass and asks his lover to check it out. The lover inserts one finger, then two, but he can't get in far enough. Finally he gets his whole hand in, feels something, and pulls out a Rolex as his partner shouts, "Happy Birthday!" The other, which R.V. told during Women's Week, is about a straight man putting the moves on a lesbian:

> There was this guy, sitting right here, at the 801 bar, up here. And he sees this gorgeous woman sitting across the bar. And he goes to Wendy [the bartender], "Wendy, I really want to buy this girl a drink." And Wendy goes, "You know, this is Key West, where the women are strong and the men are pretty!" And he says, "I don't care, I really want to buy this woman a drink." So Wendy brings the drink to the woman and she motions to the guy to come over, and they start talking for a little while, and all of a sudden she says, "Do you want to see a fabulous pair of legs?" And the straight guy goes [here R.V. puts on a deep, gravelly, dirty-old-man voice], "Oh yeah!" You know how straight men do it. So she shows her legs, she wraps them around him, and he goes [same voice], "Oh yeah, fabulous!" Couple of minutes more go on in the conversation, and she says, "Do you want to see a fabulous pair of breasts?" He goes [with even more enthusiasm], "Oh YEAH!" She unhooks her bra, takes her mammaries out, puts them in his face, he's going, "Oh yeah, oh yeah." Couple more minutes go by, she says, "Do you want to smell some fabulous pussy?" He goes, "OH YEAH!" and she goes [here R.V. exhales loudly, as if breathing in the man's face], "Hhhhhh."

The audience goes wild.

And the drag queens go further than talk. They grab and touch and strip willing audience members, both onstage and off. (David describes just two times that men waved him off when he went to touch them, "so I just walked past them." But sometimes, what with all the drinking, people go along and then have second thoughts the next day and threaten the bar with lawsuits.) Some of their numbers involve finding a man, bringing him up onstage, aggressively pulling off first his shirt and then, back turned to audience, his pants and even underwear. Patti LaBelle's "Lady Marmalade" is a typical number for this routine; three girls perform it at the "Girlie Show," two of them holding the man's arms out straight and the other stripping him. One Saturday night

Margo, who isn't usually in that show, substituted for one of the other drag queens, and David told us that he liked the idea of showing the audience "that somebody over the age of thirty can have sex."

Sometimes they ask the volunteers for shots to show something: a breast for women, the ass for men. Often there are audience members (especially, it seems, straight women and male-to-female transsexuals) who can't wait to get up onstage and bare it all. In Kylie's "Sex Show," he talks people into stripping by promising, "I wouldn't ask you to do something I wouldn't do myself," and then comes through with the last number of the evening, "Queen of the Night." "Listen, motherfuckers," she says one night after stripping, "when I take my clothes off in a wig and makeup, I expect a lot of applause. I feel like Adam and Eve."

As the drag queens perform and roam out into the audience, they will caress a woman's breasts or feel a man's genitals. Margo likes to move past a straight man seated in the front of the cabaret and then reach over into his crotch from behind. Gugi sits down on women's laps and bounces up and down looking puzzled, as if not understanding why she isn't finding a penis inside her. One night Sushi wheedled $100 out of a heterosexual man in his seventies she called "Daddy-o" by painting his penis with his wife's red Chanel lipstick onstage. Another night Sushi told someone he could lick his balls onstage for $100. During a Fantasy Fest show, Sushi pulled down a straight man's leather pants and took the man's penis in his mouth. Then the man's wife took over, right onstage. The girls love to discover that straight men are aroused by their fondling. One night Milla brought a newly married couple onstage. The man looked very drunk and also enamored of Milla. "You look *great!*" he kept saying. Later Verta talked with him and he confided to her, "I could do her!"

The sex talk and the public nudity and the groping serve as an extension of the way that the girls challenge conventional understandings of male and female, straight and gay. In their public talk about sex and the slang words for body parts and sex acts that they bring into regular use, the drag queens practice what might be called a politics of vulgarity, although they would never use this term.[4] (Sushi, for example, seemed horrified when we mentioned it. He doesn't think of their talk as vulgar at all, just "raw and honest.") In the same way that they blur the boundaries of gender and sexual categories and violate traditional distinctions between public and private, they cross the line between the respectable and the vulgar. Their bawdy talk about sex acts shocks the audience, creating an opening for the introduction of ideas about gender and sexuality that are shocking in a different sense. Such talk

Kylie, "Queen of the Night" (photo by the authors)

also implicates the audience in the performance. By listening to and having to respond to vulgar talk about body parts and sex acts, and by being fondled and stripped in a public space, the distinction between the drag queens as marginal members of society and the audience as respectable is challenged. Vulgarity has a kind of leveling and normalizing effect.

Kylie dancing on a table (photo by the authors)

The shows are profoundly political (or politically incorrect, as Scabby's show is billed), and this is no coincidence. "What we're gonna do is try to open these people's minds," Kylie announces at the "Sex Show." He asks a German tourist if he is straight, and the man replies that he's normal. "Normal!" cries Kylie. "I'm normal; you're weird." David tells us that he introduces "I Am What I Am" in the way that he does in order to educate straight people. "I think by seeing what they see and being there, they see a part of the gay community they may not in their own towns or even cities. 'Cause they're not gonna go to gay bars." He also does the number for the gay audience. "Most of the time, what I do is, I'll look at straight people, but I focus on the gays and lesbians in the audience. And I watch their reaction, and it's terrific, 'cause you see, there's pride—this is an anthem of sorts."

They talk about "Queen Nation," and one of their backdrops depicts the New York City skyline and the Stonewall Inn, with "Queen Nation" scrawled on the side of the building. Margo's show "Stonewall Tuesdays" opens with a little historical lecture. On June 29, 1999, Margo begins:

> Welcome to the "Stonewall Show"! As you know, thirty years ago this past Sunday, there was a revolution in New York City at the Stonewall Bar. At that time, gays and lesbians were harassed by the police every night—taken up in paddy wagons and arrested. One night the patrons said, "We've had enough." And they rebelled. That rebellion led to the modern gay and lesbian revolution which continues to this day. Because of those brave men and women back in New York on June 27, 1969, we are able to sit here tonight—gay, lesbian, straight, bisexual, transsexual, transgenderal, whatever, and enjoy a show. Ladies and gentlemen, this show is dedicated to the people thirty years ago who said, "We've had enough!"

Three days later Sushi gave her version. "You don't know what Stonewall was? It was a bunch of drag queens back in 1969, a whole bunch of drag queens were at this club and they said, 'Screw you. We're gonna be drag queens,' and they tried to arrest them. And the drag queens revolted. So it was my people who got the movement started. So don't forget about the drag queens."

One Christmas night Sushi was especially irreverent, claiming Jesus as a drag queen and calling for Christian love. "And whose birthday is it?" he would say, raising his eyes to the heavens. "Did Jesus wear pants? No, he wore a frock. And did he hang out with a bunch of men? Yes!" And later: "Now remember, it's his birthday. It means you love everybody, no matter where they stick it."

They talk about the gay and lesbian movement, AIDS, gay marriage, discrimination. Milla dedicates "Bohemian Rhapsody," about a boy who has thrown his life away by killing someone, to his best friend who died of AIDS. "I like to end our evening, I always like to do a number that is the heart of our people, ourselves, each and every one," Milla says. Sushi puts in plugs for safe sex: "Everyone say, 'Peace and love.' Everyone say, 'Safe sex.'" He asks the crowd, "And what do you do during safe sex? Condom, darling!" One night Sushi calls us up onstage and tells the audience we've been "married" for twenty years, "illegally married for twenty years. And they call this the United States of America, where everybody's free." Kylie uses the theme of democracy in trying to talk people into stripping: "All right, let's take a vote. Do we want to see his dick? Now see, you said you believe in democracy, so let's see it, honey." R.V. introduces "Saved," which they perform in choir robes, by saying, "Screw Jerry Falwell and the *Teletubbies,* we're gonna bring some good ol' gay religion to your lives." Sushi will talk about standing up to people who call you names. "If someone calls you 'faggot,' just say [here he gives a shimmy, and has the audience stand up and join him], 'I love it!'" Another night Sushi instructed the audience, "The next time you're in the Mall of America, or Ohio, or Idaho, and you see a drag queen and get that look of disgust on your face, just smile and say, 'I love drag queens.'" Again, he called on the audience to join in. After telling yet another night of having been a "femmy faggy boy" in high school, Sushi ended with "To all you fifty-year-old Republicans out there who made the lives of boys like me miserable, 'Fuck you!'"

They are also political about race and ethnicity. Matthew, for his "Politically Incorrect" show, says: "I want to be an equal opportunity bigot. I want to make fun of everybody. Jews, gays, lesbians, blacks, Spanish, Chinese, everybody. But Jimmy says I have to be careful of what I say." Sushi is most earnest about the issue of ethnicity, regularly calling attention to her Japanese heritage in order to encourage the audience members to embrace their own and others' marginal identities. She also plays on the eroticization of Asianness that permeates American society. "I do want to tell you that I am a gook, I am Japanese, you know," she says at the end of a Memorial Day show. "My mother was there when they dropped that bomb. She was on the corner saying, 'Only two dollar for you.' But she made her two bucks. She was in Osaka, which was like a hundred miles from Hiroshima. Thank god, honey. I wouldn't be here if she was in Hiroshima." Sushi often calls on the audience to call her a "gook" or "nip" or "chink," using these names to call attention to racism. "When I come out, don't say, 'I love you, Sushi!' say, 'I love you, gook!' Because I am Japanese and I'm proud of it!"

Milla uses her black woman persona to forge a feminist bond with women in the audience. At her show one night, Milla asked the audience, "You know I'm not black, right? I'd like to be. . . . I do ethnic. . . . I do color. I'm a woman of color. . . . Gentlemen, you can close your ears, because I don't really give a shit about you anyway. We are powerful women, are we not, women? . . . Yes, ladies and gentlemen, women are power. You wouldn't be here if it wasn't for them. . . . And that's why we spend all of our time being effeminate and looking up to women and thinking they are all that they are." Another night, in

Sushi as a "gook" (photo by the authors)

her Erykah Badu persona, Milla preached, "We are all one, and we are all too beautiful to be abused by any man, woman, he, she, it." Making it more general another night, and sounding a great deal like Sushi, Milla said: "Well, darlings, as long as you get along and love each other, one thing to remember in life is we all have to love and live together."

The lessons about race and ethnicity do not always take. Two regular fans find this kind of talk "tasteless," and in fact the impact of the embracing of ethnic stereotyping is ambiguous. While calling attention to the oppression of ethnic "others"—as they do to gender and sexual oppression—they flirt with danger in portraying black women with large breasts and buttocks, sexy and spicy Latinas, and Japanese women selling themselves on street corners. Such images are meant to poke fun at racial and ethnic stereotypes, but at the same time they might simply confirm them for audience members. Or offend people of color in the audience, although no one we spoke with had this reaction.

Finally, the show is over, and the host once again introduces the cast. Often, if not always, all or some of the drag queens appear out of drag, introduced with their real names. Matthew almost always does, Sushi never (or, at most, bare-chested but with his makeup and gaff still on). At Milla's show one night, all the rest of the cast came out in boy clothes: "Ladies and gentlemen, at this time I'd like to present to you the talents of, you knew her as Scabola Feces, now I'd like you to meet him as Matthew!" Matthew is dressed in jeans and a tank top. "You knew her as the oldest living drag queen in captivity, the one who farts glitter dust, now at this time I'd like to present to you the talents of David!" David has on an island shirt and shorts. "And of course, one of my dearest friends, you know her as the Swedish meat— oh, bombshell, bomb site, meatball, whatever, the incredible talents of, you knew her as Inga, please meet Roger!" Roger is in cutoffs, a black shirt, with his hair in a ponytail; he gives Milla the finger. "OK, you know who she is, she climbs the rafters just like a monkey, here's our tightrope-walking diva, you knew her as Kylie Jean Lucille, please, this time meet her as Kevin!" He sports shorts and a tank top. "I didn't have time to change, my name is Milla." Roger pulls off Milla's wig. "Tomorrow night I'll be wearing my own hair, 'cause it's so sexy." One night Desiray came out in makeup, corset, and panty hose and asked an audience member to unlace the corset. She stripped down to her gaff before she went back to the dressing room. Another summer night the kind of torrential downpour so typical in the tropics began just after the introductions, so Timothy (R.V.) and David did a number together out of drag, lip-synching to male voices. At the end of the evening, it's the final performing of protest. As if we could have forgotten that they are men, through all their use of their real male voices, their gestures to and discussions of genitalia, their choice of songs and moves of their bodies, and, most obviously, through their direct talk: "Remember we are drag queens! We do have dicks and two balls!"

☆ ☆ ☆

The cabaret is, indeed, a big chunk of life for the hardworking girls, and it is also a performance about gay life, a performance to which the audience contributes. As we have seen, the drag queens' personae, the music and monologues, their interactions with the audience all trouble and subvert conventional understandings of gender and sexual categories. How is it possible to continue to think of male and female as the only two, and opposite, genders in the face of these performances? How can one see homosexual, heterosexual, and bisexual as distinct ways of experiencing desire? The drag queens perform protest by raising these questions and making political commentaries on gay life in the United States. Although those who have studied drag have taken different positions on the question of whether it confirms or challenges traditional notions of gender, we think there is little doubt about this case. Certainly this is what the girls intend. What impact these performances have on the audience is a question that we take up shortly.

But first we look at the ways that the cabaret builds community, especially for the drag queens and, to a lesser extent, for the audience as well. And that, too, is a form of protest.

SECTION IV
"WE ARE FAMILY"

"We Are Family" is, of course, the kind of gay anthem that can get a crowd of lesbians and gay men smiling and dancing. It may be a cliché, but it's a cliché that continues to resonate for a lot of people. It's a proud song that covers what is sometimes the pain of losing our biological families while also celebrating the joy of finding new ones, a song that expresses a bond that is both the goal and the glue of the gay/lesbian movement.

Families, both the biological kind and the constructed ones, are also often dysfunctional, and we do not intend to gloss over that aspect of what it means to be family. We begin this section with a look at some of the families from which the drag queens came, not because we offer any kind of psychological interpretation of why men become drag queens, but because these stories provide context for what happens in the 801 family. We tell here about the girls' complex relationships with one another: more about Kylie's and Sushi's long-standing friendship, the ways they take care of each other, the family roles they play. Also their betrayals and fights. We consider the ways that their relationships extend to other drag queens, to what they call Queen Nation, and how, in the shows, the girls create an 801 community.

What is significant about the construction of family is that the group functions not only as a survival mechanism and emotional support for the embracing of drag-queenness, but that it also serves to express and confirm both a gay collective identity and a broader collective identity among audience members.

ELEVEN

"CRAZY WORLD"

The worlds from which the drag queens came to the 801 family were, sometimes, the crazy world that Julie Andrews sang about as the woman pretending to be a man pretending to be a woman in *Victor/ Victoria*. Kath Weston's book about the families gay people construct is called *Families We Choose,* and certainly that is what the "drag mafia" at the 801 is.[1] But in order to understand the families we choose, it is helpful to know something about the families we didn't choose. (Or, in David's case, an earlier family he chose.) Some of the girls had very difficult, even abusive, relationships with their families of origin. Others remain close to their parents. But in almost every case, it is easy to understand why the 801 family is so important in constructing a collective identity and providing social support.

Dean's (Milla's) story is one of physical abuse from his father and sexual exploitation by a trusted theater director. He adores his mother but had a very conflicted paternal relationship until just before his father died in 2000. Even his description of his parents' marriage expresses his hostility toward his father, a navy man who met Dean's mother in Italy. "He married my mother, an Italian woman, didn't speak any English whatsoever, had never been out of her country. And he takes her and brings her over here. . . . He took my, this woman that I love so dearly, and put her in such a, you know, a culture. It was such a culture shock." Having retired from the navy, his father worked as a maintenance manager at an apartment complex in St. Petersburg. Dean says flatly: "He was abusive. He was an alcoholic." He was verbally and physically abusive to Dean and his sister, getting drunk and hitting them. "He should have never had kids," says Dean.

Dean fought back. "I was very angry and very rebellious. I mean, I was like a street kid." His mother would try to protect him, to keep him from being beaten by hiding whatever he had done—such as wearing her panty hose—that might make his father angry. Dean says his father hit his mother only once or twice. Once he slapped her and Dean begged her to get in the car and leave. One night his father threw his sister against the wall for using the telephone in his bedroom, and Dean attacked him. After that, Dean fought back, "to the point, I mean, I tried to kill him once." That time he lost control—"saw red," as he puts it—and the two of them trashed the house. Dean broke a vase over his father's head just as the police arrived, and he ended up in a psychiatric hospital. He found escape in music and then drinking and drugs.

He isn't sure how old he was when he first got involved with the director of his children's theater group. He met him at a summer camp that specialized in theater. This was one of those confusing situations, not clearly sexual abuse, but certainly an abuse of power and very hurtful to Dean. Dean's introduction to the story makes this clear: "I called him my boyfriend; I was being molested they say." The man—or boy—in question was eighteen, Dean at first says he himself was fourteen, then remembers that he was twelve, going into the sixth grade. It went on for three years. Brian "made me feel so special. In a very father figure kind of way. I looked up to him; whatever he said I did." The first time they had sex, they were sleeping in a bed with Dean's best friend. "Brian started to touch me. And I said, 'What are you doing?' and he said, 'I'm just showing you how I love you. This is how you show love.' . . . And he did love me, but he was taking advantage of me," Dean says now.

What was so painful—"shameful," Dean says—was that Dean felt so special, so loved. "I mean, I turned into just a diva. You couldn't tell me anything, I thought I was the shit. I had my man who loved me, I was in the theater, I had the lead role in a play. . . . I really thought that I was somebody." Dean loved the sex: "I was hungry for it—every time I would see him, I'd just grab him and just maul that man." Brian told him not to tell anyone, and he didn't. But then Dean found out that Brian was having sex with "everybody he could get his fucking hands on," including Dean's best friend and best friend's mother, who got pregnant and had his baby. Dean knows it sounds like a soap opera: "And the night that it happened . . . he had just finished . . . fucking me in their living room, and then went in her bedroom while her husband was [out]."

And this woman was the person that Dean decided to trust with his secret, not knowing what was going on. She of course confronted Brian, who denied it. The end came in a Pizza Hut, in the company of all the other boys with whom Brian was having sex. Brian leaned over to Dean and whispered, "You know, I don't like you anymore. I don't want to be around you." Dean fell apart, ran crying and screaming through the streets, and ended up in a mental health facility. This was the first time. "I was in such deep depression, such a darkness, that I just didn't want to, I didn't want to live, I wanted to die."

Dean survived this and his abusive childhood. Even before he forgave his father, he would occasionally return to St. Petersburg, sometimes when he was trying to get off drugs. The turning point in their relationship came after his father had a heart attack around 1995. Dean thinks it mellowed his father, made him realize what it would be like to die, helped him to manage his anger. Dean insists that he loved his father, although he doesn't deny that he's hated him a lot in his life as well. Dean's parents and his sister and her husband all came to Key West over Thanksgiving 1997 for a family reunion that was very important to Dean. "They drove down here, picked me up, we spent the day together, they came to see my show, they sat there, they sat right up front. . . . Afterward, the taxi driver drove them around, treated them just like royalty, they were so consumed by this, they were so proud. And I found out that I had a family after all these years. I had a family! I have a father, a mother, but I have a family now." He even tried for the first time to tell his father about the sexual abuse, and he felt that he understood. When his father was diagnosed with cancer, Dean went out of his way to go and visit, and he spent a lot of time with his mother after the death. He forgave his father, but he recognizes the cost of this relationship: "The men that I choose in my life . . . happen to be my father . . . abusive, or less than I should have."

Dean does see his childhood as having something to do with Milla. He credits the feeling of being exceptional in his relationship with Brian with creating Milla, who really is that special. And he sees his relationship with his father as shaping his own choices and desires, since he tried so hard not to be like his father, and therefore not like a man.

Matthew (Scabby) had a much less traumatic upbringing, but, like Dean, he talks about how much he loves his mother, and he agrees with Dean's feeling of wanted not to be like his father. "You're supposed to be like this, you're supposed to act like *me*." He tells about his parents "freaking out" when they found out he was gay. "My father spit at me, punched me in the face. My father didn't talk to me, he'd grunt and growl, but he actually never made a sentence until after Michael died. And that was almost ten years later." Matthew, whose younger brother is also a drag queen, reports matter-of-factly that his father's favorite was his other brother, Eddie, "because, you know, he was a boy." Matthew and his mother "were real close. Because my mom was sick a lot" (she had two major heart attacks when he was growing up). Whenever he talks about his mother, it's clear how much he loves her. But she doesn't know he does drag; she thinks he's a bartender. When she called the 801 and asked for Matthew, "I knew it had to be either a friend from home or a family member because they're the only ones that call me Matthew. So when I got on the phone, I realized it was my mother, and I'm, like, it's a good thing they didn't know my real name and say, 'Oh, you mean Scabby. Or Scabola.'"

Sushi, too, really loves his mother. He often talks about her in his show, and once we ran into him at the local Kmart, buying pillows and Martha Stewart pillow cases in anticipation of her moving to Key West. We told him how good he looked, and he replied, "It's because my mother's coming. I love my mother." He planned to drive out to the West Coast to pick her up, but then she fell and broke her hip and put off the move, and eventually she decided she didn't want to leave. It's clear from the stories Sushi tells to the audiences at the 801 that his mother, still in some ways a proper Japanese woman, can't quite believe some of the things he does. In one show Sushi announced: "My mom told me she was going to disown me. Not because I was gay, not because I wanted tits, not because I was a drag queen. She said she was going to disown me because I was going to get naked and do a porno magazine. Can you believe that? She's fine with me being a drag queen, me being gay, doing drag. She just can't stand the fact that she read something about me wanting to take my clothes off."

Gugi also talks about how much he loves his mother. He grew up in a family of six kids, two his stepsisters. He had met his biological father for the first time during the summer of 1998, and he had just lost his stepfather when we first interviewed him in 1999. Both events were clearly painful for him. About meeting his father, he says: "He starts talking about how one of his sons had gotten killed last year and how he wished he went to the funeral, he loved his son so much. 'I have to go now.' Like what am I, chopped liver?"

One of his stepsisters came out first, and that helped him to have the courage to be more open with his Puerto Rican family, which he describes as "kind of like being an Orthodox Jew." But he didn't actually tell them, although he knew they knew. When he broke up with his first lover and asked if he could come back to live at home, his mother told him, "You know what, you're my son, I love you, you will always be my son no matter what." She had a little harder time with his doing drag. One Halloween when he was at his mother's house, he dressed in drag to go to a contest, "and my mother saw Gugi for the first time.

. . . Her mouth dropped. She said I was an embarrassment to her, walking out of the house like that." But the next day she apologized. "She was watching TV; she goes, 'That's a pretty dress, isn't it?' After that we'd go shopping and pick out what she would wear."

Kylie has very little contact with his family. "I don't really have anyone, any family that I am close to. I mean, I do love my grandmother. My dad's dead; my mother I can obviously live without—I mean, she lives halfway across the country." He doesn't have much of a relationship with her; he told us once that she never calls him, even on his birthday. His grandmother made him spend some time with his father before he died of lung cancer in the late 1990s, and he realizes how much he would have regretted it if he hadn't made peace. His father beat his mother and his brothers, but he and his sister escaped, Kylie because he was the youngest, because his father had mellowed by that time, and because "I just didn't do the same things that my brothers did, so I just didn't rile him up as much." When Kylie started to go wild in high school, dressing in freaky clothes and then drag, his parents weren't terribly concerned, because his brothers and sister had been into drugs and much more serious trouble. Kylie describes his behavior as wanting attention. "I wanted love really." He thinks his childhood is "probably part of the reason why I have a hard time getting into a relationship, because I don't trust people that easily and that quickly."

R.V. had a troubled adolescence but remains close to his parents, who divorced after twenty-seven years of marriage but seem to have an amicable relationship. He grew up in a small town in northern Ohio, where his parents ran a canoe livery. His father, a retired steel worker, "says he doesn't condone the lifestyle, but if anyone ever said anything bad about me, he would be right there to back me up." "My dad was great. He just let it be. My family has always been very supportive," R.V. told *Southern Exposure,* the monthly entertainment guide to gay Key West.[2] When R.V. won the title Miss Hog Town Hussy in Gainesville, his father bragged about him in the steel mill. R.V.'s mother reports that his father even joked about opening a drag dress shop.

When R.V. graduated from high school, his mother, Ann, laid down the law: stop smoking marijuana and live by the rules of the house or leave. She explains that she couldn't have him influencing his fifteen-year-old sister. R.V. left, off to make his career at Disney World. But he wasn't exactly kicked out of the house. Rather, Ann, who had met Disney people at trade shows, took him there to get a job, since he loved the theater and was obviously very talented. When they arrived in Orlando after a two-day drive, they found out that Disney had just experienced a hiring freeze. So Ann took out a loan, bought him a trailer, and within a month he had a job at the trailer park, and when Disney started hiring again, he tried out and made it.

R.V. tells of coming out to his parents when he was in a treatment center while working at Disney. It was family week, R.V. had been working in therapy on admitting to himself that he was gay, and then he had to tell his parents. Ann remembers that he didn't tell them then, but called her up about six months later. "I said, 'I know.' He goes, 'What?' I said, 'I know.'" In another context, she says, "I think a mother just knows." What really upset his mother, according to R.V., was that the first man he had had sex with was a friend of the family who molested him. Now a married man with children who continues to visit with R.V.'s family, the man, the same age as R.V., was in a program that brings city kids to the country for the summer. As R.V. tells it, "he kept threatening me if I didn't have more sex with him every time he came down. So it almost became a rape situation." His mother "freaked out" when she found out about this, but R.V. said to "just forgive him like I have. It's done, it's over with. I'm gay."

Even though his parents knew he had won the Miss Hog Town Hussy title, it was a big step for R.V. to tell them that he was doing drag for a living. "They were kind of quiet for a little while. 'Oh, you're wearing a dress.'" Interviewed for the Key West newspaper, R.V. admitted, "It's a hard thing to do, tell your parents that you wear a dress for a living."[3] Ann isn't sure exactly when he started doing drag. For her, the big thing was coming out as the mother of a gay man. "People would ask me, 'How are Timmy and Stacy doing, and are they married?' And at first I would say 'no.' Finally, it took me about a year after he came out, and I remember the first time somebody asked me were they married. I said, 'No, to be perfectly honest, they're both looking for Prince Charming.'" She reports that the man she is seeing is homophobic and that is one of the reasons she will probably never marry him.

Now, she says, she talks openly about R.V.'s drag. And she loves to see him perform. The first time, "he had me in tears. He did Bette Midler's song, something about your mother." R.V. tells the same story: "And she was sitting right there and I did the one song from Bette, 'In My Mother's Eyes,' and I dedicated it to her. And she was just, tears were streaming down her face." Ann says, "It didn't take a whole lot of getting used to, seeing him that way. And Tim's a loving kid." The only thing she doesn't like is his foul language. About R.V.'s favorite word, "fuck," Ann says, "In my opinion, you just don't have enough smart things to say, or funny things to say, when you use that word. Which is a typical mother's reaction."

But she is so proud of him. She tells of stopping off in Provincetown when R.V. was working there and she was on the way to a conference. But she had forgotten his address, so she called a gay friend back in Ohio to ask him to look up in a gay publication to find out the name of the club where R.V. was performing. He told her to look for a rainbow flag and ask anybody there for R.V. And that's how she found him. "It amazed me that that many, that I could do that, that he was that popular. . . . It's like he's come into his own."

Ann was eighteen when R.V. was born, and she thinks she made some mistakes early on, so she seems really happy that R.V. talks about how supportive she is. "I don't think I did such a great job in the beginning. . . . Maybe I did better than I thought because my daughter says the same thing. You know, you raise your kids and then they get involved in drugs and stuff like that and you think, 'Oh shit, where did I go wrong?' And then they kind of grow up to be adults and have values that are very similar to yours and certain beliefs that they have and they attribute it to the way you brought them up and I think, 'Wow, maybe I didn't mess up.'"

David's (Margo's) family story isn't about growing up, but about creating a family before he became the elder statesman of the 801 Girls. In the mid-1960s, he moved from New York to St. Thomas, where he managed a guest house, restaurant, and bar. One day around dawn, he was sitting around drinking and talking with a bunch of friends in his room in a guest house when Daphne, a Trinidadian woman who lived in a nearby room, burst in, in hysterics. Her visa had expired and she didn't want to go back to Trinidad since her boyfriend, the biological father of her six-month-old son, lived in St. Thomas. They all talked about various solutions. "But the bottom line is she has to marry a U.S. citizen in order to stay. . . . Everybody looks at me. I nod my head and that began the engagement that lasted four days until we were married."[4]

The happy couple didn't fool the immigration authorities for long, since it was public knowledge that he was gay and she ran around with men, but they attempted to keep up appearances for a while by living together. David went "absolutely nuts" about the baby, Kendrick (Kenny), and when he found out that Daphne didn't want to raise him and had left six other children in Trinidad with her grandmother, he agreed to take responsibility. When Daphne died suddenly in 1999, David wrote that she "gave me the greatest gift I have ever received—

her son. My son. Our son."[5] In the early 1970s, David went to New York with Kenny for the summer, but they never went back. David wanted him to have a good education and other opportunities he felt would be denied him on St. Thomas.

So, as a white single Jewish gay man in 1970s New York, David raised a black son. At first he didn't work so that he could take care of Kenny, then later he entered him in a black independent school, where the administrator talked David into taking a teaching job. He taught reading, writing, math, science, social studies, and African and Caribbean heritage, and he learned Kiswahili so he could teach that as well, staying just one lesson ahead of the two- to five-year-olds he was teaching. When David moved to Key West, he left Kenny, now grown up, in his apartment. In 1999 Kenny got married. In his *Celebrate!* column, David reported that Kenny called one day to say that his wife, Linda, might be pregnant. It turned out to be a false alarm, but, David wrote, "during the course of that conversation, I found my mouth saying that, if they wanted, after the baby is born, I would move back to New York to help care for it."[6]

The summer before the wedding, David told us that he had asked Kenny whether he wanted him to wear a tuxedo instead of a dress to the wedding. Kenny opted for the tuxedo, but David claimed that he would wear it with red high heels. "He's seen me do drag. He loves it," David told us. We don't believe he really went through with it, but the story illustrates how successful David was at creating a family and raising a son he continues to call "perfect."[7]

David's world is a little crazy, by some standards, but his story could also be told to the strains of Louis Armstrong's "What a Wonderful World." Although some of the drag queens' family tales might seem to reinforce the notion that distant or abusive fathers and loving mothers create gay men (or drag queens), that is not at all what we mean to suggest here. Rather, these stories show the importance of family, of whatever kind. Which brings us to the 801 family.

TWELVE

THE 801 FAMILY

Occasionally, at the end of the Broadway show, the girls perform "We Are What We Are," a rousing drag queen anthem from *La Cage aux Folles*. One night Sushi introduced the number this way to a very mixed audience:

> Did you love being gay? Did you love being straight tonight? You know, that's where we came from. Well, maybe a few bisexual mothers and fathers. This is our last number. It means a lot to us. So please, welcome to the stage, your family!

They then went on to perform, mouthing lines about how much they love causing confusion, how their "muscles and tits" prove that, proudly, they are what they are. What is especially significant about this number is the "we," a pointed revision of the famous "I Am What I Am." Such drag queen "we-ness" not only confirms the sense we've already seen of a drag queen identity, but it also speaks to the collective nature of what goes on at the 801.

There is no question but that they have constructed a family, if at times a slightly dysfunctional one. Making friendship into kinship is typical of the gay and lesbian world in general, but there is even more going on here.[1] The family extends beyond their own little group to other drag queens in the community, to the regulars at the bar, and even, if only momentarily, to vacationers caught up in the spell of the show. By creating family ties with one another, they construct a collective identity as drag queens, and by building a community that draws in the audience, they reinforce a collective gay/lesbian identity. And then they go beyond to affirm that we are all "one human family." As we shall see, this is part of what drag has always meant.

At the center of the 801 family is Sushi as house queen, and the core relationship within the family is her longtime friendship with Kylie.

As we have seen, and as Sushi announces at every show, she and Kylie have been best friends since high school in Oregon. "Welcome to the stage my best friend for sixteen years, the one who convinced me to be who I want to be—to wear orange high heels. Welcome to the stage my sister, Kylie Jean Lucille," Sushi announces at the show one Christmas night, when the shows have a particularly family-like quality.

Sushi/Gary and Kylie/Kevin have been through a lot together. Gary describes what it meant to meet Kevin, who was wild and crazy, "and that's what I liked about him because I followed all the rules." He tells about Kevin asking to watch him defecate:

> He asked me, he goes, 'I wanna watch you take a shit.' And I was like, 'Why?' And he said, 'I don't know, just 'cause I've never done it before.' And I said, 'All right.' And so he made me, it wasn't just like watching me—I mean, he literally made me stand up and he looked as it came out my ass, and he was, like, 'Oh my god, girl, here it comes!' And then he made me watch, and then I was like, 'I want to see you do it,' you know? And after that, it was like a bond between us. I mean, how many people actually look at somebody else's asshole?

After Kevin moved to Los Angeles from their hometown, Gary went to visit and lived undetected for three weeks in the closet of Kevin's family's two-bedroom apartment. He drank during the day and slept at night, but then Kevin's parents discovered him and kicked him out because they thought he was a bad influence. Kylie has a less clear memory of this than Sushi, although Sushi claims he can't remember a lot of detail because of all the drugs he's done. "Did he come for a visit or did he move? See, at the time I didn't realize that these things were so important to him. . . . I don't see Gary as the type of person that's really emotional, that shows his emotions too much, so it's kind of hard to gauge when something is making a big impression on him, so he tends to remember these stories much more than I do." Kylie does say that his parents didn't like Gary because "when we got together, we did drag and stuff." He adds that "they told me, 'Well, you know, he's got to get out of the closet.' Which is really funny."

After this, Gary went to Santa Monica and lived on the streets and panhandled and sold sex to men. He lived behind a Dumpster and changed in the bathroom of a fast-food joint, walking in as a boy and out as a woman. Kevin went along when Gary sold himself, hopping into the car and saying, "It's two-for-one night, buy one, get one for free," so Gary wouldn't have to go alone. "I wouldn't do it alone at the beginning. We'd do it together. We were scared," says Sushi. Kylie describes himself as naive about the hooking. "He was on the street and I felt so—I felt I couldn't leave him there alone and I would be with him, and then it was so easy for him to do that, to hook, and as stupid as I am or was at the time, I thought that it was appropriate for me to do the same things. Not only to be with him on the street but actually also be with him doing this job too. . . . I don't think it was a healthy thing at all." Sushi sometimes tells this story at the show: "I think I will introduce the person I used to prostitute myself with in L.A. We just graduated from high school, 1986. We were down on Santa Monica Boulevard, smoking unfiltered cigarettes, and they were delicious. We were young; we were fabulous. She was the one who told me it's worth more than two dollars. . . . Well, anyways, my oldest friend in the world . . . my soul mate friend, Miss Kylie Jean Lucille!"

Sushi almost always tells the audience how long she and Kylie have known each other. One night she added, "Never fucked each other in the ass. Or wanted to. But we've had sex together. With another man." Kylie explains: "We had sex with the same man at the same time." Sushi continues: "You were grabbing the right ball and I was grabbing the left, right? Remember that man who got us stoned in L.A. in that Lincoln Continental? And he was, 'Grab those balls, you girls!' We yanked him so hard." Kylie: "All that for twenty-five dollars."

Before Gary met Greg and moved to Key West, when he was bouncing around from L.A. to Portland to Maui and back, Kevin begged him to live with him. As Sushi remembers it, "Kevin hated me, he hated me at that point. 'You're leaving, I hate you, why do you have to leave? Why don't you stay here with me?'" And when Gary and Greg left for Key West, their first stop was L.A., where they stayed with Kevin for a month. "I wanted to show him how good I was doing and I was so proud, I fell in love, I'm on my way to Key West." So it's not surprising that after a few years Sushi talked Kevin into retiring and moving to the Rock. Kevin stayed at the grocery store where he worked until he could get his pension. He worried that he would move to Key West only to find that Gary and Greg would break up and Gary would move back to Oregon and leave him stranded there. But he did it. Kylie says that if he gets tired of drag, he'll leave, but, he says, "I've known Gary for how many years and I'll still see him. That wouldn't change." And of course Sushi and Kylie have outlasted Sushi and Greg. When Sushi and Greg broke up, Greg moved out and Kylie moved in. One night at dinner, Sushi complained that Kylie couldn't possibly understand what he was going through because he had never been in a real relationship. Kylie responded that he was obviously a lot smarter about relationships than Sushi. They argued as lovers do and then let it go.

"He is my family; he's closer than my brothers are," says Sushi. Kylie at first describes his relationship with Sushi as an "obsession," but then rethinks this: "Well, actually, that's what it is, in a nutshell, it's family. . . . I don't really have anyone, any family that I am close to." When Sushi left Key West for the summer to make costumes in North Carolina, Kylie told us how much he missed Sushi, since "she's the only one I can really talk to." Talking about Sushi, Kylie says, "She feels like she gets walked on a lot and that's her own fault. . . . If someone comes on to you and you like them and everything and you're so desperate for love, it's very hard to take that first step and say, 'Nope, I see this is not good for me' and walk the other way. And that's what I think she needs to learn." After Sushi and Greg broke up, Kylie told us that Sushi would moon over photographs of men he had had sex with, one of them a porn star: "And I can just see her thinking, 'They liked me!' As if that's what gives her worth." Kylie comes off as having a lot more self-confidence, and he seems to want to protect Sushi. Certainly their love for each other is deep and palpable.

Dean (Milla) and Matthew (Scabby) are also close friends, although they've had their ups and downs. Dean at first lived in one of three rooms with a shared bath ("A nightmare for drag queens!" says David) over the Valladeros news agency, where David is pretty much of a permanent resident amidst other drag queens in transit. When we first interviewed Dean and Matthew, Matthew told us, "I, like, love her; she's my best friend right now. She really is. And right now she's kind of my backbone 'cause I'm going through a bad time." Matthew's parents sent him plane tickets to get out when Hurricane Georges was hurtling toward Key West, but he refused to go. "It was Milla's birthday! I wasn't leaving my best friend on her birthday in a hurricane!" Then they had a falling out: Dean blamed Matthew and his boyfriend Ricky for stealing money from Mama. Some of the other girls thought the whole thing was silly. Kylie, resorting to her typical cynicism, dismisses the episode: "Everyone except Milla knows that Scabby is a liar and a thief." "I can't believe he would do this to someone in the family," Dean kept saying to us. When Dean left town with Jared, his new young boyfriend, he was still deeply hurt. But then Jared turned out, at least according to Dean, to be responsible for the theft; as Scabby put it with his usual dramatic flair, Dean "realized Jared was an ax murderer." So

Dean landed back in Key West, alone, and before long back in the show. And back with Matthew as well.

They tend to live in family groups, as the changing roster on David's floor, what he calls "Drag Haven," suggests. Kylie, Milla, Scabby, and Desiray have all lived in the rooms next to Margo at different times. From there, Dean and Matthew rented a house together with their boyfriends. A little later, the two of them went to live in a compound rented by Elmer and Kimberly, a straight couple who spent almost every night at the bar. Dean at first called Elmer and Kimberly "Dad" and "Mom" and said he really loved them because they took care of him and loved him just for himself. "It makes me feel human," he told us. Later that relationship went rather awry. But Matthew was the first to move out, telling us that Elmer and Kimberly didn't like that he didn't "conform to their lifestyle," although others said that he wasn't paying his rent. What upset Matthew the most was that it was Dean who asked him to move out. So Matthew moved into Inga's house, and Inga and Gugi moved into Elmer and Kimberly's. When Elmer and Kimberly left Key West, Inga and Gugi stayed on in the house. By then both were working at Diva's instead of at 801. At one point Gugi went up to Bowling Green, Florida, where Elmer and Kimberly had moved, to try to make his relationship with his boyfriend work, but before long he was back in town. When Dean came back after going away to Providence with his boyfriend, with the same hopes of making it last, he first moved back in with Matthew. Then R.V. and Matthew were living together. And Desiray moved into Sushi and Kylie's two-bedroom apartment, where she sleeps on a love seat in Sushi's bedroom. And so it goes.

Sushi's dream is to buy a drag queen house where they all can live. He's no fool: he knows that, Margo not withstanding, one can't make a living as a drag queen forever. A drag queen house would mean security, a place to live, and people to take care of each other. From the start, Sushi believed in this book not only because he wanted us to "tell the truth" about them, but because he hoped that the royalties we promised to share with them would be the start of a fund for the house (we warned him they wouldn't be much!), that if they had a little they could talk Jimmy into giving them more. First Sushi found an abandoned school in Bahama Village, but that didn't work out. Later he began negotiations with Joey Schroeder to rent-to-buy a house Schroeder owns. Whether this dream will ever work out is an open question. Dean never liked the idea and constantly challenged Sushi's insistence that any money that came to them from the book would go to Gook Productions and a drag queen house. Dean thought they should all just get their share. Sushi retorted that then some of them would just put the money up their noses.

Even when they don't live together, they often gather in family groups to celebrate special occasions. At the show one evening, the girls gave Kylie a microwave onstage for her birthday. Many spend holidays such as Thanksgiving and Christmas together. One year they all ate Christmas dinner at bartender Tommy's house. Another Christmas we asked what they had planned, and Sushi told us they were going to have a slumber party at Inga and Gugi's on Christmas Eve after the show and then they would get up and have presents in the morning. During Hurricane Georges, Dean and Kylie went to Greg and Sushi's house to sit out the storm. They used the giant plywood cutouts of the girls that decorate the bar to board up the windows. After Fantasy Fest in 1998, Elmer and Kimberly got married in the garden behind Bourbon Street with all the girls in attendance. Gina Masseretti of the No Name Drag Players, a local group, performed the ceremony. Angelica Duval, another local drag queen, photographed the event. Milla was the maid of honor, Inga a bridesmaid, R.V. the flower girl, Mama the ring bearer, and Matthew was the father of the bride. Kevin and David came as guests and then Margo, "International Social Columnist," wrote a tongue-in-cheek account for *Celebrate!*, the local gay/lesbian newspaper. At that time we barely knew Elmer and Kimberly, but they had seen us in the bar and Kimberly insisted that we come. Along with Emma, we even had to pose in the wedding photographs, and we made it into Margo's column: "Among the guests Margo spoke to were Leila Rupp and Verta Taylor, who are in and out of Key West with the frequency most of us take showers. . . . They, of course, brought Emma who is carried in a shoulder bag by Leila. She's a dog. Emma, that is."[2] It was truly a family affair.

The drag queens, like family, worry about each other, too. One summer Milla and Scabby went north on an extended trip, and shortly after they left, at a drag queen meeting, Kylie announced, in the sarcastic tone only Kylie can muster, "I'm glad Scabby thinks so much of us that he called to let us know that they got there all right." David told us that he at one point was living with a young hustler with a rough streak and the girls were afraid for him, afraid the boy would hurt him. "I said, 'I know he won't.' And it was like, which was kind of sweet, like if he tries anything, we'll kill him." Even when they talk negatively about each other, for example, worrying that someone's drinking has gotten really out of control, it is obvious that they care. One time at a meeting, Sushi didn't show up on time, which is not like her, and they started to worry:

"What on earth happened to her?" asked Milla.

"Don't you think Jimmy would have heard [if something happened to her]?" offered R.V. "Someone would have called Jimmy."

Finally Milla reached her by phone. "You guys, go ahead and start the schedules. She OD'd, I mean she took a Xanax," she reported. When Sushi finally turned up, very groggy, they applauded.

The one they really worry about is David, who has had bladder cancer, a heart attack, and an aneurysm, among other things. All of this without medical insurance, and of course when he is ill or recovering from surgery, he can't work and thus has no income. After his surgery during Georges, they made extra space for him in the shows. At one drag queen meeting, Dean was planning his show and asked if David needed money. "We discussed it, and until you feel like you're on your feet, whatever you need is what we're going to give you." At the time, David wasn't old enough for Medicare. Sushi raised the possibility at one meeting that David might be able to get the health benefits Joe Schroeder supplied for his construction company workers, although we don't think that ever happened. Eventually Medicare paid his medical expenses and his social security covered his rent and the girls gave him $40 or $50 a week for cigarettes and food.

They have had two benefits for David, one in 1999 and the second in 2000. The first time, he was bleeding internally but told us the urologist wouldn't treat him until he paid his $3,000 bill from the previous surgery. The girls collected all sorts of donations—gift certificates for dinners and services and cruises and such—and Ma Evans auctioned them off. Jimmy promised to match what they raised and gave Sushi $350 to bid up the items. They were all there. Matthew and Dean came in boy drag; Sushi, Inga, Gugi, Kylie, and Destiny, as well as local drag queens Krystal Klear (Queen Mother XVI), Mama Crass (who later joined the 801 Girls), Charlena D. Sugerbaker, and LaLa Belle performed. R.V. organized the event and Ma Evans served as the master of ceremonies. Here's how Ma introduced the evening: "Drag is drag to some. To the Drag Mafia it is family. A family of talented sisters dedicated to the call for help. When needed, we totter onto our heels and we do just that. We help."

In between the bidding and performances, the girls roasted Margo. Sushi told the story of seeing Margo in drag for the first time at Atlantic Shores:

> She was sitting there with this big white hair, really bad makeup. I have to say right now, it was really bad. I love you, girl, but it was

bad. And that turquoise spandex tiger suit. It was not working for you. Her little Nerf ball titties were hanging out there. And all the other girls that I've had for five years, they were saying, "Oh my god, look at that old creature, honey, what the hell is she thinking?" And I said, "Remember this, girls, that's what you're gonna look like in about fifty years." . . . I said, "I love her, I'm gonna hire her for my little family here at 801." I love you, Margo. Come on up here, girl. I want to thank everybody that has come tonight and supported this. You know, the government is not going to take care of us.

They raised $3,000 and ended with "We Are Family." The next year David fell ill again, needed several surgeries, and couldn't work for months. They had another benefit and, when Margo could finally come back to work, staged a special early show, "The Return of Margo." Throughout his ordeals, David wrote movingly in his columns about what friends did for him: "When I returned from the hospital in October of last year, I have never seen anything like the outpouring of love and generosity that were shown to me. People brought and bought me food, gave money, gave time and reaffirmed my thoughts that, all things considered, there is still a hell of a lot of good in this world."[3]

And David is not the only one to experience the largesse of the "drag mafia," as we have already seen in considering the centrality of drag queens to fund-raising in Key West. When Ma Evans fell and injured her arm outside the bar, the community put on a benefit at Diva's to help pay for her medical bills and physical therapy. During Pride Fest 2001, LaLa Belle—aka L.A. Meyers, the reigning King of Fantasy Fest—had an esophageal hemorrhage while performing in the "Pride Follies" and nearly died. A first benefit, held at Atlantic Shores, raised over $10,000, and it was followed by several more in other bars around town.

As is already evident, they talk about themselves as a family. "We have a hell of a lot of fun back here, and what we are, we can do it because what we are, are family. We are family," announces Margo one night at the show. Another night, introducing Gugi, Sushi says, "I picked her up about eight months ago, brought her into my family. We consider ourselves family, darling." Desiray tells a reporter, "This is my family; we take care of each other. That's Drag Family. If ya mess with one of us, you mess with all of us, and trust me, you don't want that."[4] When R.V. left Key West to spend the summer in Provincetown in 1998, David, in his regular column, shared the "little tear-stained note" she left behind: "To my family and friends of Key West," it began.[5]

Although David has another family, he calls the girls at 801 "my family in Key West."[6] As he told the Key West newspaper, "We nurture each other, interact with each other, care for each other and do love one another. . . . When one of us is upset, we all are . . . when one of us has a joyous occasion to celebrate, we all share this joy. The girls of 801 are a family, a unit, and very proud and supportive of each other."[7]

They sometimes assign different family roles to each other. Jim Gilleran often serves as the father. Sometimes he pays medical bills or loans them money or bails them out of jail if they get in trouble. "The boss is Dad, he's the dad that is like the dad that we've always known on TV, the one who has the newspaper in front of his face, but when needed, when needed, he's there," says Dean. "This is somebody that I love, and I love him, I really love him, because . . . he's like a father, he's really like a father." Jimmy's wife, Cathy, talked to us about his role as father. She thinks that the fact that he is straight and has his own children is important to the role. R.V. makes much the same point: "He's the straight one and he already has the kids and the wife and all that. And he just looks at us sometimes, what we do and just starts shaking his head. 'I can't believe this.' He just acts like a typical dad, too. He really does. . . . It's one big family." Only David doesn't see Jimmy as Dad, naming him a "Hunk of the Week" and admiring his "appealing little-boy looks. . . . Every time I see him I want to give him a glass of milk and a plate of cookies and pat him on the head."[8]

Matthew describes Jimmy as the daddy and Sushi as the mommy. Verta asks, "And then you're all?" "The girls," Matthew responds without missing a beat. "I love the people I work with; I've got really good friends. I've got a really good family here; my friends, the people I work with, I consider them family." Matthew describes Margo as "like a grandma," "I relate better to her like if I have a problem or something." The night Leila watched them dress, they got into elaborating their family roles:

Kylie: Milla's the bad kid.
Milla: I'm the black sheep. I always get myself in trouble, I don't get you guys in trouble.
Kylie: Scabola's the crazy one who belongs in an institution, that no one ever talks about. [laughter]
Milla: We had to let her out, we had no choice, the insurance ran out. [more laughter]
Scabby: So they let me wander the streets.
Milla: The insurance company dropped us.

Kylie: I'm the baby, the brat.

Milla: The genetics come from Mama. [Scabby laughs his wicked laugh.]

Scabby: And Jimmy. [laughter] Jimmy and Mama.

Kylie: Margo's mad but we have to take her in because they were going to throw her out on the street.

Milla: Because we lost the insurance because of her [pointing to Scabby], and we couldn't pay.

Scabby: It's all my fault we lost the insurance!

Milla: And we couldn't pay for the old lady's care.

Scabby: Social security didn't pick her up.

Kylie: Ma Evans is, what's her name? Mrs. Crabtree?

Milla: She's the neighbor, she lives in the hallway. [Everyone talks at once.] She's [gesturing to Gugi] the fucking maid, the Puerto Rican maid, that's all she is to us.

Kylie: Exactly! Actually, she's just an exchange student we're taking in for a year.

They also have drag family relationships, crediting whoever helped them become a drag queen with being their mother. R.V. claims Gugi as her daughter: "Give it up for my daughter, the fabulous talents of Gugi Gomez!" Milla calls Gugi her sister, although R.V. is not Milla's mother. Gugi, in turn, is Desiray's mother. "She's my drag mother!" Desiray tells a reporter for *Celebrate!* "My immediate family is my drag mom Gugi Gomez; she floated over here on a raft from Cuba. . . . My grandma is R.V. . . . Destiny is my auntie. . . . And Baby Drag, she's my cousin. . . . And the rest of the girls are my sistas."[9] Desiray explains to us that "the family is about who is your mentor. . . . The reason Gugi's my mom is that she painted my face for the first time." One night Desiray's mother was visiting and Gugi was in the bar in drag, and Desiray dedicated a song "to my mother and my drag mother." Both were in tears.

Like all families, things are not always perfect, as we've already seen. Some of them accuse one or two others of having stolen tips on occasion, although one of the girls said that all was forgiven. One night Sushi and Milla got into a fight in the dressing room because Milla told Sushi she was being an asshole onstage, and Milla tore off one of her fingernails, fake nail and real one both. "Drag queens start out fighting like women and end up fighting like men," Milla told us. Another time Kylie complained that one of the other girls wouldn't let her perform one night and then demanded to be in the show another night. "But that's her way—she's very selfish, a very selfish, controlling person. I have a hard time liking her all the time." "It can be vicious at times," R.V. says, and "you can scream at each other, but you make up in about an hour or so or less than that." When Roger went to work at Diva's, he told *Celebrate!* that he liked not having to put up with the "bitching and fighting" of seven drag queens in a small room, and he reported that his friendship with the 801 Girls was better "because we don't work together."[10]

When Sushi banned Mama from the upstairs bar for two weeks and from the dressing room forever for getting drunk and Super-gluing the zippers on Ma Evans boots, he simply announced, "There was an incident, and we all know what happened, and I don't think it was appropriate, I don't think it ever should have happened, and I dealt with it, I dealt with the people involved, and so that's it, I don't want any more jabbering and talk about it, it's over, it's done with, the two people who were involved are all right with it, and I dealt with it." That, in other words, is that.

Gugi, who says it's "like a family," adds, "Like any family, it gets divided once in a while in certain situations. And, they should remain nameless. [He laughs.] Overall, no, we stick with each other through thick and thin and make shows." Gugi was referring to the time when Inga and Milla didn't get along because Milla took up with Joey. While this feud was going on, Matthew described Inga and Milla as the only two who were competitive, "because they have personal problems that they bring to work." Gugi continues about this incident: "I love Milla to death. I mean, she's been there for me. She's the one I'm closest to, her and Inga, I can't decide which one. But I couldn't believe she did that. It was sort of a shock. It is just such a no-no, something you don't do. Like anything like that, it changed the relationship forever." But it didn't, really. Joey later left Milla for Inga, then "ran off" again, as Roger (Inga) put it, then returned for a while to Inga, who had taken over Milla's apartment. Dean (Milla) described performing with Inga after things had settled down: "We turned and with no practice, totally unrehearsed . . . she turned and I turned and we had it down, and it felt so good because it had been so long since we had that. And I was beaming, I was thrilled! That meant that she loved me." It is striking that although they have their conflicts and bitter memories, they never are competitive about their performances.

Not that they don't play with drag queen bitchiness. They do, onstage, R.V. grabbing the wig off Milla's head or Desiray giving someone the finger. The height of such antics came in a fabulous feud in the gay paper between Margo and "BellaDonna," *Celebrate!*'s "Society Writer," whose identity was at the time a secret, part of the intrigue of the exchange. Margo and Bella began trading swipes in the columns of *Celebrate!*—insulting each other for being old, ugly, pathetic, and desperate. Bella, for example, described Margo at a leather party "down on her knees (with knee pads shoved into her support hose) demonstrating how to put a condom on a man with her mouth. Did you leave your teeth in, girl?" David responded in his column that "the only times Margo has seen Bella, Bella has her face buried in a twinkie. And I don't mean the twinkies that are available on your grocer's shelf. I mean the twinkies that end up costing a hell of a lot more plus the bar tab they run up."[11] For several months they traded such digs, David ending his "Kiss kiss, hug hug," in true catty gossip-column style.

The feud hit its peak when Margo described slipping a drug into BellaDonna's drink one night when Edward Ditterline, then editor of *Celebrate!* (and BellaDonna's alter ego), was to take both of them to the opening of a new club on Marathon Key. Margo claimed that Bella-Donna fell asleep on the bar at 801.[12] But the next week Edward Ditterline told a different story: that Margo by mistake gave BellaDonna Viagra intended for David Felstein, causing Bella to tear off her clothes, run into the backroom bar, and molest thirty-eight gay men. Interviewing Bella, Ditterline was astonished to learn that Margo was actually Bella's mother. Bella embroidered a campy tale about "BellaDonna Margarita Porcini alla Cioccolatte della Stella D'Oro," born to Margo in Paris in 1947. Newly fired from the Folies Bergère and married to Bela Lugosi, after whom Bella was named, Margo had had affairs with Tennessee Williams, Ernest Hemingway, and Liberace, one of whom was Bella's biological father.[13] David took up the story with gusto, reporting that "Margo is more concerned than ever about the apparent disappearance of her treacherous, foul-mouthed daughter," urging everyone to "keep up the search for that horrible, viper-mouthed, evil-minded daughter."[14] In its campy style and over-the-top silliness, the feud played out all the stereotypes of bitchy old drag queens at each other's throats.

In real life the drag queens do engage in some of these kinds of antics. David's columns in *Celebrate!* are replete with in-group disputes. In one, he warned of a "bitter, disenchanted queen . . . her life a mass of nothing," spreading false rumors about drug dealing and drug use. "Anyone who frequents the 700–800 blocks of Duval Street knows who this person is."[15] In another he took to task, without naming names, a local amateur drag queen whose fund-raising techniques and desire to win Queen Mother he found annoying, and then reported that "according to her warped mind, the reason that I seemingly attacked her, as well as another craver of Queen Mother, is that I want the Queen

Mother crown and want to edge out the other contestants."[16] When Ms. D, the drag queen in question, finished for the third year in a row as first runner-up, just barely losing to Mama Crass, then a 801 Girl, a letter to the editor of *Celebrate!* accused the contest of being fixed since five of the six judges, the writer wrongly asserted, were associated with the Bourbon Street/801 complex.[17] The letter—and another complaining about the vulgarity of emcee D.D.T.—caused a minor furor in the paper. Ms. D responded to the whole uproar in true drag queen style. For her performance at the Miss Firecracker Pageant, she appeared in a straitjacket, wig and makeup askew, and to Patsy Cline's "Crazy" grasped at a crown dangled just above her head. She brought the house down and won kudos in David's next column.[18] (She finally won Queen Mother in 2002.)

The gossip and backbiting are just the other side of community. In the dressing room, as they sling insults at each other, Milla turns to Leila and says, "And you know what? This is all love. It really is." Leila tells them that one of the reviewers of the book proposal said we seemed to see them through rose-colored glasses, that we missed the bitchiness. Milla responds, "We actually do like each other that much; that's why we can bitch like we do." "We're trying to get over all that," Sushi tells Leila. Scabby adds, "We fight like you would with your brother or sister and then get over it." Milla concludes, "You know what? I bet our family is more functional than most." One night at dinner with Sushi and Greg, Kylie says, "It's like with any family, when it's outside of the pack, you start closing ranks. There's a need for family. That's why you preserve it, even when you hate someone in the family. You still close ranks when someone from outside attacks because you need that unit to stick together. If I don't have this one [gesturing to Sushi], or even this one [meaning Greg, although this is a stretch!], I don't know what I would do. I wouldn't be here, frankly."

If the girls make up a family, the bar functions as a kind of home for them. They often come to the shows when they aren't working. One day when Dean was down because a boyfriend stole his tip money, he came to the 801, practiced some numbers, held our dog Emma, and set the wigs. "It's home," he says simply. David describes the 801 as "my home away from home."[19] Both Gugi and Inga, after they left to work at Diva's, regularly turn up at 801 after their shows. Roger told an interviewer that he went up to say hello every night on his way to work.[20]

They stick together, and that is the meaning of what they call "Queen Nation." Sushi once talked about never having had women friends, just a few in high school: "And nothing close like with my drag queen friends. I guess you gravitate to your own kind." Sushi told the Key West newspaper that they stick together because "nobody else cares. We're a real subculture; most of us only have a high school education because we've always been outcasts."[21] When Miss Q, the outrageous English drag queen who performed with R.V., died of AIDS in London in the summer of 2001, the girls, and especially R.V., mourned her. "I'm smoking a lot of pot tonight to try to forget," R.V. told Verta at the benefit for LaLa Belle.

The 801 family is based on their shared work and shared identity, and it extends into the larger world of drag queens. One evening before the show, a drag queen in her sixties set up a portable sound system outside the bar and began to tap dance on the sidewalk. Sushi rushed over to announce for her and pass the hat. Later they told us that this queen, who was hoping to have surgery to become a woman, had killed herself. Another night Sushi brought a white-haired old man walking with a cane onstage and reverently introduced him as "Queen Mother IV, Mona Celeste." When La Te Da closed for a while, throwing the drag queens there out of work, the girls made space in their show for some of them. Occasionally they invite queens who show up in the audience to perform a number and keep the tips. That's how Gugi became part of the show. Having just returned from a stint in Chicago, she accepted the girls' offer to perform a number. The next week she came to the drag queen meeting and signed on to work as many nights as she could.

But as much as Queen Nation is about drag queen power, there's something else that happens in the drag shows as well. As we've already seen in looking at the shows, the drag queens both affirm gay/lesbian identity and at the same time break down the differences among people in a way that brings everyone—straight as well as gay, women as well as men, tourists as well as locals—into the family, if only for an hour or two.

Like celebrities, the girls elicit devotion from some of their fans. People send them photographs and letters thanking them for the show. People feel as if they've gotten to know the drag queens and think of them as friends. Often the girls don't remember such people at all, but they are good at pretending. The ubiquitous "darling" covers such situations well. Gugi describes people telling them that they've changed their lives, "they stood up to their mother or broke out and did their own thing because of us." He, too, comments on how strange it is that such things can happen and they don't even know the people on whom they have had such a big impact.

Some audience members really do become friends. Kylie tells us about Roxanne, who lives in Fort Lauderdale and comes down regularly with her husband and twin daughters. "She is like a friend. . . . I talk to her and she tells me about her family, and so it's like she comes because she is a friend now." Elmer, of the Bourbon Street garden wedding, describes meeting Sushi, Kylie, and Milla at the Atlantic Shores. They "sort of hit on me. And I told them I was straight, then they invited me to the show. So I came to the show and developed, actually, friendships with a couple of them. They have been close relationships." Kimberly, who married Elmer, adds, "Very close. And then we got married and when we met, we just started coming every night. He already started and he took me here the first night we met and then we came every night after that." Just before Elmer and Kimberly rented the house where they lived with Dean and Scabby, Elmer put it plainly: "It is family."

A young straight local woman describes meeting Sushi when she was eighteen. "Sushi made me feel really special and she pulled me out of the crowd and told me to, you know, she kind of noticed that I was latching on to my mom and she said I had to be my own person and I never forgot her for that, and so as soon as I came back down to Key West, I sought her out and . . . just started coming watch her perform and very quickly developed a close relationship." She tells of going shopping and seeing things that are just right for the girls. "After Christmas I cleaned out my closet and I found this little black dress that says 'Easy' on the front and I said, 'This has Milla written all over it.' And I brought it in and I gave it to Milla, and I had a white lace dress that I said, 'That has Sushi written all over it' and I gave the girls the dresses."

Two gay men from New York come once or twice a year and go to the shows every night. They describe getting to know the girls. "First of all you never see them. They're only there when the show is on or you rarely will see them during the day, but that's what happened, and one by one we started to get to know each of them." His partner adds, "And of course we sit dead center at the bar." Trying to explain why they don't do other things in Key West, one says, "I think we go because . . . right from the beginning, we just seemed to click with them, and we like them as people." They stay at a gay guest house and always try to recruit others to come along, because "we want to share the relationship with them."

The girls' relationships with audience members become part of the show. One night, a straight woman friend brought her baby. Kylie announced, "Let's hear it for bringing your baby to a drag show. Especially one this sexy." (It was Saturday night.) "We've all baby-sat him one time or another." R.V. added: "Remember, Sanderson saw this show from the womb. The first words out of his mouth are gonna be 'Fuck you, bitch.'" (R.V.'s once-upon-a-time call-and-response line.)

In addition to the relationships that develop between the drag queens and audience members, there's something that happens each night to create a bond, if only temporary, among audience members. Kimberly says, "I just enjoy coming now because now I love not only everyone onstage, I love everyone else who comes in here. It's like that family and then the other family out here." Another straight local woman says, "I know everybody in the bar and I look at the show and I go home. I really enjoy it." The young woman who met Sushi at eighteen adds, "It's about community. . . . The way I see it, we're all here because we love the girls and we come to support the girls . . . and that gives every single one of us sitting at this table a link. That's what brings us all together and that's the beginning of our community." Not all at this group of locals agreed. One gay man, who was married and has daughters and whose identity as a father is very important, found it "a little bit too much to call that family." But the others described not only getting to know regulars and forming friendships, but having meaningful interactions with visitors they met during the show. This has a great deal to do, of course, with the interactive style of the show. One gay tourist describes it as "a family affair," "everyone is involved and having a good time."

The 801 is not unique in creating this kind of home-away-from-home atmosphere. As we will see shortly, drag shows have a long history of creating community among gay and lesbian people. A local Latino man from Atlantic City, who had also lived in New York, noted that "drag shows were all over the place so this was just natural. This was like home for me to come to a drag show like this." Two lesbian tourists came to the show because they knew "we would be in an atmosphere where we could be ourselves and not have a problem." A young local gay man, sitting in the cabaret at one of our focus groups, says, "Like right now, I feel like I'm in my living room. And it's just been a home." Asked to explain how he went from walking into the bar to feeling as if he were at home, he explains, "It was the frequency of my visits initially." (He was living in his van and came every night.) "It was just setting up kind of friendships between different people. I've never felt unsafe here. I've never felt unwelcome."

What is special about all the family and home and community talk at the 801 is that it expresses all the contradictory things that we have seen going on in the shows. The foundation is their personal relationships among themselves and their belonging to Queen Nation. Their ties to one another—sometimes replacing bonds to their families of origin, sometimes complementing them—are a particularly strong example of gay men's friendships in contemporary American society.[22] In the shows they create a world in which being gay and lesbian is the norm: they foster the collective identity that is so central to the gay/lesbian movement. Some in the crowd articulate this as the clear message of the show: over half of our focus group members described the shows as nurturing a gay/lesbian collective identity. Describing what she took from the show, a lesbian entertainer from Orlando proclaimed, "I am what I am." A gay male New Yorker made the same point: "The message really comes across as it doesn't matter who you are; you have to be able to laugh at who you are and enjoy being who you are." At the 801, as another man put it, "Everybody is equally fabulous."

But at the same time, the drag queens bring straight people in the audience into that gay world. Three-quarters of focus group participants saw the 801 community as crossing categories of sexuality. And nearly half thought the shows both affirmed gay identity and forged bonds between gay and straight people. As Milla once confessed to us, "What I love the most is that all these people come to our shows—professors, doctors, lawyers, rich people—and they're as fucked up as we are." This complexity is captured in yet another of Sushi's introductions of her soul mate Kylie: "This is the person that created, well, started to create this person that I am tonight. Told me that I was special and that every single one of you is special." Starting with her relationship with Kylie, Sushi reaches out to gay and lesbian audience members and then beyond, drawing connections across gender and sexual categories, making everyone special, everyone part of the family.

SECTION V
"FREE YOUR MIND"

Finally, the show is over and the audience drifts out of the bar. What do they take home with them? Why do all of these different people—brides-to-be and their female friends and family members, newly married straight people, gay male locals and tourists, lesbian couples, college students on spring break—come to the show and sometimes return again and again? Given the ways that the drag queens deliberately trouble gender and sexuality, and the ways that the bar creates a kind of community among audience members, in what ways does the drag show have serious political consequences, in what ways is it an important part of the gay and lesbian movement?

Returning to the girls' favorite number for opening Kylie's "Sex Show," we explore here the ways that the performing of protest frees the minds of audience members. But first we put the drag show in its historical context, for there is both something old and something new about what goes on at the 801.

THIRTEEN

IN A LONG TRADITION

One Sunday afternoon Sushi called us in Columbus. The girls were sitting around sewing costumes (or so we thought) and somehow the question of the origin of the term "drag queen" came up. Sushi told us later he didn't know why they started talking about it, "but we were really fucked up." Scabby, Sushi reported, thought it came from Stonewall, when the queens were dragged out of the bar by the police. No, we assured Sushi, both "drag" and "queen" had longer histories than that, although we weren't sure about them, and we had never even thought about when the two terms got put together. Leila rushed to look the words up in her copy of the *Oxford English Dictionary* but found nothing about these particular meanings. It wasn't so easy, we found out, to locate the origins of the terms.

But what is particularly interesting is Scabby's creative explanation. For increasingly, people, at least gay and lesbian people, connect drag queens with Stonewall and the origins of the modern gay/lesbian movement. And it's this that we want to explore here: drag as a long tradition of resistance and challenge to the dominant order. For what the 801 Girls do is a new form of drag in one sense, yet in another it continues the potential that drag has long held in same-sex communities.

To return to the question of terminology: we put out a query to the list serve of the Committee on Lesbian and Gay History and received a slew of helpful replies, and for those we are grateful. As we thought, "drag" in the sense of men wearing women's clothing dates back to the mid- or late nineteenth century. A young Englishman wrote to Ernest Boulton, who was convicted of conspiracy to commit the crime of "buggery" in 1871 because he wore women's clothing in public, "I am sorry to hear of your going about in drag so much." One witness in the case explained to the police, "I know what 'in drag' means; it is the slang for going about in women's clothes."[1] Theater historian Laurence Senelick traces the origins of the term to criminal slang meaning "slowed down," from the drag of a carriage that was used as a brake, then applied to the effects of long skirts trailing on the ground, definitely a slowing factor compared to trousers! There doesn't seem to be any evidence to support the rumor that "drag" comes from "dressed roughly as a girl" (as Richard, aka Ms. D, Miss Key West for 2000, told us) or from the related notion that it was used in stage directions in Elizabethan England to mean "dressed as a girl" ("drab" meaning "dressed as a boy").[2] Of course, the whole question reminds us that printed sources may not always be the best source for understanding slang terms in an underworld subculture.

"Queen," originally "quean" in the queen's English, is a much older term, originally meaning "whore" and used, according to Rictor Norton, in late-seventeenth-century England to refer to "mollies," the term for effeminate sodomitical men.[3] This is in line with much of the terminology for gay men in English, which moved from female prostitution to the male same-sex subculture because both were part of the same urban underworld. The *Oxford English Dictionary*—the current edition of which does, it turns out, have this meaning of "queen"—gives as definition number 12 "a male homosexual, esp. the effeminate partner in a homosexual relationship," but dates the first usage to 1924.[4] The terms "drag" and "queen," which might logically have come together sooner, seem to have joined no earlier than the 1930s. The first usage in print anyone has found to date is 1941.[5] The meaning was clearly a gay man dressed as a woman for purposes of entertainment: "A professional female impersonator; the term being transferentially used of a male homosexual who frequently or almost invariably wears women's clothing, often for purposes of homosexual contact. . . ."

Cross-dressing for a wide variety of purposes—religious, theatrical, political, social, sexual—has taken place across time and around the world. From Native American societies to Siberia, gender transformation is or has been associated with special spiritual powers.[6] In cultures in which it has been considered scandalous for women to appear on the stage, from Shakespeare's England to seventeenth-century Japan, men or boys have played the parts of women, and in other contexts women played what were called in seventeenth-century England "the breeches part." Men in early modern England sometimes put on women's clothing during riots or protests, drawing upon a tradition common in community festivals, in order to mock authority and hide their identities.[7] Women in Australia in the nineteenth century, as in Europe in earlier centuries, sometimes donned the clothing of men in the interests of geographical and social mobility, gaining the freedom to travel and access to better-paying jobs. And in many cultures, men might dress in women's clothes to express their desire to have sex with other men. Increasingly, in the Western world, male cross-dressing except in limited circumstances came to be associated with same-sex desire.

Take, for example, the "mollies" of eighteenth-century London. Like men in subcultures in other large European cities, including Paris and Amsterdam, mollies were effeminate men who frequented taverns, parks, and public latrines, sought out male sexual partners, and shared a style of feminine dress and behavior.[8] An agent of the English Societies for the Reformation of Manners entered a London club in 1714 and found men "calling one another my dear, hugging and kissing, tickling and feeling each other, as if they were a mixture of wanton males and females; and assuming effeminate voice, female airs."[9] The agent's trial testimony continued: "Some were completely rigged in gowns, petticoats, headcloths, fine laced shoes, furbelowed scarves, and masks; some had riding hoods; some were dressed like milkmaids, others like shepherdesses with green hats, waistcoats, and petticoats; and others had their faces patched and painted and wore very extensive hoop petticoats, which had been very lately introduced."[10]

In the context of eighteenth-century European urban life, men dressing in women's clothes in public establishments represented an assertion of sexual desire and a sign of membership in a community. The same was true rather later in the United States, where cities did not grow large enough to shelter same-sex communities until the mid-nineteenth century. A physician in 1871 described "restaurants frequented by men in women's attire, yielding themselves in indescribable lewdness," and another in 1893 reported that an organization of African American men in Washington, D.C., decked themselves out in "low-necked dresses . . . feathered and ribboned headdresses, garters, frills, flowers, ruffles, etc. and deport themselves as women."[11] The Bowery in New York by the end of the nineteenth century was home to what were called "resorts" or saloons that sheltered a flamboyant "fairy" culture, where "boys [who] have powder on their faces like girls and talk to you like disorderly girls talk to men" hung out.[12] Fairies might wear makeup, wear outrageous clothing, and adopt feminine mannerisms, but they only dressed in women's clothing in secure resorts or the much more public drag balls that flourished in cities such as New York and Chicago.

This association between gender transgression and same-sex desire can be found throughout time and around the globe, so it is no surprise that when scientists of sex in Europe and the United States, known as "sexologists," first began to write about people who desired others with biologically alike bodies, they conceptualized this state as gender "inversion." As one doctor put it, "Men become women and women men, in their tastes, conduct, character, feelings and behavior."[13] At first, same-sex desire was a symptom rather than the defining characteristic of the deviance the doctors called inversion. Later Freud unhooked the two, arguing that the most masculine of men might desire other men. Other sexologists conceptualized a mind/body split, a female spirit trapped in a male body or vice versa, and portrayed such individuals as members of a third or intermediate sex.

It is in this context that we need to understand the history of drag performances. What is clear from the history of drag is that it has long served a community-building function, since drag shows and drag balls were places that women and men with same-sex desires knew they could meet others with the same interests. At the same time, drag as a theatrical spectacle has also attracted the attention of straight onlookers, whose presence can legitimize the performances. Thus the tension between marginality and celebrity that the 801 Girls experience and the disagreement about whether the 801 cabaret is gay space are foreshadowed in the history of drag.

Drag as we know it today had its origins in the mid-nineteenth century, when glamorous female impersonators first appeared onstage.[14] A half-century earlier, the only men who wore women's clothes onstage were "dame comedians" who burlesqued old women for a laugh, making no attempt at either verisimilitude or pulchritude. Such portrayals evolved into glamour drag via all-male school theatricals, the circus, and minstrel shows. But in addition to these respectable origins, female impersonation onstage had connections to the subculture of cross-dressing men looking for male sex partners. Ironically, what could get men arrested on the streets won applause in the theater. Yet that very connection made female impersonators in the theater insecure. At the height of his popularity in the first decades of the twentieth century, Julian Eltinge, a female impersonator with impeccable offstage masculine credentials, carefully guarded his privacy and tried to portray himself as a man's man and heterosexual who disliked his profession. In fact, he seems to have had a male lover, which may explain why he vigorously separated himself from "the usual creeping male defective who warbles soprano and decks himself in the frocks and frills of womankind," who, tellingly, besieged him at the stage door.[15]

At the same time that respectable audiences, largely composed of middle-class women, enjoyed the talents of entertainers such as Julian Eltinge, cross-dressing entertainers also flourished in more disreputable places that catered to gay crowds. By the 1920s, with the advent of Prohibition, speakeasies began introducing mixed audiences of middle-

and working-class patrons—and in Harlem, white and African American patrons—to drag. This was also the high point of public drag balls, where men might use the cover of masquerade to dress in women's clothing and dance with other men and where straight people came to gape. New York's drag balls came to rival those of Chicago, New Orleans, and even Berlin. At the Hamilton Lodge Ball or Masquerade and Civic Ball, known by the late 1920s as the "Faggots' Ball," "effeminate men, sissies, wolves, 'ferries,' 'faggots,' the third sex, 'ladies of the night,' and male prostitutes" gathered "for a grand jamboree of dancing, love making, display, rivalry, drinking and advertisement."[16]

In part because of the popularity of the balls, and in part out of club owners' desperation to attract business as the depression thinned the crowds of paying customers, New York's Times Square experienced a "pansy craze" in the early 1930s. Nightspots featuring female impersonators and "professional pansies," that is, effeminate men who dressed in men's clothes, attracted not only gay patrons but also "night riders and gadabouts . . . seeking new thrills."[17] But then the repeal of Prohibition, with its flouting of law-abiding, middle-class codes of behavior, meant an end of the speakeasy life that had brought drag out of the subculture. The creation of a liquor control board, in New York as well as other states, gave the government more leverage than ever over drinking establishments, leading to a ban on homosexual behavior in reputable bars and clubs and, ironically, the growth of exclusively gay bars.[18]

During the Second World War, drag found a surprising home when soldier drag queens, both African American and white, put on elaborate shows to entertain their buddies. The army provided scripts, music, lyrics, set designs—even dress patterns![19] And drag survived the postwar crackdown on gay culture, in part by catering to straight audiences. In San Francisco, where the tourist industry touted the city's reputation for sexual license, gay men and lesbians mingled with heterosexual tourists at the drag shows at Mona's and Finocchio's.[20] Finocchio's, which closed its doors in 1999, worked to keep its shows respectable, partly by separating the audience from the performers and partly by keeping the shows clean. As a performer interviewed about the club's closing noted, "The show is not about being gay. It's not about sex."[21] The Jewel Box Revue, although born in a Miami gay bar in 1939, also aimed at a straight audience.[22] With an ethnically mixed cast unusual for the time, the troupe toured the country for thirty years. The Revue's elaborate show of what were advertised as "impressions" rather than impersonations featured performers mimicking stars such as Bette Davis, Marlene Dietrich, Mae West, and Katharine Hepburn. The rise of the mass media made such gay-heroine-divas immediately recognizable across the country.[23] Similar performances graced the stages of clubs such as the Moroccan Village and 82 Club in New York, the My Oh My Club in New Orleans, the Club Flamingo in Hollywood, and the Garden of Allah in Seattle.

But despite the persistence of such clubs, the postwar environment took its toll on drag performances. The Boston Licensing Board banned female impersonation in cafés, restaurants, and other establishments in 1947, and in 1951 Cardinal Cushing added the Catholic Church's condemnation. In a number of cities, wearing drag on the street was illegal, so female impersonators had to carry cabaret cards to prove that they were performers. Only on Halloween could men get away with dressing in drag, so traditional drag balls, like the African American–sponsored events in Chicago, continued to flourish throughout the 1950s.[24]

But the clubs where drag queens performed suffered, and their increasingly precarious financial situation led to a revolution in drag performances. Traditionally, drag queens actually sang, accompanied by live music. First the clubs introduced recorded music, then drag queens began to lip-synch rather than sing. From the perspective of the female impersonators who sang and danced, the change allowed untalented amateurs into the business.[25] Esther Newton's classic book *Mother Camp* captured the process of transition from live to mimed performances in the drag world of the 1960s.[26] "Stage" impersonators, who sang and regarded their performing as a profession, looked down on lip-synching "street" impersonators, usually younger, more marginal, more visible and confrontational, and more likely to do drugs.

The other development in the 1950s that changed the nature and perception of drag shows was the increasing viability and public awareness of transsexuality.[27] The possibility of men actually changing into women cast drag in a new and more deviant light, and some drag queens did in fact take the step to changing sex.[28] The famous Black Cat Café in San Francisco lost its liquor license in 1963, and the Jewel Box Revue was banned in Reno and picketed in Harlem. Drag performers, some of whose acts included stripping down to a G-string, differentiated themselves from and resented the competition of transsexuals, who did not have to be mistresses of illusion.

As drag changed in dramatic and less dramatic ways up to the explosion of gay and lesbian activism in the 1970s, two things remained constant: drag both built community among gay and lesbian people and challenged, if more or less politely, the dominant gender-divided and heterosexual order. José Sarria, who performed in drag at the Black

Cat in San Francisco and ran for city supervisor in 1961 as part of the struggle against police harassment of the gay bars, formed the Imperial Court System in 1965, arguably the first drag queen movement organization.[29] The court system (now known as the International Court System, with chapters scattered over the western part of the country) raises money for the gay community (and other charitable purposes) through drag shows, but more importantly provides a "family" and respect for drag queens, the heart of the Court. The Imperial Court System, by bestowing family names and royal titles on its members, made concrete the community-building impact of drag. As a regular at the Garden of Allah in Seattle remembered, the bar was paradise: "In it we found love, understanding, companionship, friendship, and a common bond. We were more or less one big family."[30]

If drag historically has created community, it has also always carried the potential of challenge. Even the tourist shows at Finocchio's or the Jewel Box Revue had a potentially political edge. Although comedy and de-wigging at the end of the show reassured the audiences that this was good clean fun, the drag queens engaged in a lot of the same antics that we see at the 801. As a steady patron of the Garden of Allah recalled, "Billy might go out in the audience and sit on some sailor's lap and wiggle his false boobs in the poor sailor's face." A performer at the Garden told of using such lines as "A hard man is good to find," or, taking out her falsies, "These are great. I scrubbed the floor and washed the car with these today and I'm wearing them tonight."[31] Performers doing comic drag gestured to their genitals at the mention of the word "love," imitated sexual intercourse, and used double entendre.[32] In 1965, at a Chicago bar called the Shed, drag queen Skip Arnold folded political commentary into his farewell show: "The same jokes that are going around, that they now call Polish jokes, were once Jewish jokes, Puerto Rican jokes, Negro jokes. . . . I can't wait until next year, when the Mattachine turns all those same things into queer jokes, you know? Oh, if you think we're not gonna march *then*, you're out of your mind. We've suffered the slings and arrows . . . which ain't bad, if you're S and M."[33]

For the assimilationist "we're just like you" tendency of gay and lesbian activism, from the homophile movement of the 1950s to the present, drag queens have been an embarrassment. But in the more confrontational wing of the movement, drag has played a central role. The four Harlem drag queens sentenced to sixty days in the workhouse in 1928, who called out to the arresting officers as they were led away, "Goodbye dearie, thanks for the trip as we'll have the time of our lives," were resisting gender conventions and compulsory heterosexuality.[34] Like butch and fem lesbians walking the street arm in arm in the 1950s, drag queens have represented "sexual courage."[35] As Margo regularly reminds the audiences at the 801, drag queens led the charge at Stonewall. "I'm not missing a minute of this—it's the revolution," shouted Sylvia Rivera, who began life as a transvestite prostitute in Times Square and continued her activism until her death in February 2002.[36] Drag queens have also stimulated pride. As Key West author Leigh Rutledge put it, in a tribute to "old queens," "They are, they have always been—whether famous or merely sitting next to you at the bar—the spotlights of gay life. They have always known exactly where to shine: on the very best, the very funniest, the most delicious aspects of being gay."[37]

But their resistance has also been important to the organized gay and lesbian movement. From José Sarria, drag queen and political candidate, to the drag queen chorus line challenging the police the night of the raid at the Stonewall Inn in 1969, drag queens, however ambivalently viewed by the movement, have been there.[38]

In the flamboyant zap actions of the early days of gay liberation in England, men wore dresses in public as an act of confrontation and donned women's bathing suits to picket the trial of feminists who had disrupted the Miss World Contest. In the aftermath of Stonewall, groups in the United States such as Street Transvestites Action Revolutionaries (founded by Sylvia Rivera, a heroine of Stonewall, among others) and Flaming Faggots, along with men who identified as "radical fairies" and "effeminists," as well as butch women, challenged gender conformity within the movement. But such gender revolutionaries fought an uphill battle with gay liberationists and radical feminists who dismissed drag as politically incorrect.[39] Not until the 1980s, when groups such as the Sisters of Perpetual Indulgence and Church Ladies for Choice took up comic drag in a serious political struggle with the religious right, did transgender presentation again play a more central role in the movement.[40] The San Francisco Sisters, sporting beards and mustaches and riding motorcycles in nun habits and rosaries, showed up at protests and fund-raisers around gay issues. Church Ladies for Choice, on the East Coast, put on dowdy dresses and sang such lyrics as "This womb is my womb" at anti-abortion rallies.[41] Although not strictly drag, these gay groups paid homage to the tradition of drag resistance.

Drag at the turn of the twenty-first century has taken on a wide variety of forms, but all of them are foreshadowed in drag history. There are talented artists who impersonate female icons or create their own personae; there are street queens who live a marginal life; there are professional and amateur drag queens who lip-synch and adopt a range of styles, from female impersonation to campy drag to voguing; there are movement activists who adopt drag for explicitly political purposes; there are mainstream celebrities such as RuPaul and Lady Chablis, who began their careers like other drag queens but made it big-time. Perhaps nothing illustrates the rags-to-riches possibilities of drag so much as the fortunes of Wigstock, the Labor Day drag festival in New York that began in 1984 with an impromptu performance by tired drag queens leaving a club at the end of the night and grew over the years into an international extravaganza attracting tens of thousands of spectators and official recognition from the city.[42] Although drag has also gone mainstream, with actors from Dustin Hoffman to Wesley Snipes to Terence Stamp wearing dresses in the movies, such commercialization mirrors the popularity of Julian Eltinge and the pansy craze rather than signifying the death of drag as a strategy of protest.

The gay ambivalence about drag that has always characterized parts of the gay and lesbian movement certainly surfaces at the 801. While none of the women we talked with at the bar articulated the feminist critique of drag as mocking women by exaggerating femininity, we talked with lesbians in Key West who did. For obvious reasons not at the show, they dislike drag queens because they don't like femininity in women, so have no use for it in men, and on top of that resent the male privilege that they see drag queens as men enjoying. Some gay men also find drag a bit unsettling. Or more. Several gay men told us they find the 801 Girls too "in-your-face," "aggressive," or "sleazy, trashy, and vulgar." Others expressed ambivalence. A gay male teacher admitted to uneasiness about drag when he first came out. "It kind of frightened me to a certain extent. And part of that was just, you know, maybe a lack of security with my own identity. Does this mean I want to be a woman?" His lover, a physician, who confessed to being less secure about his sexuality, still found drag troubling. "Maybe because I have a more feminine side, maybe, I don't know what it is." He talked about the stereotypes of homosexual men he took in as a young boy— the effeminacy, furtive anonymous sex—and his continued concern that straight people view gay men that way. "I'm not as secure," he concluded.

Other gay men in the audience, too, mentioned gay male fear of or hostility to drag. "You know, it's the 'don't act too gay because it gives us a bad name,'" said one. "It puts forth this image of gay people as just out there, you know, weird, freaky people. And so they don't want to identify with that. They want to be, you know, nine-to-five, corporate, have the job and raise the kids and live in the house in the suburbs. . . . And those are the people probably most afraid of drag shows."

His lover agreed, but described being "revolted" when he was first coming out and went to drag shows. "I mean, I remember thinking, 'What are these freaks doing up there? What's wrong with them?' . . . And then I would try and think, 'OK, what psychological problems do they have that they feel confused? They really want to be women.'"

One gay man remembered that when he lived in San Francisco, only tourists and older gay men would go to the drag shows. "The cross-dressing and all that stuff seemed to be part of the heritage of the '50s and '60s. It wasn't something current men would do." But he found it interesting to think of "how the drag queens break things open and think about how they started the Stonewall riot as well, the drag queens out there with their courage and their fire, breaking everything open."

The 801 Girls, then, follow in a long tradition. Their various routes to dressing in drag, their simultaneous centrality and marginality in their community, their varieties of drag performance, their outrageousness, their creation of community—all are foreshadowed in the history of drag. What is, perhaps, new, at least since Stonewall, is their proud assertion of belonging to "Queen Nation."

One big question remains: How does what they do onstage affect the people who flock upstairs to see them? That's what we wanted to find out.

FOURTEEN

"WE'RE NOT JUST LIP-SYNCHING UP HERE, WE'RE CHANGING LIVES"

Interviewed in the Key West newspaper for a story about drag queens in Key West, Sushi commented, "We're not just lip-synching up here, we're changing lives by showing people what we're all about." Despite the fact that drag shows are, most centrally, entertainment, the intentions of the drag queens to free the minds of audience members do pan out. The diverse individuals who flock to the 801 come away with an experience that makes it a little less possible to think in a simple way about gender and sexuality or to ignore the experiences of gay, lesbian, bisexual, and transgendered people in American society.

Finding out what audiences think was no simple matter. We decided to conduct focus groups and solicited the aid of Josh Gamson, who had used this method in his study of talk-show portrayals of gay and lesbian people.[1] He showed us how they were done and also helped recruit gay men, who we were afraid might be less likely to come talk to us. We would go to the shows with flyers "good for one free drink," which bar owner Jim Gilleran kindly donated to the project, and walk around trying to persuade people to come back the next afternoon to talk about the drag queens. Sometimes, when they remembered, the girls would tell the audience about our study and urge them to come talk with us. Sometimes, when Sushi would introduce Verta and Leila as "professors of lesbian love," this didn't really help. Generally we would get about fifteen or twenty people who would swear they would come. But of course people were drinking, some were on vacation, and no more than six ever turned up, and that was at the height of the season. As the crowds thinned and tourists from all over the country (and some from abroad) gave way to less affluent Florida visitors (what the drag queens are wont to call "white trash on vacation"), our groups got smaller and smaller, finally dwindling away, one day, to nothing. Nevertheless, our response rate was typical for focus group research.[2]

Over the course of the year we did the focus groups, we talked to a diverse set of people. In addition to the planned focus groups, we spoke less formally to another fifty-five people about the show. The focus groups consisted of forty people, exactly half of them women and half of them men. If this reflects the general population, the other characteristics of the group do not. The crowd was far more gay, lesbian, or bisexual (70 percent), less racially and ethnically diverse, younger, wealthier, more highly educated, more likely to be Jewish or nonreligious, and heavily Democratic or independent in politics.[3] Nevertheless, the groups included a range of sexual identities (including bisexual and transgender people), ethnicities, ages, classes, educational levels, religions, and political affiliations.

What is striking, of course, is that this group of people gathered in a gay bar to see the show. Actually, there is some dispute about whether the cabaret upstairs is gay space or not. A young straight woman who had never been to a drag show described it as "scary going into a gay bar," because "you walk into a gay bar, you're gay." The older straight woman friend who took her to the 801 commented, "I feel like I'm walking through the gay bar to go up to another venue. I don't think of upstairs 801 as really a gay space." A bisexual local man had the same take: "This is not really a gay bar. I mean, if you have a problem with gay people, then you shouldn't be up here. But it's not a gay bar. It's everybody's bar." As Kylie put it one night at the "Girlie Show," "This is a cabaret, not a gay bar. Downstairs is a gay bar." Nevertheless, it's a big commitment to go through what clearly is a gay bar downstairs and go up the stairs to the cabaret. "I'm a tad uncomfortable," the older friend of the young woman told us, "because I feel like I'm in someone else's space." "There is only one way down at 801. You're up there, you're stuck, it's very small, it's very intimate, so yeah," explained the young woman, "it is a little more intimidating" than someplace like Diva's, where you can easily walk in and out off the sidewalk. Sushi notes that "we have a wider variety of people coming to our shows now than we did over at Bourbon Street because Bourbon Street was so packed with boys, boys, boys, boys."

Mama, the Brazilian drag queen who hangs out at the 801, insists that straight visitors to Key West are guests on a "gay island" and the 801 is "not their place," so they should respect the rules of the game. The young straight woman would agree. "I think my initial thought when we were going in was, 'I am entering someone else's territory.' . . . And I felt like I needed to play by their rules." But then, when the drag queens acknowledge the diversity of the crowd through doing shots and their talk, "after the show got started, it didn't matter if it was a gay bar."

Of course the bringing together of straight and gay people has some-thing to do with Key West. As a forty-three-year-old straight male real-tor from Naples put it, the mixed audience is "definitely a statement about Key West. I mean, we talked about that today and what a diverse city it is and how accepting everything is here versus a lot of other places, and it was really neat, I thought." A gay man recently moved to Key West pointed out that "the girls here have a much more diverse audience than they would have in many other cities, because of the tourism here you have a lot more straight people on average coming in here." Roger (Inga) likes the fact that there are so many straight people because "maybe it's the first time they've seen something like this, or it's something they've seen only on TV. . . . It's so new to them; they enjoy you so much." R.V. describes attracting "straight people looking for that *Jerry Springer* atmosphere."[4] Sushi, as we have seen, talks at the show about bringing everyone together. As Inga puts it, "It's from the worst faggot to the butchiest lesbian to the happily mar-ried couple with the kids, the honeymoon people, the people who hate gays but maybe thought it was something interesting—it's such a big thing." A gay male tourist talks about the show's "really big mass appeal to a cross section of everyone. I mean, there were a lot of straight people and gay people, men and women, and they came across with that very well . . . pulling people up onstage the way that they did." Or as a straight professional woman put it, "I thought it was more about here is, like in this whole world there's black, there's white, there's whatever. It's just a flavor of the world to me. And it's OK. That's what I thought."

On the other hand, complicated things go on when straight people come to what is at least to some extent a gay space. Although the drag queens appreciate their straight audiences, Kylie also says, "Straight people don't know how much gay people love to see us make fun of them." The gay men in the audience enjoy, as one said, that the drag queens "get some guy up there trying to take his shorts off and things like that. Especially because they always get the straight boys up there to do that." Another gay man commented, "I mean, I love it when they hassle straight men." And there is a lot of hostility directed at straight men.

So why do straight people, or gay people for that matter, attend the drag show? They come, of course, to be entertained. "People want to see a number; they want to see the next costume," as Roger (Inga) says. "They want to get entertained." And in fact some audience members said just this. "I didn't think there was any point. I just thought it was a fun thing," said a straight male advertising executive. A local gay male attorney thinks of the show as "a continuing part of the gay community's entertainment." Asked what they liked about the show, two young lesbian tourists responded quickly, "It was funny"; "Definitely funny"; "Entertaining." But of course, as Josh, who helped us out with the focus groups, commented, they wouldn't find a man dressed as a man and lip-synching to a song by a male performer particularly entertaining.

And in fact even those who thought first of the entertainment value of the show almost always went on to talk about other qualities. Almost 90 percent of focus groups members described something beyond sheer entertainment about what they had experienced. One of the women in the lesbian couple quoted above, a computer consultant, noted that the show kept their attention, "you were watching the whole time. . . . You have to be pretty open-minded to enjoy it." Her partner, a gym teacher, added, thinking about the impact on straight people, "Maybe it would change their view a little on what it is." Another young lesbian couple, asked why they came, responded, respectively, "Community"; "Entertainment." A straight Moroccan woman from Montreal started by saying, "It's like a show. I'm not thinking about drag; I think it's a show and it's so nice and it's fun." But then as others in the focus group began to talk about straight women falling in love with drag queens, she wondered, "But what does this mean?" A straight woman part-time resident, in her forties, said, "It's just a form of entertainment," yet discussed all sorts of ramifications of the show, including opening the minds of straight visitors. A lesbian visitor from Orlando gave her main reason for coming: "Well, I find it entertaining. The show's very entertaining," but very quickly commented on how much "I Am What I Am" meant to her as she struggled with self-acceptance.

Coming to the show for its entertainment value, some audience members note the quality of the show. A local straight woman, born in France, liked "everything." A straight man from Fort Lauderdale who comes to the show regularly with his wife and daughters found it "really comfortable" from the beginning; "it was something special." A gay man visiting from Philadelphia came back after having seen the show the year before because "we were just blown away by how wonderful and fun it was." His partner thought that "there's, like, really incredible performance art going on. . . . These girls are more than just lip-synching. They're really involved. They're coordinated. It's choreographed and just seems like they're having so much fun and the audience is having so much fun." A local working-class man who attends two or three times a week liked the cabaret style, the group numbers, the way they work together, the spontaneity. As we've already seen, a number of people mentioned that it's the best show in town.

"One of the best drag shows I've even seen," pronounced a local gay man.

Audience members, of course, have favorites among the girls. Lesbians in the audience definitely tended to have a thing for Milla. A French lesbian physician liked her because she "had something very sexy. . . . She was very professional and she had something very, I don't know, sensual, sexy; she had beautiful legs. . . . And knowing that she was a guy also did a lot to make it very interesting." Her lover agreed: "I liked Milla the best, too." A straight woman from Canada found Milla attractive but really liked Inga because "she's pretty and she looks like a girl and when I met her after [that is, out of drag] she looked so young. . . . He's so cute and so shy." Another straight woman tourist liked Milla and Inga best, but one of the straight men with whom she had attended the show proclaimed Inga "too Amazonish." He liked Kylie most because "she had great legs and a great butt." A gay male couple talked about how much they liked R.V., "her performance is amazing. . . . She's so, so awesome." They also loved Kylie swinging in the rafters. A young lesbian couple fell for Sushi, agreeing that she was "hot." Obviously, people have different responses to the girls, but it is noticeable that women, both straight and lesbian, tended to talk about their attraction to those—Milla, Sushi, Inga, Gugi, and Desiray—who look the most like women in drag. As one straight woman said about Desiray, revealing her shifting ideas about gender, "She is so pretty; I'm jealous of him."

During the show most audience members tend to think of the drag queens as women. "Women. Women. Definitely," says a local straight woman. A straight couple described reacting to Milla as a woman. "She was a woman," said the man. "Uh-huh, she was a woman. It never even entered my mind. She was a beautiful woman. God," responded the woman. A lesbian in the group interjected, "But there's something there. There's something that's not a woman that I don't know, I find— You know that they're not." "I know that they're not," responded a third woman, a straight friend of the first. "I think we all knew that they weren't women, but the whole point was that you're looking at them" and thinking that they're women, explained the man. A young straight woman who had never before seen a drag show explained that she thought of them as both men and women. "Back and forth, I think. Yeah, I was just confused and went back about twelve times." One gay man, as if echoing what the girls, or at least some of them, might say about themselves, said, "I don't think of them as really any of it. I feel like they're their own thing. I feel like a drag queen is something com-

pletely different. . . . It's way more than being a woman and it's definitely not being a man." In fact, what some women especially admired
was the drag queens' strength and aggressiveness, their ability to act
like men while looking like women. As one put it, "It's the freedom. . . .
I mean, they're so energetic, they get up onstage and they are energetic.
. . . If you're a woman, it's very improper to get up there and say 'What
the fuck's going on man,' you know?"

One of the big issues for audiences—an issue on which there is
great dissension—is how they feel about the breaking of the illusion
of femaleness. As we have seen, the girls themselves insist on differen-
tiating themselves from female impersonators. "That's the best part,
when the voice is all low," says R.V. Inga loves to shock the audience
by coming out at the end out of drag. "They get such shock out of
the difference . . . they get so surprised over that and they just don't
understand." It was Inga who suggested, after the first time that Kylie
spontaneously stripped at the end of her show, that Kylie leave on her
wig to contrast the hair "and the face and then the male body." An
eighteen-year-old straight woman really liked R.V "because it is obvious
that she is a he . . . and he kinda played on that. And I thought that
was really neat." Yet she couldn't sort out how she felt about Sushi
dropping her dress to show her chest. "That confused me so much. . . .
To me, it ruined the fantasy of it." One of the straight men who especially liked Kylie thought that her climbing in the rafters took away
her femininity, although the women in the group, both lesbian and
straight, disagreed. In another group, a gay man described this as "neat
to see a woman expressing all sides of her—it's a man but I mean—
no, I mean it's a woman who can explore her masculine side. Can jump
through the rafters." A straight woman in yet another group thought
it was "fun" and "a good part of the show," but didn't like that it destroyed the illusion. Yet she enjoyed R.V., although "it is part of his
shtick not to try" to look like a woman.

There were also conflicting reactions to the girls' tendency to call
attention to their male—or lack of female—body parts. A straight man
commented that it was a "turnoff . . . when they bent over and you
could actually see their penis and balls tucked up underneath," even
though he knew they were men. A straight woman who had attended
the show with him had the opposite reaction, "I just thought it was
kind of neat that, you know, that he talked about his balls and tucking
one under and I thought that was really cool." A gay male professional
couple both liked the breaking of illusion; as one put it, "It sort of ties
it all together. I mean, you know that it's a man behind the costume,
but you can't help but wonder, 'Are those breasts real?'" A young les-

bian woman liked R.V. "moving his boob over" and "loved the end when they all came out undressed" (she meant dressed as men). "I mean, I thought that was great because—" and here her lover interjected, "Yeah, I mean, I like to see the person behind, who's actually there." One thing that seemed to attract people to the focus groups was the possibility of meeting the girls out of drag.

Some audience members really pondered the significance of this breaking of illusion. A gay male hairdresser was both shocked and awed in a way he found hard to articulate when Kylie stripped at the end of the Saturday show. "I mean, I don't know what that does for people, but it sure does something." His lover thought that "one of the most interesting things about drag is seeing the performers out of drag . . . meeting them just who they are." They both liked "that constant reminder that 'we're men, you know. And don't forget it, you know. We might be fabulous and look wonderful, but we're men.'" An older straight woman found Sushi's stripping behind the scrim "awesome." "You're sucked into, these are men portraying women and all of a sudden, you're brought back to reality. And maybe that's part of it, that's the point. You know, we want you to see that this is who we really are, but it's part of the show."

R.V.'s rendition of "What Makes a Man a Man?" for many audience members took on great meaning. A lesbian speech pathologist from Orlando described getting "choked up" because "there was a feeling of acceptance and I was really struggling with acceptance and I just felt a connection and I think that's what made me want to keep coming back, is feeling that connection." A straight local woman commented, "I mean, it just makes you cry. The whole thing, it really touched me." "Awesome number," proclaimed a local gay attorney. "It's really an emotional song," said a local working-class gay man. A lesbian tourist "thought it was great." She speculated that if straight people really listened to the words, "then maybe they would start thinking about it. . . . I think that they could get it." A gay male local described "a lot of older married couples sit there with their jaws hitting the floor. Especially when the eyelashes come off and the wig and the makeup just disappears like that. . . . And it's a great song, it's a great number, it's a great act, it says a lot in that one song. And they're like, I think they're still shocked when they leave that way like, 'Oh my god, I don't believe it.' They want to believe that they're women and it's hard for them to accept that they're not."

Above all, the crowds tend to love the interaction with the audience that sets the 801 apart from drag shows in other places. Kylie tells us that when people ask what kind of show it is, he says, "It's an audience-participation show." A gay male tourist reported going to at least fifty drag shows around the country, "but never anything like this. Never, never with this much audience participation." A self-described queer male physician from Boston described his surprise that the drag queens "not only sort of expect but almost demand that the audience actually participate in some way and give a little bit of themselves." Interestingly, a forty-eight-year-old straight female tourist who had never been to a drag show before thought there was "very little audience participation," although she enjoyed what there was. An upper-middle-class lesbian from New York considered the audience involvement a clever way "to get everybody engaged and keep people engaged and not too focused on one group or another." A young local gay man with theatrical interests said, "I'm really drawn to the audience interaction. . . . It's very in-your-face and there's an interaction between the audience and I love that. You know, while I've seen some of these numbers fifty times, quite literally, every night it's fresh."

As this comment suggests, the participatory aspects are what draw people back night after night. In a focus group of locals, a young gay working-class Latino man said he goes to the shows every night "just to see what's going to happen next. To see if Kylie's going to climb the rafters again." A straight woman who was very close to the drag queens added, "Or get totally nude." The Latino man continued, "You never know what's going to happen next. . . . It's never the same. . . . Something happens." A young straight woman added, "Yeah, I think the audience definitely changes everything." A young gay man, newly moved to Key West, said, "There's nothing I don't like about the show," but admitted that "my favorite part of the show that keeps bringing me back is the audience is always different. . . . They're always doing something different to somebody else and it's—some nights it's so hysterical. . . . It depends on the crowd." The Latino man really enjoyed "the first-timer who comes here, never been to a drag show ever, and just gets into the show . . . and they get brought up onstage and 'What is your name and where are you from' . . . and then we know they're going to come back. We just know it because it happens time and time again." Confirming that, two gay male interior designers from New York who attend the show every night during their stays commented on the fact that the show is very set but the audience provides new material every night. "I think what is enjoyable about it is how people, some people are free enough to let their guard down. And enjoy it and be made fun of and be brought into the ensemble for those couple of minutes."

One older woman who knew the drag queens well but rarely attended the shows did not like the audience interaction, finding it demeaning to the people brought up onstage. But she was pretty much an exception. The interior designers, big fans of the show, called the shot segment "a stupid interlude," "it goes on forever and ever and usually it really isn't that interesting," but they found it "really a lot of fun" to watch the people up front "sort of toying with fate, wanting to see if they're going to be singled out and brought up onstage or not." As these comments suggest, the show is not for everyone. Occasionally the drag queens really upset audience members by playing with them or, worse, inadvertently kicking them in the face or hurting them in another way. One of our research assistants, Stephanie, witnessed two straight couples at the show one night, one couple smiling and laughing and enjoying the sex talk and the other clearly uncomfortable. When Sushi tried to bring the reluctant man onstage, he resisted, and then both couples got up and left, prompting Sushi to comment, "It's not for everybody." One former tourist who had moved to Key West and loved the show told about a conversation in the bar downstairs with a straight couple "from Middle America." They were drinking heavily and the woman told him that she had gotten divorced from a transvestite. He explained that transvestites and drag queens are different and finally convinced them to go up to see the show, but they didn't like it. "The first people I've seen up here that did not enjoy the show." A straight woman in one of our focus groups told us that she was going to bring her husband to the show, and when we ran into her a year later and asked what he had thought, she said he wanted to leave after one drink: "I think he was a little homophobic." Two straight women who loved the show nevertheless were made uncomfortable by the overt sexual interaction in the bar after the show. For them, that was "crossing the line." One night a straight man in a Harley-Davidson T-shirt and ponytail, drinking heavily and sitting up front with his wife, refused disgustedly to touch a dildo that Kylie waved at him. It was Saturday night, so Kylie warned him that later he was going to strip and that he'd dangle his real penis in his face. When Kylie disrobed, the man leapt up, flung his chair away, and hurriedly left the bar.

But generally the people brought up onstage or played with in some way enjoy it. A group of gay men think they all "enjoy their little fifteen seconds of fame." A lesbian physician who volunteered for shots liked the experience. A gay male visitor reported that the girls tried to drag a straight man onstage, "and he's like, 'No, you stripped me naked last time.' And I thought, 'Isn't that funny, that he's here right up front.' . . . Here he was right up front with his friends at the show. Even though last time he got, you know, naked." One night a forty-six-year-old married professional woman from Boca Raton, at the show with her husband and another couple, went up for shots. She was wearing a short dress and no underwear, and when Kylie flipped up her skirt, the crowd went wild. In a focus group she said that it was a memorable experience (as did everyone else!), and her husband loved the look on Kylie's face when he raised her dress and saw that she wasn't wearing any underwear.

But sometimes people really are embarrassed. A young local woman who felt very close to Sushi (and who had been naked in front of the girls because Sushi was making her a dress and she would come to the dressing room for fittings) described how upset she was when Sushi tried to take her bra off onstage one night. "It was the only time that I've ever felt really uncomfortable in that part of the show." Sushi couldn't understand her resistance—"I've seen your tits before, girl!"—but in fact there is a big difference for most people between being naked with friends and naked onstage. One night Sushi pulled up Verta's top and exposed her breasts, and she was humiliated. Although she did notice that he said, as he was doing it, "I love you, darling," as if to thank her for being part of the show. They regularly say thank you to the people who let them take off their clothes, and sometimes offer them a free drink, as if to say, "What a good sport" and "Don't feel ashamed." And in fact afterward several audience members, both women and men, came up to Verta to be supportive and make sure she felt all right. (The next night, in a restaurant, a local woman saw Verta and said, "I saw your breasts last night!" which was a little embarrassing!) Occasionally someone will complain to the management, usually in the clear light of the next day, and then the girls have to ask permission before they strip someone or tone down their interactions for a while. A few times people have sued the bar or filed assault charges.

There is no question that people will do things they wouldn't ordinarily dream of at the show. Inga calls it "a way to get away from being a responsible person. Get drunk and go to the drag show." A focus group of gay men attributed the behavior at the show to the fact that Key West is a resort and a wild one at that. "Like the old saying, what happens on the rock stays on the rock—whatever we do in Key West stays in Key West and you can do pretty much what you want, and you don't have to worry about it," said a thirty-three-year old man from Chicago and Key West. Other gay men in the group agreed that audience members drink too much, do crazy things, and never admit it at home. A straight woman wondered what possessed people to strip at the show and then answered her own question: "Part of it is that they're drunk." "Daddy-o," the straight man in his seventies who let Sushi put Chanel lipstick on his penis onstage, was in fact quite drunk and had been groping the drag queens earlier in the show. His wife turned to us as the painting went on and whispered, "We're really nice people; I don't know why things like this happen to us!" Some audience members really liked the naughtiness of the show: "It's naughty, it's nasty, you just don't do that. It's not conventional. I like that," as a straight professional woman put it. "They're bawdy, they're very, very bawdy," said a gay man approvingly.

The public sexuality does have an effect on audiences. As Kylie says, "The things we talk about most people would never talk about even with their partners." One gay man admitted, "I like the shock value of the sexualness." At a drag queen meeting, Kylie describes one Saturday night when "it got so crazy I just didn't know if I could handle it, 'I don't know if I can keep this audience in line.'" Sushi agrees: "They were literally crawling on the stage; we didn't even need to take off their clothes." A straight local man described coming to the bar because it was "the easiest place to pick up women that I've ever seen in my life." Not only was there no competition, but "the women seemed to get excited by the show." A straight local woman confirmed this, describing her homophobic boyfriend's refusal to go to the 801 but his eagerness to send her. "Because I get so turned on, I go home and bang his brains out. We've had some of our best sex after these performances."

Confirming the impact of the public sexuality on heterosexual desire, we witnessed one night a straight woman lap-dancing on her boyfriend. Inga reports seeing a straight couple having sex in the back of the bar. "Oh, I would love that, if I saw someone fucking!" says Kylie. Roger reminds Kylie of a straight couple that tried to pick him up as Inga. "Wanted to have a threesome." "Swingers. We get a lot of swingers too," adds Sushi. After a long time away from the subject, Kylie returns: "I can't believe people, a straight couple, would come up here and fuck during a drag show. That astounds me." "They get caught up," Roger explains. And Kylie, who announces one night at the "Girlie Show" that "we're gonna try to make you horny if we can," decides that what happens is that "it's exciting! That it is so confusing, so different." The intense sexuality was too much for Verta's twenty-year-old southern Baptist niece Sara, who came to the show shortly before she was married and told us that she couldn't take it, never having had sex herself. "Well of course, fucking is scary," said Dean when we told him why we had to leave. As Sara pointed out, she was probably the only person in the bar who had never had sex.

A central part of the show, from the perspective of the drag queens, is the arousal of straight men. Roger, in an interview in *Celebrate!*, admitted that he knows that both men and women get crushes on Inga, but also expressed surprise that "straight guys can come up and get all hot and bothered."[5] At one drag queen meeting, Sushi and Kylie talked about a couple who had gotten in a fight because the man got an erection when Sushi grabbed his penis. The woman was drunk and started crying. "When she woke up in the morning, I'm sure she felt a lot different about it. Stupid," says Kylie. "But they didn't come back," Sushi says, evidently worried. "Maybe they were leaving the next day," Kylie reassures him. A young woman at her first drag show felt sorry for a young straight man brought up for shots—the one paired with the leather man who was at first afraid and later hugging everyone. "I thought for him it had to be confusing because the drag queen that was coming on to him was, to me, the prettiest, and I kept thinking, 'God, that's a guy, that's a guy!' . . . And I thought it had to be confusing for him because, there you're looking at this woman who is attractive and he's probably thinking, 'God, she's hot.' Forgetting that she's a he. And I think when she got on top of him, he was probably embarrassed because he was turned on. So I felt sorry for him."

In some cases, people see the show as a place to experiment with sexuality. A man at one show told Verta, when she was recruiting for our focus groups, that he was married and didn't want his wife to find out that he came to the shows all the time. One night when we were visiting with the girls on the street, a German couple approached us and the woman said, "I want to know what it is to be gay?" Everyone laughed, but she persisted: "No, I want to know tonight. I want to try." Scabby told her people are just born gay, and Leila joked, "Well, you could always practice." And she responded, seriously, "Yes, that's what I want to do." Just then her husband came back to her side and she said, "Oh dear, now I can't finish this." Another time we met two Mormon women on vacation without their husbands. One of them asked us all sorts of questions, announced that it was all right with her if we were lesbians, and then confided that, if she were going to be with a woman, she'd be with her friend. More than once presumably straight women in the bar have expressed interest in lesbians. When our research assistant Stephanie went onstage one night for shots as the lesbian, a woman there with her husband came up to her and said, "I'm totally straight, but that just turned me on" and kissed Stephanie on the mouth. Another night the straight woman onstage seemed eager to have the lesbian sitting on her and said she was "willing to try pussy-licking." Certainly the drag queens meet a goodly share of presumably straight men who are eager to have sex with them. The fact that a lot of audience members talked about having come out by going to drag shows suggests that such sexual encounters may be either casual experimentation or an expression of suppressed desires.

As we have seen in looking at the shows, this is all about what scholars call the "troubling" of gender and sexuality. The drag queens make it impossible to think of the categories of man/woman and gay/straight in any simple way. They know this. Gugi says, "Last night—though this happens almost every night—[this woman] goes, 'I'm straight, I'm a woman, I'm not a lesbian, but you're so beautiful, I find you so attractive.'" At the same time, he describes "a straight guy, has been straight for like fifty years or something like that. And he could not keep his eyes off me. He finally had the nerve to come up to me and goes, 'You know, I've been straight all my life and I know you're a man, but you're so beautiful, you are so . . .' He goes, 'I can't keep my eyes off you.'"

And in fact audience members describe these very feelings. A straight woman tourist loved when the girls fondled her husband: "It's like here's this man touching my husband, it's like really cool. And he's standing there letting him. He's letting his feminine side come out, which was really neat because we all have those sides to us." She found this the "sexiest" part of the show, "there was something crackling the most. . . . The line was crossed the most at that moment. . . . And I liked it." Her husband described his own response: "I'm sitting there and there's a little bit of me saying, 'This is sexually exciting' and there's another part of me saying, 'Wait a minute, don't do this. You're not supposed to be sexually excited, this is a man, you know,' so there's a little conflict and nervousness when they came over to me."

A lesbian woman described feeling very attracted to Milla: "She was very sexy," and a straight woman agreed: "I was very drawn to her sexually. I felt like kissing her. And I'm not gay at all." Asked whether she thought of her as a woman or a man, the "not gay at all" woman responded that she was attracted "because she was a woman. She was a woman. She was a beautiful woman." Another straight woman told about her friend, also straight, who fell in love with Milla. "She saw Milla and she started falling in love with her. . . . And Milla kissed her with the tongue and she was like, 'She kissed me, she kissed me!' . . . She says, 'I want to make love with her.'"

What many audience members conclude is that the labels of "gay" and "straight" (or "female" and "male") just don't fit. Almost 90 percent of our focus group members made reference to this aspect of the shows. For one gay man, "You leave them at the door." Another gay man thought the show "really pushes gender identity and gender role and homophobia issues with straight people. To have that kind of interaction with drag queens." Because straight men are supposed to suppress any femininity, "the drag show really gives them an opportunity to kind of delve into, ever so slightly, that side of their personality." A straight male tourist put it this way: "I think that one of the beauties of attending a show like this is that you do realize that you . . . shouldn't walk out and say, 'I only like men,' and you shouldn't say, 'I only like women,' and it all kind of blends together a lot more so than maybe what we want to live in our normal daily lives." A young gay man thought that "they're challenging the whole idea of gender and so forth and they're breaking that down."

This, we think, is profoundly political. Certainly the drag queens see it that way, confirming an intentionality to their performance of protest. "I intend to challenge people," Kylie tells us. "I'm not just doing a number," says Sushi.

> Anybody can just do a number. . . . And my drag shows, I'm trying to make more of an experience, a learning thing. Trying to preach love, not hate. . . . And I have a platform now to teach the world. We have so many people from everywhere in the world. Even less than five minutes of talking to somebody, just that little moment I share with somebody from New Zealand or Africa or your college professor or whoever, they go back to their hometown. They remember that five-minute conversation, they realized, "I'm not gonna call this person a fag," you know what I mean? It's just a little part that I am a real person.

Dean and Matthew, at dinner one night, make the same point, talking about a young straight married couple who brought their four-year-old son to the show and came back in the dressing room to talk. "Parents can bring their child into a show . . . start educating them at such a young age . . . 'Listen, this is OK, this isn't a problem, these are people too, and you have to respect people for whatever and whoever they are.'" Much later in the evening, talking about the importance of "crossing boundaries," they return to the incident. "Opening up people's minds. And I think last night was a perfect example of that, when that young couple brought their child up there." Gugi describes people who are "freaking out," thinking, "'Oh my god, I'm in a gay bar, I'm seeing men in dresses.' And after that, you know, halfway through the show, I jump on their laps, they're having a ball, they give you twenty bucks. Tell you, 'This is the first drag show I've ever seen in my life.' Just opening up people."

R.V. is in some ways the most directly political in the shows, although Sushi and Kylie are too. "I love going up to the straight people when I find out who they are and going, 'When did you come out to your parents that you were straight?' I love doing that. It's those little innuendoes. I mean, it proves a point and lets them know, 'Hey, we're OK also.' You know, especially after the Matthew Shepard thing and all that."

Kylie insists that he wants to make people think. During one focus group, he showed up to get dressed and talked with two gay men about why he strips on Saturday night. "We're drag queens. We dress as women, in fact at the end I thought it was perfect to let everyone know with the face, a face with makeup on and a wig and yet a male body is, it confounds people. It baffles them and it does make them think. They have to think about something." Asked what he hoped they would think about, he responds, "Whatever they want to. Life isn't always what it seems, maybe that's what I want them to think."

The show also spotlights gender and racial/ethnic oppression. Dean talks about Milla's songs being "about being victimized by men, and pain and anger. But they're all different women, and that's why there is that black girl in the audience, maybe I don't see her, but she's in that audience and I become her. I'm what she can't do. Maybe I helped her. Maybe she went home that night and told that muthafucker to get out of her goddamn house. . . . Maybe I changed somebody's life." Dean talks about performing Alanis Morissette's "You Oughta Know," about a woman's anger at the lover who dumped her, and "talking to my father . . . to every motherfucking man that ever hurt me, and to every man that ever hurt anybody." Gugi, who also performs that number, says much the same thing about the way it expresses his anger. Kylie sees some of his songs speaking directly to women. He performs "Passionate Kisses," for example, because it's about a woman wanting to have it all, and "I am asking the audience, 'Is it too much to ask?'" And in fact women in the audience respond to the drag queens as powerful women who, hurt as they might be, act in ways they admire.

In addition, Dean sees Milla as political because she can arouse women and men, gay or straight. "We are attractive to everybody. We have taken gender and thrown it out of the way, and we've crossed a bridge here. And when we are all up there, there is no gay/straight or anything."

Does it make a difference? Or is this simply an evening of (possibly drunken) entertainment? Certainly many audience members believe that the shows have the potential to change people. A local gay Latino man says, "You see one person, they've been to Key West for the first time, never been to a drag show before, they're from square America and there's just like, 'I've never seen a man in a dress before, especially looking better than me,' that's what you hear from a lot of women. A lot of straight women. . . . And then sure enough, next vacation they're back in Key West and they're back up here again." One local gay man thinks the impact of the show is 20 percent permanent but 80 percent temporary, because people go home and resume their normal lives. A very thoughtful gay male tourist used the metaphor of shattering glass to describe what the show does to thinking about gender. "Certainly this has been a stirring experience," he commented. "And I still question, if everyone in America or the world shattered everything, would we be able to survive that? I think not. I frankly think not and I certainly know that I couldn't, but little fractures here and there that ask questions that I have to somehow be responsible for is good."

For some the impact is literally life changing. One local straight woman found that she could only be attracted to very feminine men. "Every time I go out with a guy, I dress him like a woman." One of the gay men in our focus groups—who responded to the man who worried about how much shattering we can take by saying that he had moved to Key West because he loved that everything was shattered—ended up becoming a drag queen and winning a regular slot on the 801 roster. Joel came on vacation with a lesbian friend, wandered into the bar, fell in love with the show, and decided to move to Key West. When Sushi found out that Joel was sleeping on a lawn chair behind Bourbon Street, he got him a job as a cocktail server. Joel approached R.V. about getting in drag, but R.V., according to Joel, was interested in a relationship and refused. Then Gugi taught him how to make up and, voilá, Joel became Desiray.

These are, of course, the exceptions, but that doesn't mean that people don't take something away from the show. It's true that those who were willing to come to the focus groups were probably more likely to see the show as having meaning than those who refused, but even the people we talked with casually tended to reinforce the idea that the shows open their minds. A gay male physician from Vermont, whom we first met and talked with on the street and who later came to a focus group, compared the drag show to traditional forms of sacred cross-dressing in different parts of the world: "I don't know what it is that it does, but it does something where we have an opportunity to see something different about ourselves or to see the world through different eyes or to relieve tension or I don't know what it is. . . . I see this phenomenon that is beyond just dressing up and pretending you're a different gender, there's something gutsy about it. 'Gutsy' meaning it's visceral, it's important. And it's also really scary because it's me up there being dressed as a woman." His lover commented that "we all play so many different roles in our lives, and I think one of the most basic roles we sort of pick up at birth is our gender. And so that's what I think the drag show really does is it flip-flops. . . . I can play the woman if I want. . . . It's a message about roles. We play them and we don't even realize we play them." Another gay man had the same thought. "We're very complex individuals and we're made up with all these different aspects to our personality. We have our feminine side, we have our butch side, we have our hilarious side or our mean side."

A young straight woman commented, "It does make you think about a lot of things you don't usually think about." "Do you think about what makes a man a man?" Verta asked. "Exactly. Where is the line, because obviously they cross the line." The performance made an older straight woman incredibly curious. "The whole time I was thinking, 'What's going on in these people's minds?'—you know, 'What are their lives really like, what do they look like when they're not in drag, how'd they get where they are?' Just really in-depth thinking about the whole thing and them and their personalities and stuff. And thinking, you know, 'Now is this really a business for them . . . is it just a business for them or is this really their sexuality?'"

Not all audience members think the show has the potential to change people. More dubious than most, a gay male doctor from Boston couldn't imagine "that the straight people go home . . . and say, 'Gosh, isn't it nice that the gay people have a way of expressing themselves.' Or, 'Wow, maybe the world is full of different people.'" Yet others believed just that. A gay hairstylist could not figure out why straight people would come to the show. "I mean, the first time, if you come once, it's entertainment definitely, but if you really come more than once, you come a lot to drag shows, there's definitely got to be some sort of questioning or something because you can see this type of performance in the heterosexual world without any gender crossing." A gay male teacher from Vermont thought that the performances "show more or less to the straight people that we're not as bad as the media makes us out to be." A young lesbian remarked that people who come in thinking, "It's stupid, and what a fag . . . you know, if they have an attitude like that, maybe if they came to the show, they would actually see that they're not like [that]. . . . Maybe it would change their view a little on what [drag] is." A straight woman living in Key West for the summer, who didn't herself think there was a message in the show, then contradicted herself, hoping that "if somebody were to go to the show . . . they would take with them, because most of the people I would take would be from Ohio and would be from sheltered lives with very little exposure to the gay community. So I would like for them to be open-minded and not be offended." And in fact more than once straight people at the show turned to us and volunteered that they "don't care" or that it's "all right" with them that we are lesbians, suggesting both the depth of heterosexual privilege and the possibility of increased tolerance as a result of exposure to gay culture.

The drag queens themselves think this is the case. Matthew describes straight people coming in "feeling intimidated like, 'Oooh, I don't know that I really want to do this, but it's free and it's something to do on vacation. So let's go in.' They come in like really almost shy and scared in the beginning. And nine times out of ten, they stay till the very end because they're having so much fun. And they leave with a little bit more knowledge about being a homosexual, even being a drag performer." R.V. thinks that when straight people leave the bar, "they have a better, more tolerant understanding of what we're all about, what gay people are about. We change their lives." Sushi says, "They come from all over and fan out, to Idaho and Oklahoma, and we make a difference. We liberate them a little bit." As her comment about not just lip-synching makes clear, she sees what she does as a mission and not just a job.[6]

Jim Gilleran thinks that tourists experience something they never would in their normal lives and that "they take that home and they may affect, if they affect one other person, and it's not about gay or straight, it's about just accepting other people, discrimination." Even a group of local gay men who suspected that straight tourists wouldn't talk much at home about their experiences at the 801 thought they wouldn't be exactly the same. "They opened up a little bit." "Right, they have a whole new perspective. Maybe they've learned something," responded another. "And I think that helps open up a lot of people's eyes as far as they go back home and run across somebody and they find out they're gay, they're going to be a little bit less judgmental of that gay person." Added another, "It's like taking the blinders off the horse. They get a wider field of vision." Or, as the straight male photographer who turned our color negatives into black-and-white photographs for the book put it rather less seriously, "I'll never look at my daughter's Barbie doll in the same way again."

That drag shows in general might have lasting impact was suggested to us by a conversation we had one day with a cabdriver taking us to the airport in Columbus. He was a straight-looking man in his fifties who, hearing about the research we were doing, told us about going to a drag show in San Francisco when he was seventeen. He couldn't remember the name of the club, but when Leila asked if it had been Finocchio's, he said "Yes!" right away. His father was the vice president of a car dealership in the city, and the receptionist there, who made the drag queens' costumes, took him and his girlfriend to a show one night. "They were incredible," he told us all these years later. "I fell in love with them. Your eyes see women and in ten minutes you forget they're men." (Well, maybe that couldn't happen at the 801!) "Some guys came in not knowing and they perceived them as women, and when they found out they were men, they couldn't deal with their emotions." We were struck by how powerful this memory was for him.

Summing up the hopes and dreams of the drag queens, and putting into his own words the notion of drag as performing protest, a young gay man with theatrical ambitions explained that the show "signifies for me . . . that we have these differences but here we are all together within this small space. Communing, interacting, being entertained, having a good time and everything is going well. . . . And I think the idea being to make some sort of, like, utopia or this is the way it could be. Once we all leave this bar, if we can all see four different people that are different and commune together, or at least respect each other, then when we leave this bar, wouldn't the world be a little bit better place?"

☆   ☆   ☆

That, of course, is what the drag queens hope: that they help to make the world a better place. Drag has a long history within gay life and the gay movement, and despite persistent criticisms that it demeans women or embarrasses men or reveals the seamy side of gay life or undermines the notion that "we're just like you," drag has the potential to serve as an effective political strategy. Although scholars disagree about the relationship of culture and politics, about the effectiveness of cultural strategies for bringing about change, we think that there is little doubt about the political nature of drag. (We take up this question in the final chapter, where we discuss for those who are interested the theoretical significance of our study.) As one of the few ways that straight people encounter gay culture—where, in fact, straight people live for an hour or two in an environment where gay is normal and straight is other—drag shows, especially in a tourist town like Key West, play an important role for the gay/lesbian movement. Precisely because drag shows are entertaining, they attract people who might never be otherwise exposed to gay politics. As one female audience member put it, they "take something difficult and make it light." Through a complex process of separating people into gender and sexual identity categories, then blurring and playing with those boundaries, and then bringing people all together again, the drag queens at the 801 do indeed free people's minds, open their minds, remove their blinders, change their lives. It is a stunning performance of protest.

FIFTEEN

A NIGHT AT THE 801

And so we reach the end of our story. As we watched the girls transform themselves in the dressing room, we considered the road each had taken to this particular life and the different meanings being a drag queen held for him. Like others who have explored the lives of people who do not fit easily into polarized categories of male or female, masculine or feminine, men or women, we argue for the expansion, rather than elimination, of categories. "Drag queen" is one, although even this is too broad to encompass all gay men who perform in women's clothing in public. Sushi's traumatic self-realization that she may be a transgendered person rather than a drag queen suggests that we ignore at our own peril the categories that are so important to the ways people think about themselves.

We have also explored the role of the 801 Girls in their unique community. Their celebrity contrasts oddly with their own occasional sense of themselves as freaks or outcasts, which comes partly from the hostility they can encounter on the streets but also from the difficulty they tend to have maintaining relationships with lovers. Despite the quirkiness of the Conch Republic, perhaps the best of all possible worlds for drag queens, the ambiguity or marginality of their place in the community mirrors the role of drag in national gay and lesbian worlds.

Most important, we argue that the drag queens are performing protest, are part of the gay and lesbian movement's efforts to make the world a better place for those of us with same-sex desires. Through their dress, gestures, routines, dancing, talk, comedy, and interaction with the audience, they make understandable the concept that people and desires and sexual acts and emotions cannot always be simply categorized into one of two or three possibilities. In making this argument, we are suggesting that cultural forms such as drag performances are political, and that the fact that they are cast as entertainment may make them especially effective in reaching people and changing the ways they think.

Finally, we see the consequences of the drag queens' performance of protest. In a very complicated way, they affirm gay/lesbian/bisexual/ transgender identities in contrast to heterosexual ones; but they also break down those differences and assert the common interests of all people. That they do indeed make people think and that they do indeed have the potential to change minds, if not immediately the world, are confirmed by what audience members take away from the shows.

What happens at an evening at the 801 is, we think, a story about more than one particular bar. That is partly because of the sharing of drag queen repertoires across the country, including through such major national events as Wigstock, the annual New York drag extravaganza that ended a seventeen-year run in 2001, and the multitude of local and regional drag queen contests and competitions.[1] The 801 Girls even announced one year a plan to sponsor "Drag Queen University" in Key West. An article in *Celebrate!* describes familiar scenes at Diva's, where Inga and Gugi went to perform:

> It is a place where gender blurs and reality is relative. . . . Straight men clamor to press dollar bills into Inga's cleavage or rush to the stage to offer homage to Vogue, whose flawless rendition of Tina Turner's stage moves makes your heart pound. Lesbian ladies find themselves all fired up by Gugi Gomez's spicy Latina sensuality and straight women ignore their dates to steal a kiss and run their hands along Colby's taunt [sic] thighs. Somehow, the talents of these performers take the audience outside of themselves. At Diva's, you can be anyone you want to be.[2]

You can be anyone you want to be—and you are challenged to think differently about what you thought you were.

This is more than the story of the 801 Cabaret in yet another sense. As our concluding chapter explains in more detail, we think that what happens onstage has implications for the larger question of what makes certain types of cultural expressions political. Drag shows are entertaining, as we have seen. They attract a whole slew of people who might never venture out to watch, much less join, a gay pride celebration or a demonstration. Yet they elicit strong emotions, even sexual responses, which are likely to have a powerful impact on people. Such visceral moments make change possible. We suggest that what makes drag shows—as well as other cultural performances—political is that they subvert the traditional (in this case, gender and sexual) order, that the performers intend them to have these consequences, and that they build and affirm a gay/lesbian collective identity and also broaden the meaning of community by linking diverse audience members to the performers and to each other. Drag shows help us to see how social movements have an effect, how social movements matter.

☆   ☆   ☆

At the end of the night, the show is finally over, the house music comes on, and some of the girls come out to have their pictures taken or to talk with friends. Some stay in drag; some have changed. Those who are still in drag then go back to the dressing room and visit as they take off their makeup and clothes. We've been privileged to be there a few times, and it's very special. The time we were in drag, Sushi really let down her hair, metaphorically, and we felt especially close. Sometimes we've been there until two or three in the morning, just talking.

Another time Sushi said that we should then come out with them for the rest of the night. He also wanted us to drink so much that we threw up, but we passed on that right away. We were tempted to see their social and sexual adventures firsthand, but we passed on that too. Instead we have heard tales. And we have imagined. Not too explicitly, we must admit!

But we have pictured the end of the night, which is actually morning. As the "good people" of Key West, as Sheryl Crow would have it, are going to work or exercising or beginning to go about their days, the girls are going home to sleep. We imagine them watching the sunrise, perhaps at the Conch Flyer, the bar at the airport that is open all day and night. We imagine them coming home, perhaps sleepy, perhaps not. We imagine them getting in bed, perhaps alone, perhaps not, perhaps falling asleep the minute they hit the sheets, perhaps needing a little help. We know they often sleep through the morning, into the afternoon, sometimes into the evening, their upside-down days, as well as their complex identities, making it hard for them to have relationships with men who sleep at night and work during the day.

But what we also imagine—or, rather, hope, because we know it is romantic, but we have come to love them so much—is that they have pleasant (not sweet, since Sushi objects to the feminine sound of that) dreams. We hope they know in their own way that they have, by being raw and honest, performed protest; that they have, by broadening the meaning of community, expressed Key West's commitment to the idea that we are all one human family; that they have, by making people experience new desires, led them to feel just a little differently what it means to be gay or straight, what it means to be a woman or what it means to be a man.

SIXTEEN

THEORETICAL CONCLUSIONS
Thinking about Drag as Social Protest

Drag, as we have seen, triggers burning questions about gender, sexuality, and social movements. The recent resurgence and commercialization of drag in American society—from Wigstock to RuPaul to *Hedwig and the Angry Inch*—has spawned an ongoing debate among scholars of gender over whether performances in which gay men dress in women's clothing have political significance. On one side are scholars who treat drag in the context of the gay community primarily as transgressive action that destabilizes gender and sexual categories by making visible the social basis of femininity and masculinity, heterosexuality and homosexuality, and presenting hybrid and minority genders and sexualities.[1] On the other side are those who consider drag performances more as enacting and reinforcing dominant assumptions about the dichotomous nature of gender presentation and sexual desire because drag queens appropriate gender displays associated with traditional femininity and institutionalized heterosexuality.[2]

We clearly side with the former, although our position differs from those such as Marjorie Garber, who sees drag as political solely because it disrupts the two-gender binary by introducing a third category, or Judith Butler, who locates the subversive nature of drag in the way that it reveals gender as artificial and performative, the way it constitutes an imitation of something for which there is no original.[3] We do think that drag as performed at the 801 opens a window to multiple and confusing genders and sexualities. By portraying ambiguity and in-betweenness, drag successfully invites audience members to consider what it means to be a man or woman, what it means to desire someone of a particular sex, as more complicated than they would ordinarily think. But what we bring that no one else has to the study of drag is the concept of drag as a form of strategic collective action that is part of the larger repertoire of contention of the gay and lesbian movement, historically used to articulate political ideas that challenge conventional understandings of male and female, gay and straight, to create new collective identities, and to disrupt existing collective identity boundaries. In viewing drag performances as a political strategy, we draw on Mary Bernstein's concept of identity deployment, which she defines as "expressing identity such that the terrain of conflict becomes the individual person so that the values, categories, and practices of individuals become subject to debate."[4]

The debate about drag poses for us the larger question of what makes certain types of cultural expressions political. We do not suggest that all drag shows, across time and around the world, challenge conventional ideas in the sense we argue here. On the contrary, our goal is to identify the characteristics that determine to what extent not just specific drag performances, but other cultural practices as well, function as protest tactics. This is exactly the question that Judith Butler raises when she notes that "there must be a way to understand what makes certain kinds of parodic repetitions effectively disruptive, truly troubling, and which repetitions become domesticated and recirculated as instruments of cultural hegemony."[5] We have taken up this challenge by analyzing a specific set of drag performances and—what no one else has done—audience responses to them.

Viewing drag as protest adds to recent developments in social movement theory. The study of protest events—or repeated collective public displays used by a challenging group to make claims against opponents, authorities, and other groups—has been one of the defining features of the resource mobilization and political process traditions, which are the dominant approaches in social movement scholarship.[6] Scholars such as Doug McAdam, Sidney Tarrow, and Charles Tilly have emphasized the dynamic nature of political contention by pointing to important historical variations in the tactics or specific types of protest actions used by relatively powerless groups seeking to challenge the status quo.[7] Nevertheless, in defining what counts as protest, it is customary for students of social movements to concentrate on a set of standard forms—marches, demonstrations, rallies, public meeting, boycotts, strikes, and so on—that emerged in response to such developments as state building and changes in capitalism.[8]

By paying attention to the role of culture in mobilizing protest, several studies have pointed to the wide range of cultural strategies used by activists to influence allies and opponents.[9] Music and theater, for example, have long served as a means of articulating grievances in the labor movement, the civil rights movement, ethnic movements, and the feminist movement.[10] In the 1980s carnival, spectacle, and parody emerged as major tactics of the gay and lesbian movement in the campaign to raise public awareness of AIDS.[11] Such studies open up novel ways of thinking about protest by bringing to light the cultural forms of political expression used by groups denied access to ordinary politics and by social movements seeking change primarily in cultural codes and institutions.[12] The move to embrace cultural politics raises an important question that must be addressed if scholars of social movements are to be convinced that these more unorthodox forms of politics should be counted as protest. How do we know when cultural forms such as music, comedy, ritual, art, theater, and spectacles are rituals of affirmation, when apolitical entertainments, and when actions geared toward changing or opposing change in institutions of social life? When is cultural performance a form of protest?

In considering these questions, our analysis draws upon, extends, and bridges three areas of theory and research: social constructionist approaches to gender and sexuality, social movement literature on collective action repertoires, and performance studies. Although their foci differ, all of these literatures employ the metaphor of performance. By bringing social movement theory together with cultural studies and performance studies approaches, we are able to understand just why and how drag performances can be truly troubling.

Social constructionist perspectives treat gender and sexuality as historically variable categories of difference overlaid onto external markers, behaviors, bodies, desires, and practices that typically function to reinforce major structures of inequality.[13] Most research on gender and sexuality focuses on the processes that create and maintain a binary and hierarchical gender system composed of two genders, male and female, and a heteronormative sexual system consisting of two sexual identities, heterosexual and homosexual.[14] Recent writings by gender scholars, influenced by the thinking of queer theorists, have called attention to "performative" gender transgressions such as drag, cross-dressing, female masculinity, and other boundary-disruptive tactics used by feminist, queer, transgender, and other social movements.[15] In such protests, the body of the performer highlights the social basis of gender and sexuality and becomes a weapon to contest dominant heterosexual gender codes. This type of claims-making is what feminist philosopher Nancy Fraser has analyzed under the rubric of "recognition struggles," by which she means social movements that view injustice as a consequence of lack of respect for group differences, or cultural domination.[16] We have applied this approach—largely missing from existing social movement research—to examine the gender and sexual meanings deployed in drag shows.[17]

If gender and sexuality theory deals explicitly with the processes involved in signaling, negotiating, and regulating gender and sexual identity, social movement theory directs our gaze to the strategic decision-making involved in protest performances.[18] Despite some points of difference between the various perspectives that have developed over the past twenty-five years to explain collective action by subordinate groups, social movement theory is concerned with the interactive nature of protest and the construction of collective identity and solidarity that takes place through protest action.[19] Here, again, the metaphor of performance appears. Historical work on political protest has demonstrated the various forms of resistance and the specific tactics subordinate groups use to express dissent and critique power in real-life situations. Social movement scholars use the concept of collective action repertoires developed by Charles Tilly and Sidney Tarrow to describe the distinctive forms and constellations of tactics and strategies, developed over time and used by protest groups to act collectively and make claims on individuals and groups.[20] Like its theatrical counterpart, the word "repertoire" implies a limited set of routines, or forms of action, targets, and modes of expression, that are "learned, shared, and acted out through a relatively deliberate process of choice."[21] Tilly's "repertoires" notion implies that all forms of protest—whether strikes, sit-ins, or guerrilla theater—can be understood as performances in which ideological and political discourses are promoted by vying groups.

The significance of recurrent tactics of protest is that they induce individual participation in collective action by building solidarity and oppositional consciousness among members of aggrieved groups, which furthers the potential for resistance and political action. They are easily learned, adapted, routinized, and diffused from one set of individuals to another who are not necessarily known to each other, creating the possibility for more widespread resistance.[22] We have adapted the collective action repertoires concept to understand the way drag shows can be a form of strategic collective action that has an impact by promoting new collective self-representations of gay, lesbian, bisexual, and transgendered individuals and providing a forum for the expression of ideas that subvert and undermine conventional notions of masculinity and femininity and heterosexuality and homosexuality. Viewing drag shows as a protest tactic allows us to understand them as part of what scholars of social movements would describe as the larger "repertoire of contentious politics" of the gay and lesbian movement.[23] Our interactive view of protest performances, which is in line with recent developments in social movement theory, turns our attention to the relationship between the performers and the audience, who represent different identity groupings, and to the way their interactions transform and create new forms of identity and community.[24] Finally, a social movement approach directed us to the political intentions of the performers and to the culturally encoded ways different groups express opposition, providing a lens through which we can view drag as a collective boundary-crossing strategy aimed deliberately at changing gender and sexual systems.

The artificial distinction between expressive and instrumental politics that permeates the literature on social movements and contributes to the lack of attention to cultural repertoires is called into question by social scientists and scholars of cultural studies who research political performances.[25] Earlier attempts by cultural historians and scholars of performance studies to classify countercultural expressions such as theater, music, poetry, dance, religious ceremonies, and other performances as either politics or culture have given way to a more complicated reading of performances as almost always partaking of both aspects, such that politics and entertainment are deliberately interwoven with the goal of winning acceptance of the message.[26] Further, cultural performances typically are staged to elicit strong emotion and are experienced by the audience as play rather than serious, which allows them to attract participants who might not otherwise attend a political event.[27]

Research in performance studies also suggests that performances can be simultaneously divisive and communal.[28] In cases where performers draw audiences composed of groups with different and competing identities—such as drag shows—performances have the potential to promote the internal articulation of collective identity among the performers and segments of the audience who share interests with them. At the same time, as we have seen, cultural performances can contribute to the external articulation of collective identity between members of the different groups who gather to participate in the event, on the one hand, and the larger community, on the other.[29] They provide free spaces where subordinated and dominant groups can come together to produce and create a shared culture of opposition.[30]

Our analysis here, then, links theories of gender and sexuality construction, which conceive of some drag performances as transgressive attempts to deconstruct the gender and sexuality systems; social movement theories of collective action repertoires, which suggest that some cultural performances may be a means of deliberate contestation and of building collective identities and solidarity; and research in performance studies, which suggests that cultural protest may be simultaneously strategic and expressive, divisive and communal. Viewing drag performances from the standpoint of social movement theory provides, as we have seen, an entirely new angle of vision. It allows us to think of some drag shows, at least, as what social movement theorists would consider one form of collective action within the larger repertoire of contention of the gay, lesbian, bisexual, and transgender movement. A major theme of this book has been the way one group is using the performance of identity to challenge the status quo, to reinforce a sense of group identity by accentuating participants' commonalities and differences, and to alter another group's values and political interpretations.

Our examination of drag as a form of protest, however, has led us to the conclusion that there is need for a broader conceptual definition of social movement tactics or collective action repertoires that allows us to understand how and when the distinctive cultural forms, practices, and institutions created by subordinated groups are, in fact, being used for political purposes. In this book we have highlighted the way drag performances serve as a vehicle for changing people's beliefs about gay, lesbian, bisexual, and transgendered people. To varying degrees, however, cultural expression is used by all social movements. Based on our examination of this case, we close by offering a general model that points to three criteria that distinguish a cultural performance as oppositional or political.

First, and most important, is the degree to which a performance is demonstrably a site of *contestation* where symbols and identities are forged, negotiated, and debated by groups with different and competing interests. The second criterion is *intentionality,* or the deliberate, conscious, and strategic use of cultural entertainment as the medium of expression for political ideas. Third, we have argued that cultural repertoires of protest are distinguished from other nondeliberately political forms of cultural expression by the fact that the performance is staged by a set of actors for whom, in however transitory a manner, culture serves as an arena for the enactment, reinforcement, or renegotiation of *collective identity*. We conclude by elaborating these three dimensions of cultural repertoires.

Contestation suggests that the discourse—or the symbols, identities, and cultural practices—conveyed by a cultural performance subverts rather than maintains dominant relations of power. In reality, evaluating the public displays of social movement culture is more complicated than determining whether they are hegemonic or oppositional, since protest groups typically mobilize by drawing upon identities, practices, and symbols that are already meaningful from the standpoint of dominant ideologies and frameworks.[31] We see this in the ways that the drag queens' routines appropriate mainstream popular music that has one set of meanings, drawing upon hegemonic and counterhegemonic gender and sexual symbols to inflect these songs with new meaning.[32] Drag-queenness, as have seen, like other oppositional identities, may draw upon conventional gender and sexual categories, but it also expands and problematizes identity by taking bodies and practices that are culturally encoded as feminine or masculine or as heterosexual or homosexual and combining them in ways that create new gender and sexual meanings. Further, the performance of identity at the 801 Cabaret promotes resistance to domination by incorporating key discourses and practices of a variety of oppositional movements, such as gay/lesbian, feminist, transgender, and racial and ethnic movements, to produce a range of alternative gender and sexual identities.[33]

As we have conceived it, *intentionality* is also a key to identifying cultural performances as political. That is, in assessing the political potential of performances conveyed as entertainment, we should be interested in the same question that we ask with respect to the multitude of other forms of protest used by social movements. To what extent are drag queens intentionally thinking and acting consciously about goals and strategies for challenging dominant constructions of masculinity, femininity, and the gendered heterosexual family? Prior research in the field of social movements suggests that a challenging group's selection of tactics from the available repertoires of collective action reflects both learned conventions and strategic choices adapted to the political context.[34] While a performance can arguably be political even without conscious intention or awareness on the part of the actors, it is useful to distinguish performances on the basis of intentionality, because doing so reveals what both the performers and audience interpret as political about the performance.

Drag shows, like other staged performances, are a form of "playing," but the planning and staging that goes into them marks an underlying rationality.[35] The drag queens work hard and are able to get their message across in part because of the quality of their performances. In addition, their use of comedy, satire, music, campy humor, and improvised interaction with the audience to voice opposition makes what they say more palatable. The drag queens' strategic performance of identity, their use of the stage as a platform for political expression, and their role in the gay and lesbian community and movement all address the question of intentionality. As the work of performance studies scholars suggests, cultural action that has the kind of strong emotional component that we have seen in the 801 shows can, nevertheless, be as intended and strategic as seemingly more conventional forms of political action.[36] Indeed, a major theme of this book has been that emotion is an important element in protest action. Our examination of the drag queens' use of music to evoke strong emotion and the audience members' complex emotional reactions to the shows at the 801 is consistent with recent work by social movement scholars who argue that emotions can be used strategically by groups seeking political and cultural change.[37]

The formation or affirmation of *collective identity,* "the shared definition of a group that derives from members' common interests and solidarity," is the final factor that distinguishes a cultural performance as political.[38] Collective identity, or a sense of "we-ness," is activated through interactions among members of marginalized groups in networks and free spaces outside the surveillance of dominant groups.[39] Performance studies scholars demonstrate that cultural forms have the potential to construct and affirm collective identity and solidarity at two levels: *internally* through articulation of boundaries and community among those engaged in the performance; and *externally* through the formation of transcendent collective identities that redefine the meaning of community.[40]

The tactics used by social movements to advance their aims vary, from the use of irreverent and vulgar language, costumes, and music, which we have seen in the drag shows at the 801 Cabaret, to more disruptive actions such as marches, strikes, boycotts, petitions, sit-ins, riots, and acts of violence.[41] Participating in various forms of protest is, in fact, one of the major ways that individuals come to identify themselves as part of a group that has been treated unjustly by virtue of their shared characteristics and to recognize that they have a common interest in opposing injustice.[42] As we have seen, the performances at the 801 serve this function. For the audiences who attend the shows, they are sites for the articulation, definition, and redefinition of group boundaries. For gay as well as heterosexual audience members and for women as well as men, the shows ends up deconstructing and destabilizing historically negative and stigmatized identities and constructing and expressing new and more positively valued ones.[43]

The drag queens manage to forge a collective identity that manipulates, modifies, and reinterprets group boundaries by drawing (and then crossing) lines between gay/lesbian/bisexual/transgendered people, on the one hand, and heterosexual women and men, on the other. We have also seen that the drag queens' critique of mainstream heterosexuality and gender norms is not subtle, and that the performers draw on a larger drag queen legacy of oppositional culture and consciousness. The performances acquire their political edge, in large measure, through the fact that the shows involve participants from the heterosexual mainstream that the drag queens both draw in and mock. The interactive nature of the performances depends on the diversity of the audience because the shows at the 801 use the collective enactment of identity displays and sexual desires and the audience's embodied experiences to expand the range of possible gender and sexual categories and meanings, shaking up, questioning, and reworking the lines between "us" and "them."

Together, these elements forge a two-tiered and complex collective identity that simultaneously reinforces gay/lesbian identity and a more expansive and inclusive definition of community that encompasses gender and sexual differences. Research in social movements focuses on the way that oppositional identities and beliefs are elaborated through the protest experience itself.[44] The process in drag shows of making claims on dominant groups and of delineating the "we" whose rights and freedoms are at stake creates new forms of solidarity that result from similarities and differences within and between contending groups that attend the performances.[45]

Theatrical and other cultural performance repertoires such as music, dance, poetry, and film historically have been important local sites of sociopolitical contestation and for understanding the construction of new and multiple layers of collective identity. Like all forms of collective protest, drag has its roots in the structures of domination and subordination that affect the lives of gay, lesbian, bisexual, and transgendered people in much of the modern world. And drag derives from and sometimes overlaps with and sometimes collides with the culture of camp and cross-dressing, which vacillate between a language of opposition and a language of submission.[46] Drag is an embodied tactic that, however effective it might be, coincides with the cultural aims of the modern gay and lesbian movement to criticize, resist, and undermine conventional notions of gender and sexuality and the representations, practices, identities, and bodies that reinforce compulsory heterosexuality.

Drag shows also provide an excellent case for demonstrating a wider and more inclusive range of cultural repertoires used by social movements. The concept of contentious repertoires is one of the central elements in the major theories that have developed to explain protest actions, social movements, ethnic rebellions, and revolutions.[47] But some forms of claim-making, particularly those that rely on cultural expression and that are directed at authority structures other than the government, have been excluded from the domain of contentious politics as viewed by the dominant approach to social movements. We offer a model that is general enough to subsume a wider range of protest forms. The three-pronged theoretical approach we have used in our

THEORETICAL CONCLUSIONS ☆ 221

study adds a new dimension to existing writings on drag that have focused almost exclusively on the gender content of the performances, ignoring the intentions of the performers and the reactions of the audience that give performances their claim to politics. In addition, the literatures on gender transgression and performance studies bring a fresh perspective to the study of social movements that allows us to recognize the varied forms, targets, sites, and impact of protest in modern society.[48] We have identified three dimensions that allow us to understand the political potential of cultural performances.

This framework allows us to get beyond the view that culture and politics are fundamentally different components of social reality, with political action intended, rational, and nonemotional and cultural action unintended, nonrational, and emotional. Rather, cultural forms of expression and political issues are dynamically interrelated, with continual interplay between them. The 801 Cabaret provides a striking example of that interplay, as audience members move from talking about the entertainment value of the show to discussions of gender disturbance and acceptance of sexual and gender diversity. As we have suggested, it is because of its status as entertainment that drag succeeds as intended. Entertainment makes possible political expressions that might not otherwise find an audience. For anyone who has attended one of these shows, there can be little doubt that identity categories and sexual desires can be disrupted precisely because the show is "just play." Serious political protest enters through the lightness of nightclub entertainment. A major conclusion that we hope readers will take away is that paying closer attention to various forms of cultural expression will lead to a fuller understanding of the significant role that protest and social movement–related action play in changing society.

Drag shows do not always serve as protest forms, of course. The drag shows at the 801 Cabaret are typical of a genre of drag that has spread to most urban regions of the United States. Such shows are undoubtedly more political than female impersonation performed in other commercial venues. The framework we outline here allows us to understand exactly why that is so. It also allows us to understand how the commercialization of gay culture, which some writers have seen as dulling the political edge of the gay and lesbian movement, in fact has the potential to educate and challenge mainstream consumers.[49] The drag queens and their audiences, as we have seen, are unlikely to talk "cultural repertoires" or "counterhegemonic gender and sexual meanings" or even "collective identity," but that does not make their performance of protest any less confrontational, intentional, solidarity building—or, indeed, any less compelling.

"We Will Survive"—the 801 Girls, summer 2002. *Back row:* Ma Evans, R.V., Margo, Destiny, Kylie, Scabby, Mama Crass; *front row:* Desiray, Sushi, Gugi, Lenelle Sincere (photo by Brad Valenta)

APPENDIX: METHODS

Our research follows the tripartite model of cultural investigation used by Josh Gamson in which multiple sources of data pertaining to texts, production, and reception are collected and the intersections among them analyzed.[1] Over a three-year period, from 1998 to 2001, we gathered data in Key West. First, to assess the way gender, sexuality, and politics are deployed in drag, we observed, tape-recorded, and transcribed fifty drag performances, including the dialogue, music, and audience interactions. We supplemented these with photographs and handwritten notes of the gender and sexual displays used by the performers, and observations and handwritten field notes of about a dozen special performances and amateur drag contests.

Second, to examine whether and how drag performances are intentional and strategic tools of the gay and lesbian movement, we collected data on the production of the performances by attending weekly drag queen meetings, observing the performers in their dressing room, and conducting semistructured life histories of twelve performers. As background we also interviewed the owner/manager of the bar, the boyfriends of two performers, and the mothers of two others. All of the drag queens identify as gay men and full-time drag queens; none was a postoperative transsexual, although one occasional member of the troupe identifies as a preoperative transsexual. Our sample includes one Asian American, one Puerto Rican American, one Swedish immigrant, and nine native-born whites. They ranged in age from eighteen to sixty years, although the majority were in their late twenties and early thirties. The drag queens asked that their names be used in the research.

This study is unique in the collection of a third source of data that allowed us to assess the construction of collective identity that took place during the performance and to observe the audience members' interactions, as they were asked to interpret collectively the meaning of the gender and sexuality displays used in the performances.[2] Over a period of five months during the height of the winter and spring tourist seasons, we conducted twelve focus groups ranging in size from two to twelve participants with audience members who attended the performances. We obtained participants by distributing invitations at the evening shows and conducted the focus group sessions in the cabaret the following day. The focus groups consisted of forty people, twenty women and twenty men. The largest single group consisted of gay or bisexual men (42 percent). The women were exactly divided between heterosexual and lesbian, while only three of the men were straight. Of the forty, slightly under two-thirds were tourists and just over one-third locals. In age, they ranged from nineteen to sixty-two, with 70 percent between twenty and forty. Most (87 percent) were white, 13 percent Latino/a, other, or mixed racial/ethnic heritage.

Twice as many people in the focus groups as in the U.S. population at large identified themselves as upper class (10 percent compared to 5 percent) or upper-middle class (45 percent compared to 21 percent). The percentage of focus group members who considered themselves middle class came close to the national figures (25 percent versus 21 percent), while the working class was underrepresented (20 percent as compared to 53 percent working class/lower class).[3] Highly educated people were also overrepresented: more than twice as many focus group members had undergraduate, graduate, or professional degrees (55 percent versus 25 percent), and about the same proportions had been to college but not graduated. Just over 12 percent of the people in the focus groups had no more than a high school diploma, compared to a third of the population at large, and 10 percent (versus 17 percent) had not finished high school.[4]

In terms of religion, they were quite unlike the U.S. population, with Protestants underrepresented (20 percent versus 58 percent) and Jews and people with no religion overrepresented (23 percent Jewish compared to 2 percent, 25 percent nonreligious versus 8 percent). Catholics came to the focus groups in the same proportions as the population, while those with other religions than these were almost twice as frequent in the groups as in the general population (10 percent compared to 6 percent).[5] We added a question on politics after we had begun the groups, but of the slightly more than half who answered it, 58 percent identified as Democrats, only 8 percent as Republicans, and 34 percent as Independent, other, or none of the above.

Another less rigorous but nonetheless rich source of data was informal conversations and short interviews with an additional fifty-five audience members. To make up for the lack of male heterosexual participation in the focus groups, we sought out presumably heterosexual men who constituted more than half of these interviewees. These informal interviews also confirmed our observations and the drag queens' reports that the summer off-season audiences are less educated and more likely to identify as middle or working class.

Finally, to assess the role of the 801 performers in the larger gay and lesbian community, we examined over a three-year period all stories that contained references to the performers at 801 in the weekly gay newspaper *Celebrate!* and in the mainstream Key West media. The data were coded by the authors and two research assistants and analyzed qualitatively. All unreferenced quotations and data come from our interviews and observations. We include here our interview guide, focus group guide, and information sheet for the focus groups.

INTERVIEW GUIDE
INTRODUCTION
A. PERSONAL HISTORY
    1. When and how did you first begin to perform in drag?
    2. How did you learn to perform drag?
    3. When you perform drag, what are you trying to say to the audience?
    4. How did you decide on your drag name and persona?
    5. What does it mean to you to be a drag queen as compared to, say, a female impersonator, transgendered person, "titty queen," etc.?
    6. Could you talk about the emotions associated with doing drag? How do they affect you?
B. THE 801 SHOW
    1. How did you get involved in this show?
    2. Besides performing, what other responsibilities do you have (choreography, lighting, sets, costumes, etc.)?
    3. Do you see the 801 show as unique, or similar to other drag shows?
    4. Do you see drag as purely entertainment, or are you trying to communicate any kind of message to the audience? If so, what?
    5. Your audiences are generally mixed—straight, gay, lesbian. Does that influence what you do onstage? How? Do you prefer certain kinds of audiences?
    6. Could you talk a little bit about how the audience responds to the show?
    7. Besides the shows, the 801 Girls seem to have a special place in the community. Could you talk about some of the other events you participate in?

8. How do you see yourself in relation to other drag queens in Key West?

9. What do you think the role of drag queens is in the gay/lesbian movement?

10. David, in his column, described the 801 as a "home away from home." What about for you?

11. Are you able to support yourself financially doing drag? On average, how much do you make in tips and wages per week (seasonal differences)? How much do you spend on costumes?

12. How much time do you spend rehearsing, dressing, planning the shows, etc.? What is involved in dressing?

FOCUS GROUP GUIDE

1. Introduction: informal conversation.

2. Everyone: first name, where from?

How many times at 801 show?

How did you wind up at the show, why did you come?

3. What did you like about the show? What didn't you like?

4. What were your favorite parts of the show? least favorite parts?

5. Do you have favorite songs they perform? Explain.

6. How would you describe the show to a friend who wasn't there?

7. When the drag queens are performing, do you think of them as women or men or both?

8. Is there a "point" or "message" to the show? If so, what?

9. Do you think the show is a gay event? What can straight people get out of it?

801 CABARET DISCUSSION GROUP INFORMATION FORM

Name: _____

Hometown: _____

Age: _____

Male ❑ Female ❑

Race/ethnicity: white/Caucasian ❑ black/African American ❑
Asian American ❑ Latino/Hispanic American ❑ other (specify)
_____

Occupation (if retired, occupation before retirement):
_____

Do you consider yourself working class ❑ lower-middle class ❑
middle class ❑ upper-middle class ❑ upper class ❑ other (specify)
_____

Religious affiliation: Catholic ❑ Protestant ❑ Jewish ❑ Muslim ❑
other (specify) ❑ none ❑
_____

Do you consider yourself religious? very ❑ somewhat ❑ a little ❑
not at all ❑

Generally speaking, do you usually think of yourself as
a Republican ❑ Democrat ❑ Independent ❑ other (specify)
_____

Degree completed: some high school ❑ high school ❑
some college ❑ college ❑ graduate or professional degree ❑

Are you married or partnered ❑ single ❑

Sexual preference/identification: heterosexual ❑ gay or lesbian ❑
bisexual ❑

Have you seen a drag show before this one? Yes ❑ No ❑

If yes, where: _____

If at 801 Cabaret, how many times? _____

NOTES

CHAPTER ONE

1. Theoretical accounts include Butler 1990 and 1993; Garber 1992. Newton 1972 is a pioneering work, and we take up the task her preface to the 1979 edition left to others by carrying the story beyond the 1960s world she studied. Other empirical works on drag include Tewksbury 1993, 1994; Fleisher 1996; Gagné and Tewksbury 1996, all based on intensive interviews with professional female impersonators; Paulson with Simpson 1996, a historical consideration of a gay drag club in the 1940s and 1950s; Schacht 1998, 2000, 2002a, 2002b, 2000c, all based on participant observation in the Imperial Court of Spokane. Schacht is also completing a book-length manuscript entitled "Flawless: Doing Drag in the Absolutely Fabulous World of an Imperial Sovereign Court." Ferris 1993, Baker 1994, and Senelick 2000 all deal with the history of drag in the theater. Brubach and O'Brien 1999 is an intelligent and lavishly illustrated look at high-culture drag in New York, London, Paris, Berlin, Amsterdam, Rio, Tokyo, and Bangkok. Chermayeff, David, and Richardson 1995 is a coffee-table book of photographs and interviews. There is also an extensive literature on gender-crossing in other times and places, as well as works that deal with other forms of gender transgression and with transsexuality.

2. See Volcano and Halberstam 1999 and Schacht 2002b.

3. Bernstein 1997.

4. Gagnon and Simon 1973; Kessler and McKenna 1978; Goffman 1979; Plummer 1981; West and Zimmerman 1987; Butler 1990, 1993; West and Fenstermaker 1995; Stein and Plummer 1996; Howard and Hollander 1997.

5. Bernstein 1997; Foster 1999; Lorber 1999.

6. Tilly 1978, 1995a; Morris 1984; J. Gamson 1989; Clemens 1993; Steinberg 1995, 1999; Taylor and Raeburn 1995; Traugott 1995; Whittier 1995; Bernstein 1997; Katzenstein 1998; Mueller 1999; McAdam, Tarrow, and Tilly 2001.

7. Samuel, MacColl, and Cosgrove 1985; Cohen 1993; Phelan 1993; Berezin 1997; Fuoss 1997; Cohen-Cruz 1998; Goodwin with DeGay 1998; Stowe 1998.

CHAPTER TWO

1. On the Imperial Sovereign Court of Spokane, see Schacht 1998.

2. David Felstein, "Random Observations," *Celebrate!,* February 6, 1998, 8.

CHAPTER THREE
1. Eric Selby, "Key People," *Celebrate!,* September 11, 1998, 10–11.
2. Ibid., October 23, 1998, 14.
3. Roger Cousineau, "Key People," *Celebrate!,* October 8, 1999, 12.

CHAPTER FOUR
1. Holly Brubach 1999, xvii–xviii, distinguishes between female impersonators, who perform on stage in drag; transsexuals, who believe they were born in the wrong body and alter it with hormones or surgery; cross-dressers, mostly straight men, who wear women's clothes in private for erotic reasons; and drag queens, who dress as women in public on social occasions. These categories leave out transgendered people, whose appearance and self-conception do not match their biological sex but who do not want to alter their bodies. See Epstein and Straub 1991; Feinberg 1992; Bornstein 1993; Ferris 1993; Herdt 1994; Hausman 1995; and Ekins and King 1996. On the historical distance between straight and gay crossdressers, and between transvestites and transsexuals, see Meyerowitz 1998 and forthcoming.
2. See Meyerowitz, forthcoming.
3. Newton 1972.
4. Keith 1999, 184.
5. Roger Cousineau, "Key People," *Celebrate!,* October 8, 1999, 12.
6. David Felstein, "Random Observations," *Celebrate!,* July 9, 1999, 10.
7. David Felstein, "Face to Face with History—Part Four," *Celebrate!,* October 24, 1997, 9.
8. David Felstein, "Random Observations," *Celebrate!,* May 29, 1998, 3.
9. See Kennedy and Davis 1993, who analyze butch and fem genders; Halberstam 1998, who argues for the expansion of the category of "masculinity"; and Kulick 1998, who identifies a binary travesti gender system based on sexuality, that is, separating those who penetrate from those who are penetrated.

CHAPTER FIVE
1. Smith 1998.
2. Maloney 1876, 83, 86.
3. Quoted in David Felstein, "Random Observations," *Celebrate!,* July 31, 1998, 8.
4. Deford 1999.
5. King 1997.
6. "Same-Sex Marriages Legalized in the Conch Republic—Secretary General to Hold World Press Conference March 5," *Celebrate!,* March 5, 1999, 19.
7. Ibid., 1, 19.
8. Maloney 1876, 82.
9. R. L. Goulding, "Life in Early Key West: An Address to the Manatee County Historical Society," January 16, 1974, typescript, 11, 7, 9.
10. Quoted in Cox 1983, 7; other historical information is also from Cox.
11. Browne 1912, 99.
12. Smith 1998, 216.
13. Mark Howell, "Rub Your Pineapple," *solares hill* 24 (December 14, 2001), 1–2.

14. Sharp 1999.
15. Bragg 1999.
16. Blackford 2001.
17. Maloney 1876, 80.
18. Lee Dodez, *Memories of Key West* (no place, no date), in Key West Public Library.
19. Kuralt 1995, x.
20. Editorial, "Sending an Appropriate Message to the World from Key West," *Island News*, March 23, 2001, 8; "One Human Family," *Celebrate!*, March 16, 2001, 1–3.
21. "Bone Island True Fallacies," *Celebrate!*, February 12, 1999, 6.
22. David Felstein, "Random Observations," *Celebrate!*, October 8, 1999, 10.
23. "Bone Island True Fallacies," *Celebrate!*, February 12, 1999, 6.
24. Quoted in David Felstein, "Random Observations," *Celebrate!*, August 10, 2001, 8.
25. David Felstein, "Random Observations," *Celebrate!*, March 19, 1999, 9.
26. Ibid., April 6, 2001, 10; "Three Youths Arrested in Hate Crime," *Celebrate!*, December 8–14, 2000, 1+.
27. "Fantasy Fest '98: Twenty Year Marker and the Reality of Our Grim Reaper," *Celebrate!*, November 6, 1998, 1, 16.
28. David Felstein, "Random Observations," *Celebrate!*, December 24, 1999, 8.
29. Ginny Haller, "Sunset Celebration: Gays and Lesbians Beware," *Celebrate!*, January 19–25, 1+; "Gay Dads Harrassed [sic], *Celebrate!*, January 26–February 1, 2001, 1+.
30. David Felstein, "Random Observations," *Celebrate!*, December 31, 1998, 4.
31. Ibid., October 24, 1997, 1+.
32. George Fontana, "To the Editor," *Celebrate!*, December 12, 1997, 6.
33. "'Mother Earth' Drag Contest Scheduled," *Celebrate!*, April 11, 1997, 13.
34. David Felstein, "Random Observations," *Celebrate!*, November 12, 1999, 10.
35. Terry Schmida, "When Life's a Drag," *Key West Citizen*, June 3, 2001, 1C+.
36. Sharp 1999.
37. Ehrenreich 2001.
38. On Cherry Grove, see Newton 1993; on Provincetown, Krahulik 2000; on San Francisco, Boyd forthcoming and Meeker forthcoming. See also the community studies in Beemyn 1997.

CHAPTER SIX

1. R.V. Beaumont, Letter to the Editor, *Celebrate!*, April 9, 1999, 7.
2. Newton 1972.

CHAPTER SEVEN

1. Michelle Agee, "Local Gay Bars Form Management Group," *Celebrate!*, June 13, 1997, 9.
2. David D.D.T. Thomas, Letter to the Editor, *Celebrate!*, June 22, 2001, 7.
3. "Miss Firecracker to Sizzle at La-Te-Da on July 3," *Celebrate!*, June 19, 1998, 4.
4. Mandy Bolen, "Tonight's the Night!," *Key West Citizen*, December 31, 2000, 1A+.

5. "Kick Up Your Millennium Heels in Gay Key West," *Celebrate!*, December 31, 1999, 1.

6. David Felstein, "Random Observations," *Celebrate!*, March 6, 1998, 8.

7. Ronnie Bareitall, "Keyster Watch," *Celebrate!*, March 16, 2001, 20.

8. Ginny Haller, "The Reason for the Men in Pink Dresses," *Celebrate!*, March 23, 2001, 6.

9. Chase McClintock, "The Great Conch Republic Drag Race Down Duval," *Celebrate!*, April 24, 1998, 1, 11.

10. Ron Marriott, "Conch Republic Drag Races," *Celebrate!*, April 20, 2001, 20.

11. Deirdre Pierce, "The Night Stuff," *Celebrate!*, May 2, 1997, 5.

12. See Schacht 1998.

13. Michelle Agee, "Drag Queen Showdown May 12 to Determine New Queen Mother," *Celebrate!*, May 2, 1997, 3.

14. *Celebrate!*, May 19, 2000, 23.

15. Keith 1999, 84.

16. David Felstein, "Random Observations," *Celebrate!*, January 2, 1998, 8.

17. "Annual Survivors' Party Set for Memorial Day," *Celebrate!*, May 23, 1997, 1, 2.

18. "Miss Pridefest Pageant April 19th at the Copa," *Celebrate!*, April 14, 2000, 18.

19. Connie Gilbert, "PrideFest '98 Begins with a Mayor Toss," *Celebrate!*, June 12, 1998, 1, 3.

20. BellaDonna, "Bella Practically Parties Herself to Death!," *Celebrate!*, June 19, 1998, 10–11.

21. Michelle Agee, "Fantasy Fest and AIDS Help: A Productive Partnership," *Celebrate!*, July 4, 1997, 1, 2; Roger Cousineau, "Royal Joust for Fantasy Fest Throne Begins," *Celebrate!*, August 27, 1999, 1, 16.

22. "Bone Island Madness," *Celebrate!*, October 30, 1998, 6.

23. "Bal Masque Carnival Once Again at the New Orleans House," *Celebrate!*, October 22, 1999, 5.

24. "Bal Masque Carnival—Successful GLCC Fundraiser," *Celebrate!*, November 5, 1999, 2.

25. David Felstein, "Random Observations," *Celebrate!*, December 25, 1998, 3.

26. Ibid., May 7, 1999, 10.

27. Eric Selby, "In Defense of Drag Queens," *Celebrate!*, September 24, 1999, 6.

CHAPTER EIGHT

1. Even without the gender barrier, the mixing of sex and friendship is in general fraught for gay men. See Nardi 1999.

2. David Felstein, "Random Observations," *Celebrate!*, January 22, 1999, 2.

3. Ibid., August 18, 2000, 10.

4. George Fontana, "Key West Karacters: RV Beaumont, Queen Mother in Waiting," *Southern Exposure*, May 2000.

5. Kulick 1998; Prieur 1999. The traditional assumption is that, in certain cultures, men have insertive sex with other men because the sex of the partner makes little difference, and as long as one plays the insertive part, the act has no consequence for identity.

6. David Felstein, "Random Observations," *Celebrate!*, January 15, 1998, 9.

7. Ibid., January 30, 1998, 5.

8. Eric Selby, "Key People: The Many Faces of Matthew Keenan," *Celebrate!*, September 18, 1998, 10–11.

9. David Felstein, "Random Observations," *Celebrate!*, May 14, 1999, 8.

10. Ibid., August 28, 1998, p. 9.

11. Ibid., August 14, 1998, 13.

12. Ibid., June 22, 2001, 5.

13. On celebrity, see J. Gamson 1994.

CHAPTER NINE

1. Michelle Agee, "801: Friendly Spot, Friendly People," *Celebrate!*, July 25, 1009, 1–2.

2. David Felstein, "Random Observations," *Celebrate!*, June 26, 1998, 8.

3. Ginny Haller, "Island Style Cabaret: Va Va Voom," *Celebrate!*, December 22–28, 2000, 1.

4. Roger Cousineau, "Key People: Swedish Femme Fatale Gives the Audience What They Want," *Celebrate!*, October 8, 1999, 12.

5. BellaDonna, "Bella's Big Weekend," *Celebrate!*, April 24, 1998, 3.

6. "'Star Wars' Provides Sushi with Yet Another Smashing Hit," *Celebrate!*, May 21, 1999, 4.

7. "Key West Has a Street Bus Named Desire," *Celebrate!*, April 30, 1999, 1.

8. David Felstein, "Random Observations," *Celebrate!*, September 3, 1999, 14.

9. Terry Schmida, "When Life's a Drag," *Key West Citizen*, June 3, 2001, 1C+.

10. George Fontana, "Key West Karacters: RV Beaumont, Queen Mother in Waiting," *Southern Exposure*, May 2000; Rupp 1999.

CHAPTER TEN

1. The term "cross-ethnicking" comes from Robertson 1998.

2. David Felstein, "Random Observations," *Celebrate!*, October 15, 1999, 11.

3. This typology is based on what performance theorist Muñoz 1999 calls identification, counteridentification, and disidentification.

4. We are grateful to Joanne Meyerowitz for suggesting this term.

CHAPTER ELEVEN

1. Weston 1991.

2. George Fontana, "Key West Karacters: RV Beaumont, Queen Mother in Waiting," *Southern Exposure*, May 2000.

3. Terry Schmida, "When Life's a Drag," *Key West Citizen*, June 3, 2001, 1C+.

4. David Felstein, "Random Observations," *Celebrate!*, November 29, 1999, 15.

5. Ibid.

6. Ibid., November 5, 1999, 8.

7. Ibid., August 27, 1999, 10.

CHAPTER TWELVE

1. Weston 1991 and Nardi 1999.

2. Margo, "The Wedding that Changed the Course of Human History," *Celebrate!*, November 27, 1998, 10.

3. David Felstein, "Random Observations," *Celebrate!*, September 17, 1999, 11.

4. Robert K. Bryant, "The Southernmost Faggot: Interview with a Vamp— Desiray," *Celebrate!*, April 14, 2000, 23.

5. David Felstein, "Random Observations," *Celebrate!*, May 15, 1998, 14.

6. Ibid., August 20, 1999, 8.

7. Terry Schmida, "When Life's a Drag," *Key West Citizen*, June 3, 2001, 1C+.

8. David Felstein, "Random Observations," *Celebrate!*, June 22, 2001, 5.

9. Robert K. Bryant, "The Southernmost Faggot: Interview with a Vamp— Desiray," *Celebrate!*, April 14, 2000, 23.

10. Roger Cousineau, "Swedish Femme Fatale Gives the Audience What They Want," *Celebrate!*, October 8, 1999, 12.

11. David Felstein, "Random Observations," *Celebrate!*, May 8, 1998, 14.

12. Margo, "Margo Manages to Manipulate Marathon Magnificently," *Celebrate!*, July 17, 1998, 11.

13. Edward Ditterline, "BellaDonna: A Legend in Her Own Mind," *Celebrate!*, July 24, 1998, 12-13.

14. David Felstein, "Random Observations," *Celebrate!*, September 18, 1998, 12.

15. Ibid., February 9, 2001, 4.

16. Ibid., March 16, 2001, 5; March 30, 2001, 4; May 4, 2001, 10.

17. Joseph R. Benten, Letter to the Editor, *Celebrate!*, May 25, 2001, 7.

18. David Felstein, "Random Observations," *Celebrate!*, July 13, 2001, 10.

19. Ibid., July 3, 1998, 8.

20. Roger Cousineau, "Key People: Swedish Femme Fatale Gives the Audience What They Want," *Celebrate!*, October 8, 1999, 12.

21. Terry Schmida, "When Life's a Drag," *Key West Citizen*, June 3, 2001, 1C+.

22. See Nardi 1999, who argues that friendships among gay men challenge the gender order by transforming traditional masculinity and serving as the basis for new kinds of social organization.

CHAPTER THIRTEEN

1. Senelick 2000, 302, 321.

2. Thanks to Ms. Bob, who responded to our e-mail request.

3. Norton 1992, 103.

4. The 1989 edition on line includes this definition. Thanks to Sharon Carlson for the reference. See http://dictionary.oed.com/cgi/entry/00194663?query_type= word&queryword=Queen&sort_type=alpha&edition=2e&first=1&max_to_show= 10&search_id=fonl-Ssm4jQ-97.

5. Beale 1989, 136, says "since ca. 1930," while Lighter 1994, vol. 1, 653, cites Legman 1941, 1164. Thanks to Jane Caplan, Jonathan Katz, Steven Maynard, Randy Riddle, David Serlin, Michael Sibalis, and Martha Vicinus for their helpful replies.

6. See Ramet 1996.

7. See Cressy 2000, 109.

8. Huussen 1985; Rey 1985; Norton 1992; Merrick 1999.

9. Trumbach 1989, 137; see also Trumbach 1998.

10. Quoted in Bray 1982, 86.

11. Quoted in Katz 1983, 157; quoted in Burnham 1973, 41.

12. See Chauncey 1994, 42.

13. Quoted in Chauncey 1982–83.

14. See Senelick 2000, 239–41.

15. Senelick 2000, 310; Ullman 1995, 590.

16. Quoted in Chauncey 1994, 257.

17. Quoted in ibid., 314.

18. Chauncey 1994.

19. Bérubé 1990.

20. Boyd 1997.

21. Seyfer 1999. On Finocchio's, see Boyd 1997.

22. Senelick 2000, 380–89.

23. Harris 1997 analyzes the centrality of female stars to gay male culture. He traces drag impressions from a reverential portrayal to a mocking attack, which he associates with the decline of gay culture.

24. Drexel 1997.

25. Paulson with Simpson 1996.

26. Newton 1972.

27. See Meyerowitz forthcoming.

28. Senelick 2000, 389–93. See Brevard 2001, the story of a boy who becomes a drag queen at Finocchio's before becoming a woman and Hollywood starlet.

29. See Schacht 2002a.

30. Quoted in Paulson with Simpson 1996, 167.

31. Quoted in ibid., 35, 104.

32. Newton 1972, 52–54.

33. Quoted in ibid., 76.

34. Quoted in Chauncey 1994, 249.

35. The term is from Nestle 1981; see also Kennedy and Davis 1993.

36. Dunlap 2002.

37. Leigh W. Rutledge, "In Praise of Old Queens," *Celebrate!*, August 27, 1999, 3.

38. Duberman 1993.

39. See Kissack 1995.

40. Senelick 2000, 464; Baker 1994, 239–40.

41. Senelick 2000, 467–68.

42. See Fleisher 1996 and Brubach and O'Brien 1999.

CHAPTER FOURTEEN

1. J. Gamson 1998.

2. Morgan 1997.

3. For a more detailed description, see the appendix. Statistics for the U.S. population come from U.S. Bureau of the Census 2001 and Macionis 1999.

4. Terry Schmida, "When Life's a Drag," *Key West Citizen*, June 3, 2001, 1C+.

5. Roger Cousineau, "Key People: Swedish Femme Fatale Gives the Audience What They Want," *Celebrate!*, October 8, 1999, 12.

6. R.V. quotation and Sushi's comment in Terry Schmida, "When Life's a Drag," *Key West Citizen*, June 3, 2001, 1C+.

CHAPTER FIFTEEN

1. See www.wigstock.nu/what is/what is.html.
2. Kate Reynolds, "The Naked Eye Review: Diva's: A Divine Diversion," *Celebrate!*, April 13, 2001, 2.

CHAPTER SIXTEEN

1. Butler 1990, 1993; Garber 1992; Lorber 1994, 1999; Halberstam 1998; Muñoz 1999.
2. Frye 1983; Dolan 1985; Tewksbury 1993, 1994; Gagné and Tewksbury 1996; Schacht 1998, 2002a, 2002b, 2002c; Brubach and O'Brien 1999; Feigen 2000.
3. Garber 1992; Butler 1990.
4. Bernstein 1997, 538.
5. Butler 1990, 176–77.
6. Tilly 1978; McAdam 1982; Kreisi, Koopmans, Duyvendak, and Giugni 1995; Klandermans 1997; Rucht, Koopmans, and Neidhardt 1998; Tarrow 1998.
7. Tilly 1995b, 2001; Tarrow 1998; McAdam, Tarrow, and Tilly 2001.
8. Tilly 1978; Tarrow 1989; Kreisi, Koopmans, Duyvendak, and Giugni 1995; Bernstein 1997; McAdam, McCarthy, Olzak, and Soule 1997; Van Dyke 1998; McAdam, Tarrow, and Tilly 2001.
9. Morris 1984; Darnovsky, Epstein, and Flacks 1995; Johnston and Klandermans 1995; Taylor and Whittier 1995; Jasper 1997; Patillo McCoy 1998; Rochon 1998; Steinberg 1999; Goodwin, Jasper, and Polletta 2001; Ferree, Gamson, Gerhards, and Rucht 2002; Meyer, Whittier, and Robnett 2002.
10. Staggenborg 1998, 2001; Flacks 1999; Rhodes 2001; Roscigno and Danaher 2001.
11. Adam 1987; J. Gamson 1989, 1995; Taylor and Whittier 1995; Epstein 1996.
12. Scott 1990; Katzenstein 1998; Zald 2000; Raeburn forthcoming.
13. Plummer 1981; Connell 1987; West and Zimmerman 1987; Greenberg 1988; Lorber 1994; Martin 1998; Nardi and Schneider 1998; Murray 2000.
14. Gagnon and Simon 1973; Goffman 1979; Kessler and McKenna 1978; Plummer 1981; West and Zimmerman 1987; Butler 1990, 1993; West and Fenstermaker 1995; Howard and Hollander 1997; Schwartz and Rutter 1998; Ferree, Lorber, and Hess 1999.
15. Butler 1990, 1993; Garber 1992; Taylor and Whittier 1992; J. Gamson 1997; Halberstam 1998; Foster 1999; Lorber 1999.
16. Fraser 1989.
17. Although Charles Tilly's notion of repertoires of collective action has always relied on a theatrical metaphor, his recent work treats public performances by groups seeking recognition of their identities by political authorities as a defining feature of repertoires of contention. His view of protest tactics in contemporary societies, however, does not include what we tend to think of as more strictly cultural performances. See Tilly 2001.
18. McCarthy and Zald 1977; Tilly 1978; Oliver 1980; Jenkins 1983; Klandermans 1984; Zald and McCarthy 1987; W. Gamson 1992a; McAdam, Tarrow, and Tilly 2001. For an overview of contemporary social movement theories, see Klandermans 1997 and Della Porta and Diani 1999.

19. McAdam 1982; Morris 1984; Fantasia 1988; Melucci 1989, 1995; Mueller 1991; W. Gamson 1992a, 1992b; Taylor and Whittier 1992; Marwell and Oliver 1993; Whittier 1995; Tarrow 1998; Klandermans and de Weerd 2000; Snow and McAdam 2000; Stryker, Owens, and White 2000; F. Harris 2001; Mansbridge and Morris 2001; McAdam, Tarrow, and Tilly 2001; Morris and Braine 2001; Polletta and Jasper 2001; Simon and Klandermans 2001.

20. Tilly 1978; Tarrow 1998; see also Steinberg 1995, 1999; Mueller 1999; Beckwith 2000.

21. Tilly 1995a, 26.

22. Traugott 1995; Tarrow 1998.

23. McAdam, Tarrow, and Tilly 2001.

24. Whittier 1995; Lichterman 1996; Bernstein 1997; McAdam, Tarrow, and Tilly 2001; Tilly 2001; Mische forthcoming.

25. Stourac and McCreery 1986; Barucha 1993; Cohen 1993; Phelan 1993; Von Geldern 1993; Parkin, Caplan, and Fisher 1996; Berezin 1997; Fuoss 1997; Cohen-Cruz 1998; Goodwin with de Gay 1998, 2000; Schechner 1998; Stowe, 1998; Rhodes 2001.

26. Samuel, MacColl, and Cosgrove 1985; Stourac and McCreery 1986; Cohen 1993; Berezin 1994; Fuoss 1997; Schechner 1998; Rhodes 2001.

27. Bailey 1996; Stowe 1998.

28. Fuoss 1997; Schechner 1998.

29. Chaney 1993; Schechner 1998.

30. Polletta 1999; Molotch, Freudenburg, and Paulsen 2000; Tilly 2000; Mansbridge and Morris 2001; Morris and Braine 2001.

31. Goffman 1974; Snow, Rochford, Worden, and Benford 1986; Benford and Snow 2000; Mansbridge 2001.

32. Eyerman and Jamison 1998.

33. On the concept of social movement spillover, see Meyer and Whittier 1994.

34. Morris 1981; McAdam 1982; McAdam, McCarthy, and Zald 1988; Tarrow 1989; McAdam 1994; Taylor and Whittier 1995; Bernstein 1997; Della Porta and Diani 1999; Mueller 1999; Staggenborg 2001; Ferree, Gamson, Gerhards, and Rucht 2002.

35. Goffman 1970; Bailey 1996.

36. Fuoss 1997; Schechner 1998; Stowe 1998.

37. Morris 1984; Ferree 1992; Taylor 1995; Taylor and Whittier 1995; Taylor 1996; Robnett 1999; Goodwin, Jasper, and Polletta 2001; Gould 2001; Whittier 2002.

38. Taylor 1989; Taylor and Whittier 1992.

39. W. Gamson 1992a; Mueller 1992; McAdam and Paulsen 1993; Melucci 1995; Polletta 1999; Polletta and Jasper 2001.

40. Chaney 1993; Fuoss 1997.

41. W. Gamson 1990.

42. Mansbridge 2001.

43. Taylor 2000a.

44. Whittier 1995; Stryker, Owens, and White 2000; Polletta and Jasper 2001.

45. W. Gamson 1991; J. Gamson 1995; Rupp and Taylor 1999.

46. Sontag 1964.

47. McAdam, Tarrow, and Tilly 2001.

48. Melucci 1996; Castells 1997; Taylor 2000b; Zald 2000.
49. Chasin 2000; Hennessey 2000.

APPENDIX
1. J. Gamson 1994, 1998.
2. Blee and Taylor forthcoming.
3. Most surveys report income rather than class; the figures for the U.S. population come from Macionis 1999.
4. National statistics come from Newburger and Curry 2000.
5. U.S. Bureau of the Census 2001.

BIBLIOGRAPHY

Adam, Barry D. 1987. *The Rise of a Gay and Lesbian Movement.* Boston: Twayne.

Bailey, F. G. 1996. "Cultural Performance, Authenticity, and Second Nature." In *The Politics of Cultural Performance,* edited by David Parkin, Lionel Caplan, and Humphrey Fisher, 1–18. Providence: Berghahn Books.

Baker, Roger. 1994. *Drag: A History of Female Impersonation in the Performing Arts.* New York: New York University Press.

Barucha, Rustom. 1993. *Theatre and the World: Performance and the Politics of Culture.* New York: Routledge.

Beale, Paul, ed. 1989. *A Concise Dictionary of Slang and Unconventional English.* New York: Macmillan.

Beckwith, Karen. 2000. "Hinges in Collective Action: Strategic Innovation in the Pittston Coal Strike." *Mobilization: An International Journal* 5: 179–99.

Beemyn, Brett, ed. 1997. *Creating a Place for Ourselves: Lesbian, Gay, and Bisexual Community Histories.* New York: Routledge.

Benford, Robert D., and David A. Snow. 2000. "Framing Processes and Social Movements: An Overview and Assessment." *Annual Review of Sociology* 26: 611–39.

Berezin, Mabel. 1997. *Making the Fascist Self: The Political Culture of Interwar Italy.* Ithaca, N.Y.: Cornell University Press.

———. 1994. "Fissured Terrain: Methodological Approaches and Research Styles in Culture and Politics." In *The Sociology of Culture: Emerging Theoretical Perspectives,* edited by Diana Crane, 91–116. Oxford: Blackwell Publishers.

Bernstein, Mary. 1997. "Celebration and Suppression: Strategic Uses of Identity by the Lesbian and Gay Movement." *American Journal of Sociology* 103: 531–65.

Bérubé, Allan. 1990. *Coming Out Under Fire: The History of Gay Men and Women in World War II.* New York: Free Press.

Blackford, Mansel G. 2001. *Fragile Paradise: The Impact of Tourism on Maui, 1959–2000.* Lawrence: University Press of Kansas.

Blee, Kathleen M., and Verta Taylor. Forthcoming. "Semi-structured Interviewing in Social Movement Research." In *Methods in Social Movement Research,* edited by Bert Klandermans and Suzanne Staggenborg. Minneapolis: University of Minnesota Press.

Bornstein, Kate. 1993. *Gender Outlaw: Men, Women, and the Rest of Us.* New York: Routledge.

Boyd, Nan Alamilla. Forthcoming. *Wide Open Town: A Queer History of San Francisco, 1933–1965.* Berkeley: University of California Press.

———. 1997. "'Homos Invade S.F.!' San Francisco's History as a Wide-Open Town." In *Creating a Place for Ourselves: Lesbian, Gay, and Bisexual Community Histories,* edited by Brett Beemyn, 73–96. New York: Routledge.

Bragg, Rick. 1999. "Crowded Florida Keys a Paradise in Trouble." *New York Times* (September 28), A14.

Bray, Alan. 1982. *Homosexuality in Renaissance England.* New York: Columbia University Press.

Brevard, Aleshia. 2001. *The Woman I Was Not Born to Be: A Transsexual Journey.* Philadelphia: Temple University Press.

Browne, Jefferson B. 1912. *Key West: The Old and the New.* St. Augustine: The Record Company [handwritten copy].

Brubach, Holly and Michael James O'Brien. 1999. *Girlfriend: Men, Women, and Drag.* New York: Random House.

Burnham, John. 1973. "Early References to Homosexual Communities in American Medical Writings." *Medical Aspects of Human Sexuality* 7: 34–49.

Butler, Judith. 1993. *Bodies That Matter: On the Discursive Limits of "Sex."* New York: Routledge.

———. 1990. *Gender Trouble: Feminism and the Subversion of Identity.* New York: Routledge.

Castells, Manuel. 1997. *The Power of Identity.* Malden, Mass.: Blackwell.

Chaney, David. 1993. *Fictions of Collective Life: Public Drama in Late Modern Culture.* New York: Routledge.

Chasin, Alexandra. 2000. *Selling Out: The Gay and Lesbian Movement Goes to Market.* New York: Palgrave.

Chauncey, George, Jr. 1994. *Gay New York: Gender, Urban Culture, and the Making of the Gay Male World, 1890–1940.* New York: Basic Books.

———. 1982–83. "From Sexual Inversion to Homosexuality: Medicine and the Changing Conceptualization of Female Deviance." *Salmagundi* 58–59 (fall–winter): 114–46.

Chermayeff, Catherine, Jonathan David, and Nan Richardson. 1995. *Drag Diaries.* San Francisco: Chronicle Books.

Clemens, Elisabeth S. 1993. "Organizational Repertoires and Institutional Change: Women's Groups and the Transformation of U.S. Politics, 1890–1920." *American Journal of Sociology* 98: 755–98.

Cohen, Abner. 1993. *Masquerade Politics: Explorations in the Structure of Urban Cultural Movements.* Berkeley: University of California Press.

Cohen-Cruz, Jan, ed. 1998. *Radical Street Performance: An International Anthology.* London: Routledge.

Connell, R. W. 1987. *Gender and Power: Society, the Person, and Sexual Politics.* Cambridge: Polity in association with Blackwell.

Cox, Christopher. 1983. *A Key West Companion.* New York: St. Martin's Press.

Cressy, David. 2000. *Travesties and Transgressions in Tudor and Stuart England.* Oxford: Oxford University Press.

Darnovsky, Marcy, Barbara Epstein, and Richard Flacks, eds. 1995. *Cultural Politics and Social Movements.* Philadelphia: Temple University Press.

Deford, Frank. 1999. "The Florida Keys: Paradise with Attitude." *National Geographic* 196 (December): 33–53.

Della Porta, Donatella, and Mario Diani. 1999. *Social Movements: An Introduction.* Oxford: Blackwell.

Dolan, Jill. 1985. "Gender Impersonation Onstage: Destroying or Maintaining the Mirror of Gender Roles?" *Women and Performance: A Journal of Feminist Theory* 2: 5–11.

Drexel, Allen. 1997. "Before Paris Burned: Race, Class and Male Homosexuality on the Chicago South Side, 1935–1960." In *Creating a Place for Ourselves: Lesbian, Gay, and Bisexual Community Histories,* edited by Brett Beemyn, 119–44. New York: Routledge.

Duberman, Martin Bauml. 1993. *Stonewall.* New York: Dutton.

Dunlap, David W. 2002. "Sylvia Rivera, 50, Figure in Birth of the Gay Liberation Movement." *New York Times* (February 20).

Ehrenreich, Barbara. 2001. *Nickel and Dimed: On (Not) Getting by in America.* New York: Metropolitan Books.

Ekins, Richard, and Dave King, eds. 1996. *Blending Genders: Social Aspects of Cross-Dressing and Sex-Changing.* New York: Routledge.

Epstein, Julia, and Kristina Straub, eds. 1991 *Body Guards: The Cultural Politics of Gender Ambiguity.* New York: Routledge.

Epstein, Steven. 1996. *Impure Science: AIDS, Activism, and the Politics of Knowledge.* Berkeley: University of California Press.

Eyerman, Ron, and Andrew Jamison. 1998. *Music and Social Movements: Mobilizing Traditions in the Twentieth Century.* Cambridge: Cambridge University Press.

Fantasia, Rick. 1988. *Cultures of Solidarity.* Berkeley: University of California Press.

Feigen, Brenda. 2000. *Not One of the Boys: Living Life as a Feminist.* New York: Alfred A. Knopf.

Feinberg, Leslie. 1996. *Transgender Warriors.* Boston: Beacon Press.

———. 1992. *Transgender Liberation: A Movement Whose Time Has Come.* New York: World View Forum.

Ferree, Myra Marx. 1992. "The Political Context of Rationality: Rational Choice Theory and Resource Mobilization." In *Frontiers in Social Movement Theory,* edited by Aldon D. Morris and Carol McClurg Mueller, 29–52. New Haven: Yale University Press.

Ferree, Myra Marx, William A. Gamson, Juergen Gerhards, and Dieter Rucht. 2002. *Shaping Abortion Discourse: Democracy and the Public Sphere in Germany and the United States.* New York: Cambridge University Press.

Ferree, Myra Marx, Judith Lorber, and Beth B. Hess. 1999. *Revisioning Gender.* Thousand Oaks, Calif.: Sage Publications.

Ferris, Leslie, ed. 1993. *Crossing the Stage: Controversies on Cross-Dressing.* London: Routledge.

Flacks, Richard. 1999. "Culture and Social Movements: Exploring the Power of Song." Paper presented at the annual meeting of the American Sociological Association, Chicago.

Fleisher, Julian. 1996. *The Drag Queens of New York: An Illustrated Field Guide.* New York: Riverhead Books.

Foster, Johanna. 1999. "An Invitation to Dialogue: Clarifying the Position of Feminist Gender Theory in Relation to Sexual Difference Theory." *Gender & Society* 13: 431–56.

Fraser, Nancy. 1989. *Unruly Practices: Power, Discourse and Gender in Contemporary Social Theory.* Minneapolis: University of Minnesota Press.

Frye, Marilyn. 1983. *Politics of Reality.* Freedom, Calif.: Crossing Press, 1983.

Fuoss, Kirk W. 1997. *Striking Performances/Performing Strikes.* Jackson: University Press of Mississippi.

Gagné, Patricia, and Richard Tewksbury. 1996. "No 'Man's' Land: Transgenderism and the Stigma of the Feminine Man." *Advances in Gender Research* 1: 115–55.

Gagnon, John H., and William Simon. 1973. *Sexual Conduct: The Social Sources of Human Sexuality.* Chicago: Aldine Publishers.

Gamson, Joshua. 1998. *Freaks Talk Back: Tabloid Talk Shows and Sexual Nonconformity.* Chicago: University of Chicago Press.

———. 1997. "Messages of Exclusion: Gender, Movements, and Symbolic Boundaries." *Gender & Society* 11: 178–99.

———. 1995. "Must Identity Movements Self-Destruct? A Queer Dilemma." *Social Problems* 42: 390–407.

———. 1994. *Claims to Fame: Celebrity in Contemporary America.* Berkeley: University of California Press.

———. 1989. "Silence, Death, and the Invisible Enemy: AIDS Activism and Social Movement 'Newness.'" *Social Problems* 36: 351–67.

Gamson, William A. 1992a. "The Social Psychology of Collective Action." In *Frontiers in Social Movement Theory,* edited by Aldon D. Morris and Carol McClurg Mueller, 53–76. New Haven: Yale University Press.

———. 1992b. *Talking Politics.* Cambridge: Cambridge University Press.

———. 1991. "Commitment and Agency in Social Movements." *Sociological Forum* 6: 27–50.

———. 1990. *The Strategy of Social Protest.* 2nd ed. Belmont, Calif.: Wadsworth.

Garber, Marjorie. 1992. *Vested Interests: Cross-Dressing and Cultural Anxiety.* New York: Routledge.

Goffman, Erving. 1979. *Gender Advertisements.* Cambridge: Harvard University Press.

———. 1974. *Frame Analysis: An Essay on the Organization of Experience.* New York: Harper & Row.

———. 1970. *Strategic Interaction.* Oxford: Blackwell.

Goodwin, Jeff, James M. Jasper, and Francesca Polletta, eds. 2001. *Passionate Politics: Emotions and Social Movements.* Chicago: University of Chicago Press.

Goodwin, Lizbeth, with Jane de Gay, eds. 2000. *The Routledge Reader in Politics and Performance.* London: Routledge.

———, eds. 1998. *The Routledge Reader in Gender and Performance.* London: Routledge.

Gould, Deborah. 2001. "Rock the Boat, Don't Rock the Boat, Baby: Ambivalence and the Emergence of Militant AIDS Activism." In *Passionate Politics: Emotions and Social Movements,* edited by Jeff Goodwin, James M. Jasper, and Francesca Polletta, 133–57. Chicago: University of Chicago Press.

Greenberg, David F. 1988. *The Construction of Homosexuality.* Chicago: University of Chicago Press.

Halberstam, Judith. 1998. *Female Masculinity.* Durham, N.C.: Duke University Press.

Harris, Daniel. 1997. *The Rise and Fall of Gay Culture.* New York: Ballantine Books.

Harris, Frederick C. 2001. "Religious Resources in an Oppositional Civic Culture." In *Oppositional Consciousness: The Subjective Roots of Social Protest,* edited by Jane Mansbridge and Aldon Morris, 38–64. Chicago: University of Chicago Press.

Hausman, Bernice. 1995. *Changing Sex: Transsexualism, Technology, and the Idea of Gender.* Durham, N.C.: Duke University Press.

Hennessey, Rosemary. 2000. *Profit and Pleasure: Sexual Identities in Late Capitalism.* New York: Routledge.

Herdt, Gil, ed. 1994. *Third Sex, Third Gender: Beyond Sexual Dimorphism in Culture and History.* New York: Zone Books.

Howard, Judith A., and Jocelyn A. Hollander. 1997. *Gendered Situations, Gendered Selves: A Gender Lens on Social Psychology.* Thousand Oaks, Calif.: Sage.

Huussen, Arend H., Jr. 1985. "Sodomy in the Dutch Republic During the Eighteenth Century." In *Unauthorized Sexual Behavior During the Enlightenment,* edited by Robert P. Maccubkin, 169–78. Williamsburg: William and Mary Press.

Jasper, James. 1997. *The Art of Moral Protest: Culture, Biography, and Creativity in Social Movements.* Chicago: University of Chicago Press.

Jenkins, J. Craig. 1983. "Resource Mobilization Theory and the Study of Social Movements." *Annual Review of Sociology* 9: 527–53.

Johnston, Hank, and Bert Klandermans, eds. 1995. *Social Movements and Culture.* Minneapolis: University of Minnesota Press.

Katz, Jonathan Ned. 1983. *Gay/Lesbian Almanac: A New Documentary.* New York: Harper and Row.

Katzenstein, Mary Fainsoid. 1998. *Faithful and Fearless: Moving Feminist Protest Inside the Church and Military.* Princeton: Princeton University Press.

Keith, June. 1999. *More Postcards from Paradise.* Key West: Palm Island Press.

Kennedy, Elizabeth Lapovsky, and Madeline Davis. 1993. *Boots of Leather, Slippers of Gold: The History of a Lesbian Community.* New York: Routledge.

Kessler, Suzanne J., and Wendy McKenna. 1978. *Gender: An Ethnomethodological Approach.* New York: Wiley.

King, Gregory. 1997. *The Conch That Roared.* Lexington, Ken.: Weston & Wright.

Kissack, Terence. 1995. "Freaking Fag Revolutionaries: New York's Gay Liberation Front, 1969–1974." *Radical History Review* 62 (spring): 104–34.

Klandermans, Bert. 1997. *The Social Psychology of Protest.* Oxford: Blackwell Publishers.

———. 1984. "Mobilization and Participation: Social Psychological Expansions of Resource Mobilization Theory." *American Sociological Review* 49: 583–600.

Klandermans, Bert, and Marga de Weerd. 2000. "Group Identification and Political Protest." In *Self, Identity, and Social Movements,* edited by Sheldon Stryker, Timothy J. Owens, and Robert W. White, 68–90. Minneapolis: University of Minnesota Press.

Krahulik, Karen Christel. 2000. "Cape Queer: The Politics of Sex, Class, and Race in Provincetown, Massachusetts, 1859–1999." Ph.D. diss., New York University.

Kreisi, Hanspeter, Ruud Koopmans, Jan Willem Duyvendak, and Marco G. Giugni. 1995. *New Social Movements in Western Europe: A Comparative Analysis.* Minneapolis: University of Minnesota Press.

Kulick, Don. 1998. *Travesti: Sex, Gender and Culture among Brazilian Transgendered Prostitutes*. Chicago: University of Chicago Press.

Kuralt, Charles. 1995. *Charles Kuralt's America*. New York: G. P. Putnam's Sons.

Legman, Gershon. 1941. "The Language of Homosexuality." In *Sex Variants: A Study in Homosexual Patterns*, edited by George W. Henry. New York: Paul B. Hoeber.

Lichterman, Paul. 1996. *The Search for Political Community*. New York: Cambridge University Press.

Lighter, J. E., ed. 1994. *Random House Historical Dictionary of American Slang*. New York: Random House.

Lorber, Judith. 1999. "Crossing Borders and Erasing Boundaries: Paradoxes of Identity Politics." *Sociological Focus* 32: 355–70.

———. 1994. *Paradoxes of Gender*. New Haven: Yale University Press, 1994.

Macionis, John J. 1999. *Sociology*. 7th ed. Upper Saddle River, N.J.: Prentice Hall.

Maloney, Walter C. 1876. *A Sketch of the History of Key West, Florida*. Newark: The Advertiser Printing House.

Mansbridge, Jane. 2001. "The Making of Oppositional Consciousness." In *Oppositional Consciousness: The Subjective Roots of Social Protest*, edited by Jane Mansbridge and Aldon Morris, 1–19. Chicago: University of Chicago Press.

Mansbridge, Jane, and Aldon Morris, eds. 2001. *Oppositional Consciousness: The Subjective Roots of Social Protest*. Chicago: University of Chicago Press.

Martin, Karin A. 1998. "Becoming a Gendered Body: Practices of Preschools." *American Sociological Review* 63: 494–511.

Marwell, Gerald, and Pamela Oliver. 1993. *The Critical Mass in Collection Action: A Micro-Social Theory*. New York: Cambridge University Press.

McAdam, Doug. 1994. "Culture and Social Movements." In *New Social Movements: From Ideology to Identity*, edited by Enrique Laraña, Hank Johnston, and Joseph R. Gusfield, 36–57. Philadelphia: Temple University Press.

———. 1982. *Political Process and the Development of Black Insurgency, 1930–1970*. Chicago: University of Chicago Press.

McAdam, Doug, John D. McCarthy, Susan Olzak, and Sarah A. Soule. 1997. "NSF Grant Proposal: The Dynamics of Collective Protest." Unpublished.

McAdam, Doug, John D. McCarthy, and Mayer N. Zald. 1988. "Social Movements." In *Handbook of Sociology*, edited by Neil Smelser, 695–737. Newbury Park, Calif.: Sage.

McAdam, Doug, and Ronnelle Paulsen. 1993. "Specifying the Relationship between Social Ties and Activism." *American Journal of Sociology* 99: 640–67.

McAdam, Doug, Sidney Tarrow, and Charles Tilly. 2001. *Dynamics of Contention*. Cambridge: Cambridge University.

McCarthy, John D., and Mayer N. Zald. 1977. "Resource Mobilization and Social Movements: A Partial Theory." *American Journal of Sociology* 82: 1212–41.

Meeker, Martin. Forthcoming. *Come Out West: Migration, Communication and the Making of San Francisco as the Gay Mecca*. Chicago: University of Chicago Press.

Melucci, Alberto. 1996. *Challenging Codes: Collective Action in the Information Age*. Cambridge: Cambridge University Press.

———. 1995. "The Process of Collective Identity." In *Social Movements and Culture*, edited by Hank Johnston and Bert Klandermans, 41–63. Minneapolis: University of Minnesota Press.

————. 1989. *Nomads of the Present: Social Movements and Individual Needs in Contemporary Society.* Philadelphia: Temple University Press.

Merrick, Jeffrey. 1999. "Sodomitical Scandals and Subcultures in the 1720s." *Men and Masculinities* 1: 365–84.

Meyer, David S., and Nancy Whittier. 1994. "Social Movement Spillover." *Social Problems* 41: 277–98.

Meyer, David S., Nancy Whittier, and Belinda Robnett. 2002. *Social Movements: Identity, Culture, and the State.* New York: Oxford University Press.

Meyerowitz, Joanne. Forthcoming. *How Sex Changed: A History of Transsexuality in the U.S.* Cambridge: Harvard University Press.

————. 1998. "Sex Change and the Popular Press: Historical Notes on Transsexuality in the U.S., 1930–1955." *GLQ: Journal of Lesbian and Gay Studies* 4: 159–87.

Mische, Ann. Forthcoming. "Cross-Talk in Movements: Reconceiving the Culture-Network Link." In *Social Movement Analysis: The Network Perspective,* edited by Mario Diani and Doug McAdam. New York: Oxford University Press.

Molotch, Harvey, William Freudenburg, and Krista E. Paulsen. 2000. "History Repeats Itself, but How? City Character, Urban Tradition, and the Accomplishment of Place." *American Sociological Review* 65: 791–823.

Morgan, David L. 1997. *Focus Groups as Qualitative Research.* 2nd ed. Newbury Park, Calif.: Sage.

Morris, Aldon. 1984. *The Origins of the Civil Rights Movement: Black Communities Organizing for Change.* New York: Free Press.

————. 1981. "Black Southern Student Sit-in Movement: An Analysis of Internal Organization." *American Sociological Review* 46: 744–67.

Morris, Aldon, and Naomi Braine. 2001. "Social Movements and Oppositional Consciousness." In *Oppositional Consciousness: The Subjective Roots of Social Protest,* edited by Jane Mansbridge and Aldon Morris, 20–37. Chicago: University of Chicago Press.

Mueller, Carol McClurg. 1999. "Escape from the GDR, 1961–1989: Hybrid Exit Repertoires in a Disintegrating Leninist Regime." *American Journal of Sociology* 105: 697–735.

————. 1992. "Building Social Movement Theory." In *Frontiers in Social Movement Theory,* edited by Aldon D. Morris and Carol McClurg Mueller, 3–25. New Haven: Yale University Press.

————. 1991. "Conflict Networks and the Origins of Women's Liberation." In *New Social Movements: From Ideology to Identity,* edited by Enrique Laraña, Hank Johnston, and Joseph R. Gusfield, 234–63. Philadelphia: Temple University Press.

Muñoz, José Esteban. 1999. *Disidentifications: Queers of Color and the Performance of Politics.* Minneapolis: University of Minnesota Press, 1999.

Murray, Stephen O. 2000. *Homosexualities.* Chicago: University of Chicago Press.

Nardi, Peter M. 1999. *Gay Men's Friendships: Invincible Communities.* Chicago: University of Chicago Press.

Nardi, Peter M., and Beth E. Schneider. 1998. *Social Perspectives in Lesbian and Gay Studies.* New York: Routledge.

Nestle, Joan. 1981. "Butch-Fem Relationships: Sexual Courage in the 1950s." *Heresies* 3, no. 4: 21–24.

Newburger, Eric C., and Andrea Curry. 2000. *Educational Attainment in the United States: March 1999,* Current Population Reports P20-528. Washington, D.C.: U.S. Bureau of the Census.

Newton, Esther. 1993. *Cherry Grove, Fire Island: Sixty Years in America's First Gay and Lesbian Town.* Boston: Beacon Press.

———. 1972. *Mother Camp: Female Impersonators in America.* Chicago: University of Chicago Press.

Norton, Rictor. 1992. *Mother Clapp's Molly House: The Gay Subculture in England 1700–1830.* London: Gay Men's Press.

Oliver, Pamela. 1980. "Rewards and Punishments as Selective Incentives for Collective Action: Theoretical Investigations." *American Journal of Sociology:* 1356–75.

Parkin, David, Lionel Caplan, and Humphrey Fisher, eds. 1996. *The Politics of Cultural Performance.* Providence: Berghahn Books.

Patillo McCoy, Mary. 1998. "Church Culture as a Strategy of Action in the Black Community." *American Sociological Review* 63: 767–84.

Paulson, Don, with Roger Simpson. 1996. *An Evening at the Garden of Allah: A Gay Cabaret in Seattle.* New York: Columbia University Press.

Phelan, Peggy. 1993. *Unmarked: The Politics of Performance.* London: Routledge.

Plummer, Ken, ed. 1981. *The Making of the Modern Homosexual.* London: Hutchinson.

Polletta, Francesca. 1999. "'Free Spaces' in Collective Action." *Theory and Society* 28: 1–38.

Polletta, Francesca, and James M. Jasper. 2001. "Collective Identity in Social Movements." *Annual Review of Sociology* 27: 283–305.

Prieur, Annick. 1999. *Mema's House, Mexico City: On Transvestites, Queens, and Machos.* Chicago: University of Chicago Press.

Raeburn, Nicole C. Forthcoming. *Inside Out: The Struggle for Lesbian, Gay, and Bisexual Rights in the Workplace.* Minneapolis: University of Minnesota Press.

Ramet, Sabrina Petra, ed. 1996. *Gender Reversals and Gender Cultures.* New York: Routledge.

Reger, Jo. 2002. "More Than One Feminism: Organizational Structure and the Construction of Collective Identity." In *Social Movements: Identity, Culture, and the State,* edited by Davis S. Meyer, Nancy Whittier, and Belinda Robnett, 171–84. New York: Oxford University Press.

Rey, Michael. 1985. "Parisian Homosexuals Create a Lifestyle, 1700–1750: The Police Archives." *Eighteenth-Century Life* 9, n.s. 3: 179–91.

Rhodes, Joel P. 2001. *The Voice of Violence: Performative Violence as Protest in the Vietnam Era.* Westport, Conn.: Praeger.

Robertson, Jennifer. 1998. *Takarazuka: Sexual Politics and Popular Culture in Modern Japan.* Berkeley: University of California Press.

Robnett, Belinda. 1999. *How Long, How Long: African American Women in the Struggle for Civil Rights.* New York: Oxford University Press.

Rochon, Thomas R. 1998. *Culture Moves: Ideas, Activism, and Changing Values.* Princeton: Princeton University Press.

Roscigno, Vincent J., and William F. Danaher. 2001. "Media Mobilization: The Case of Radio and Southern Textile Worker Insurgency, 1929 to 1934." *American Sociological Review* 66: 21–48.

Rucht, Dieter, Ruud Koopmans, and Friedhelm Neidhardt. 1998. *Acts of Dissent: The Study of Protest in Contemporary Democracies.* Berlin: Sigma.

Rupp, Leila J. 1999. *A Desired Past: A Short History of Same-Sex Love in America.* Chicago: University of Chicago Press.

Rupp, Leila J., and Verta Taylor. 1999. "Forging Feminist Identity in an International Movement: A Collective Identity Approach to Twentieth-Century Feminism." *Signs: Journal of Women in Culture and Society* 24: 363–86.

Samuel, Raphael, Ewan MacColl, and Stuart Cosgrove, eds. 1985. *Theatres of the Left, 1880–1935: Workers' Theatre Movements in Britain and America.* Boston: Routledge.

Schacht, Steven P. 2002a. "Four Renditions of Doing Female Drag: Feminine Appearing Conceptual Variations of a Masculine Theme." *Gendered Sexualities* 6: 157–80.

———. 2002b. "Lesbian Drag Kings and the Feminine Embodiment of the Masculine." *Journal of Homosexuality* 43.

———. 2002c. "Turnabout: Gay Drag Queens and the Masculine Embodiment of the Feminine." In *Revealing Male Bodies,* edited by Nancy Tuana et al., 155–70. Bloomington: Indiana University Press.

———. 2000. "Gay Masculinities in a Drag Community: Female Impersonators and the Social Construction of 'Other.'" In *Gay Masculinities,* edited by Peter Nardi, 247–68. Newbury Park, Calif.: Sage.

———. 1998. "The Multiple Genders of the Court: Issues of Identity and Performance in a Drag Setting." In *Feminism and Men: Reconstructing Gender Relations,* edited by Steven P. Schacht and Doris W. Ewing, 202–24. New York: New York University Press.

Schechner, Richard. 1998. *Performance Theory.* New York: Routledge.

Schwartz, Pepper, and Virginia Rutter. 1998. *The Gender of Sexuality.* Thousand Oaks, Calif.: Pine Forge Press.

Scott, James. 1990. *Domination and the Arts of Resistance: Hidden Transcripts.* New Haven: Yale University Press.

Senelick, Laurence. 2000. *The Changing Room: Sex, Drag and Theatre.* New York: Routledge.

Seyfer, Jessie. 1999. "Cabaret's Closing Is a Drag to Some." *Columbus Dispatch* (November 24).

Sharp, Deborah. 1999. "Charm and Commercialism a Sour Mix in Margaritaville." *USA Today* (September 1), 1A+.

Simon, Bernd, and Bert Klandermans. 2001. "Politicized Collective Identity: A Social Psychological Analysis." *American Psychologist* 56: 319–31.

Smith, Dewitt C., III. 1998. "Among Touram: Community Study of Key West, Florida, a Small City at the Marginal Heart of American Culture." Ph.D. diss. University of Chicago.

Snow, David, and Doug McAdam. 2000. "Identity Work Processes in the Context of Social Movements: Clarifying the Identity/Movement Nexus." In *Self, Identity, and Social Movements,* edited by Sheldon Stryker, Timothy Owens, and Robert White, 41–67. Minneapolis: University of Minnesota Press.

Snow, David A., E. Burke Rochford, Steven K. Worden, and Robert D. Benford. 1986. "Frame Alignment Processes, Micromobilization, and Movement Participation." *American Sociological Review* 51: 464–81.

Sontag, Susan. 1964. "Notes on 'Camp.'" *Partisan Review* 31: 515–30.

Staggenborg, Suzanne. 2001. "Beyond Culture versus Politics: A Case Study of a Local Women's Movement." *Gender & Society* 15: 507–30.

———. 1998. "Social Movement Communities and Cycles of Protest: The Emergence and Maintenance of a Local Women's Movement." *Social Problems* 45: 180–204.

Stein, Arlene, and Ken Plummer. 1996. "'I Can't Even Think Straight': 'Queer' Theory and the Missing Sexual Revolution in Sociology." In *Queer Theory/Sociology,* edited by Steven Seidman. Oxford: Blackwell.

Steinberg, Marc W. 1999. "The Talk and Back Talk of Collective Action: A Dialogic Analysis of Repertoires of Discourse among Nineteenth-Century English Cotton Spinners." *American Journal of Sociology* 105: 736–80.

———. 1995. "The Roar of the Crowd: Repertoires of Discourse and Collective Action among the Spitalfields Silk Weavers in Nineteenth-Century London." In *Repertoires and Cycles of Collective Action,* edited by Mark Traugott, 57–87. Durham, N.C.: Duke University Press.

Stourac, Richard, and Kathleen McCreery. 1986. *Theatre as a Weapon: Workers' Theatre in the Soviet Union, Germany, and Britain.* New York: Routledge.

Stowe, David W. 1998. "The Politics of Café Society." *Journal of American History* 84: 1384–406.

Stryker, Sheldon, Timothy Owens, and Robert White, eds. 2000. *Self, Identity, and Social Movements.* Minneapolis: University of Minnesota Press.

Tarrow, Sidney. 1998. *Power in Movement: Social Movements and Contentious Politics.* Cambridge: Cambridge University Press.

———. 1989. *Democracy and Disorder: Protest and Politics in Italy 1965–1975.* Oxford: Clarendon Press.

Taylor, Verta. 2000a. "Emotions and Identity in Women's Self-Help Movements." In *Self, Identity, and Social Movements,* edited by Sheldon Stryker, Timothy Owens, and Robert White, 271–99. Minneapolis: University of Minnesota Press.

———. 2000b. "Mobilizing for Change in a Social Movement Society." *Contemporary Sociology* 29: 219–30.

———. 1996. *Rock-a-by Baby: Feminism, Self-Help, and Postpartum Depression.* New York: Routledge.

———. 1995. "Watching for Vibes: Bringing Emotions into the Study of Feminist Organizations." In *Feminist Organizations: Harvest of the New Women's Movement,* edited by Myra Marx Ferree and Patricia Yancey Martin, 223–33. Philadelphia: Temple University Press.

———. 1989. "Social Movement Continuity: The Women's Movement in Abeyance." *American Sociological Review* 54: 761–75.

Taylor, Verta, and Nicole C. Raeburn. 1995. "Identity Politics as High-Risk Activism: Career Consequences for Lesbian, Gay, and Bisexual Sociologists." *Social Problems* 42: 252–73.

Taylor, Verta, and Nancy Whittier. 1995. "Analytical Approaches to Social Movement Culture: The Culture of the Women's Movement." In *Social Movements and Culture,* edited by Hank Johnston and Bert Klandermans, 163–87. Minneapolis: University of Minnesota Press.

———. 1992. "Collective Identity in Social Movement Communities: Lesbian Feminist Mobilization." In *Frontiers in Social Movement Theory*, edited by Aldon Morris and Carol McClurg Mueller, 104–30. New Haven: Yale University Press.

Tewksbury, Rick. 1994. "Gender Construction and the Female Impersonator: The Process of Transforming 'He' to 'She.'" *Deviant Behavior: An Interdisciplinary Journal* 15: 27–43.

———. 1993. "Men Performing as Women: Explorations in the World of Female Impersonators." *Sociological Spectrum* 13: 465–86.

Tilly, Charles. 2001. *Stories, Identities, and Political Change*. Lanham, M.D.: Rowman and Littlefield.

———. 2000. "Spaces of Contention." *Mobilization* 5: 135–60.

———. 1995a. "Contentious Repertoires." In *Repertoires and Cycles of Collective Action*, edited by Mark Traugott, 15–42. Durham, N.C.: Duke University Press.

———. 1995b. "To Explain Political Processes." *American Journal of Sociology* 100: 1594–610.

———. 1991. "Domination, Resistance, Compliance . . . Discourse." *Sociological Forum* 6: 593–602.

———. 1978. *From Mobilization to Revolution*. Reading, Mass.: Addison-Wesley.

———, ed. 1999. *How Movements Matter*. Minneapolis: University of Minnesota Press.

Traugott, Mark, ed. 1995. *Repertoires and Cycles of Collective Action*. Durham, N.C.: Duke University Press.

Trumbach, Randolph. 1998. *Sex and the Gender Revolution*. Vol. 1. Chicago: University of Chicago Press.

———. 1989. "The Birth of the Queen: Sodomy and the Emergence of Gender Equality in Modern Culture, 1660–1750." In *Hidden from History: Reclaiming the Gay and Lesbian Past*, edited by Martin Bauml Duberman, Martha Vicinus, and George Chancey Jr., 129–40. New York: New American Library, 1989.

Ullman, Sharon R. 1995. "'The Twentieth Century Way': Female Impersonation and Sexual Practice in Turn-of-the-Century America." *Journal of the History of Sexuality* 5: 573–600.

U.S. Bureau of the Census. 2001. *Statistical Abstract of the United States, 2000: The National Data Book*. Washington, D.C.: U.S. Bureau of the Census.

Van Dyke, Nella. 1998. "Hotbeds of Activism: Locations of Student Protest." *Social Problems* 45: 205–20.

Volcano, Del LaGrace, and Judith "Jack" Halberstam. 1999. *The Drag King Book*. London: Serpent's Tail.

Von Geldern, James. 1993. *Bolshevik Festivals, 1917–1920*. Berkeley: University of California Press.

West, Candace, and Sarah Fenstermaker. 1995. "Doing Difference." *Gender & Society* 9: 8–37.

West, Candace, and Don H. Zimmerman. 1987. "Doing Gender." *Gender & Society* 1: 125–51.

Weston, Kath. 1991. *Families We Choose: Lesbians, Gays, Kinship*. New York: Columbia University Press.

Whittier, Nancy. 2002. "Meaning and Structure in Social Movements." In *Social Movements: Identities, Culture, and the State*, edited by David S. Meyer, Nancy Whittier, and Belinda Robnett, 289–307. New York: Oxford University Press.

————. 2001. "Emotional Strategies: Oppositional Emotions in the Movement Against Child Sexual Abuse." In *Passionate Politics: Emotions and Social Movements,* edited by Jeff Goodwin, James M. Jasper, and Francesca Polletta, 233–50. Chicago: University of Chicago Press.

————. 1995. *Feminist Generations: The Persistence of the Radical Women's Movement.* Philadelphia: Temple University Press.

Zald, Mayer N. 2000. "Ideologically Structured Action: An Enlarged Agenda for Social Movement Research." *Mobilization* 5: 1–16.

Zald, Mayer N., and John D. McCarthy. 1987. *Social Movements in Organizational Society.* New Brunswick, N.J.: Transaction Books.

INDEX

Page numbers of photographs are in italics.

Lenelle Sincere, 222
lesbians, 134, 136, 138, 187
Lesser, Victoria, 21
Lewinsky, Monica, 70, 100
lip-synching, origins of, 184
Little Mermaid, 137
living arrangements, 106, 162–64

makeup: learning to do, 13–15; process of
putting on, 13, 15–16
Mama, 15, 22, 43, 54, 99, 164, 168, 169,
190
Mama Cass, 117–18
Mama Crass, 70–71, 117–18, 165, 171, 222
Mardi Gras, 67
Margo (David), xvi, 72, 222; and audience
interaction, 134, 142–43; childhood of,
27; coming to Key West, 54; description of, 11–12, 91, 146; on drinking,
108; feud with BellaDonna, 169–70; financial situation of, 106, 165; first drag
performance of, 40–41, 140, 165–66;
former careers of, 40, 158; health problems of, 165–66; introduction in show
of, 113; performing, 128–31, 143; relationships of, 82–83, 85–86, 164; on
sex, 80; and his son, 157–58
Marriott, Ron, 100
McAdam, Doug, 213
Midler, Bette, 7, 11, 92, 112, 116, 156
Milla (Dean), xvi, 58, 72; and alcohol and
drugs, 108–10; and audience interaction, 138; audience responses to, 193,
201; as bartender, 94; as a black
woman, 114, 116, 126, 144–45, 203;
in charge of music, 102; childhood of,
13, 24–25, 26–27, 28, 151–53; choosing name, 33; coming to Key West, 54;
description of, 1, 10–11, 91; drag persona of, 33; on drag queens as freaks
and outcasts, 76, 77; on fame, 111; getting dressed, 14; as a hairdresser, 14–
15, 100; introduction in show, 113; as
omnisexual, 126; performing, 124, 126,
128–29, 130; as promoter, 99; relationship with Scabby, 162–63; relationships with men, 78, 82, 83, 110, 153,
162, 169, 203
Miss Firecracker, 72, 171
Miss PrideFest, 71
Miss Q, 65, 79, 93, 172
mollies, 180, 181

Mona Celeste, 172
Mona's, 183
Morissette, Alanis, 42, 91, 112, 203
Ms. D, 170–71, 180
Musty Chiffon, 35
"My Heart Will Go On," 117, 120

Needham, Greg, 34, 171. *See also* Sushi, re-
lationship with Greg
Nesbitt, Bobby, 52
New Year's Eve, 66–67, 68
Newton, Esther, 2, 6, 64, 184
Nikki, 21
No Name Drag Players, 74, 164
Norton, Rictor, 180

"The Oldest Profession," 123
One Human Family, 51
"One Man's Trash Is Another Man's Trea-
sure," 77
One Saloon, 42
Oprah, 110, 111
"Otto Titsling," 116

pageants. *See* Miss Firecracker, Miss Pride-
Fest, Queen Mother
pansy craze, 183
performance studies, 3, 216, 219
Peterson, Christopher, 52, 93
popular culture: drag in, 1–2, 187, 212;
impact of, 28
PrideFest, 71–72
pronouns, use of, 4–5, 35–36
prostitution, 19–20, 30, 32, 57, 61,
107–8, 122, 123, 160–61
Provincetown, 15, 56, 93, 157
publicity, 67, 102–3
"The Pussycat Song," 124

Queen Mother, 65, 70–71, 170–71
Queen Nation, 143, 149, 171, 188
"Queen of the Night," 140, 141
queer theory, 214

race/ethnicity, 11, 12, 16, 29, 33, 91, 114,
144–46, 183, 203. *See also* cross-
ethnicking, Gook Productions
Raven, 69
recognition struggles, 214
recruiting audiences to shows, 45, 57–64,
58, 60
relationships, 78–90